BLESSED MEMORIAL

Imaginings from Lectio Divina

PAUL MARTIN

CITI OF
BOOKS

CITIOFBOOKS, INC.
3736 Eubank NE Suite A1
Albuquerque, NM 87111-3579
www.citiofbooks.com
Hotline: 1 (877) 389-2759
Fax: 1 (505) 930-7244

Ordering Information:
Quantity Sales. Special discounts are available on quantity purchases by corporations, associations, and others. For details, contact the publisher at the address above.

Printed in the United States of America.

ISBN-13   Paperback   979-8-89391-118-3
                   eBook   979-8-89391-119-0

Library of Congress Control Number: 2024909781

To the Holy Spirit—the great arranger
To Barbara—my wife and most trusted beta reader of our life stories
To Calvin Steck, AB, MDiv, STM—the Presbyterian minister
who taught me, a Catholic, how to read the Bible

Lectio Divina—the prayer of divine reading.

Bring your question to God. Ask, "What do you want me to know about this?" and "What do you want me to do?" The Spirit will direct you to a passage in the Bible. Use any translation, Old or New Testament. Read it and listen for words that ring out to you. Imagine yourself as one of the characters.

Be quiet. Stop talking. Shut up and listen.

Reread the passage. You'll hear an answer. You'll recognize it as encouragement and criticism. An answer will come. It might come immediately or in a day or two, but it could take longer. Be patient. Sometimes it takes a while to arrange things. You'll recognize the answer meant for you as encouragement and criticism in ideal measure, and it will be an answer that means something, especially to you.

Ask your next question.

These are people, characters, and stories sent to me in answer to my questions about the great parables.

CONTENTS

CHAPTER 1

Police Records at the Flea Market: The Rich Young Man

My name is Tom Strongtree. I'm a retired woodworker, and this project frightened me initially. I still haven't decided if it's legal to write about it. It might not be. If I'd gone to the police and asked them, they would have confiscated the material and shut me down immediately. Instead I went to a couple of lawyers I know and asked for their opinion. The first lawyer is a relative of mine, a woman who does compliance work for a bank. She approved of the idea. She brought it to a friend of hers who is a probation officer. She liked the idea and wanted to hear more about it. Then I brought it to a friend who's a criminal defense attorney. He told me to stop in my tracks. He advised me to hold my hands up where everybody could see them and slowly back away from ever having thought of it. He told me if I stumbled onto someone who didn't want information coming out about their past, they would drag me into court. He said I didn't know how bad it could get. He said, "If one of those guys turns out to be a judge or a minister, you'd be done. They could take everything you own, and you'd be looking at a world of hurt for the rest of your life." That shook me. I took the yellow plastic bag that held my project and put it on a shelf, but I didn't throw it away.

I bought the project in the yellow bag a few years ago for thirty bucks. I found it one Saturday morning at the Springfield Flea Market

Extravaganza near Springfield, Ohio. My wife and I go to flea markets often. She collects broken picture frames, old maps, classic toys, and other odds and ends to use in her artwork. I don't buy much, but the atmosphere appeals to me. A day at the flea market starts with cheese omelets in cast-iron frying pans and lots of sunshine. My wife brings a pocketful of small bills, and I show up carrying a large paper cup of coffee. There's something gritty about flea markets. Cars park on the grass, vendors sell worn-out treasures from broken tables, and the sun heats the midway. There's the peculiar scent of cut grass, boiled sugar from candy apples, and the slightest whiff of sweat and cigarette smoke.

The best flea markets sell old junk. They are not "antique sales." Antiques are items that have been found and resurrected. The things flea markets sell need work. That's what we look for, odd stuff that needs attention. From time to time, my wife gets deep into matching pieces of chipped china or looking at old coats. I lose interest and wander off. On one of these wanderings, I happened by a table where a guy had a stack of police records for sale. It consisted of thirty Manila envelopes that contained "jail/booking" cards. Each card gave the date of the arrest, basic information, including social security numbers, and fingerprints with a mugshot photo stapled onto it. Notes at the bottom of the cards indicated where the case would go next. Some said "referred to court." Others said "released to parents." Random abbreviations scratched on the cards might indicate routine internal procedures or locations. The cards made no mention of allegations.

The guy had the envelopes bundled with a giant rubber band and said whoever he sold them to had to take the lot. He told me when he bought them, he thought someone might get a kick out of them and he'd make a buck, but it hadn't worked out that way. He'd paid $30 and wanted his money back, that's all.

Something intrigued me, but it felt awkward and voyeuristic reading the cards and looking at pictures of people who had just been arrested. I put the rubber band back around the envelopes and left the table.

Later, when I met with my wife, I told her about the police records. She wanted a look, so we went back. The guy selling them recognized me, and he started his pitch again for my wife's benefit. I listened a second time, hoping he'd say something he hadn't said before. My wife opened some of the envelopes, and I took a second look. This time I didn't see bank robbers or murder suspects. I saw the faces of teenagers looking back at me. I also took a closer look at their dates of birth, and something bothered me even more.

I asked the guy, "When kids are arrested, aren't they called 'youthful offenders'? And aren't youthful offender records supposed to be sealed? Why are these cards lying around on a table at a flea market? Is it even legal for you to sell these things?"

"I don't know," he answered. "I bought them from a guy who said he bought them at an auction. I never thought about it."

My wife didn't want them, and I'd had enough. I didn't want anything to do with the situation. I didn't want to call the police on the guy. He didn't mean any trouble. But that still left the records out there. Aside from anything to do with privacy, a thief could use the social security numbers, especially because they were linked to birth dates. I thought I should buy the records and burn them. It would only cost a few bucks, and I might be doing someone a real favor. I told myself I'd get rid of them and save someone the headache of identity theft. Then I told myself to forget it and mind my own business. It had nothing to do with me. I put the rubber band back and left everything the way I found it. I told the guy, "Maybe later."

As my wife and I turned to leave, the guy said, "Sure, I'll be here till five, and I'll be here tomorrow too."

His next comment changed the direction of my life. He said, "They'll be waiting for you."

I couldn't stop thinking about the police cards on the way home. I couldn't get over how they found their way to a flea market. Who'd have a pack of police records anyway? Where were they from? And why only thirty? If someone took them from a police station, wouldn't there be more of them?

I kept thinking about the cards and photos all that evening. None of it had anything to do with me, so why couldn't I let it go? My wife and I ate dinner. We walked the dog and watched a movie, but my mind kept returning to the envelopes. I kept turning them over in my brain, and I woke up at three in the morning with new questions.

In the early darkness, I wondered what had happened to those kids. If I had a chance to talk to them, I'd ask what they remembered about being arrested. At their age, when they'd been detained, fear kept me out of trouble. While I studied for history and chemistry tests in high school, these kids tangled with the police. I did what the teachers told me. These kids didn't. Has it made any difference? The more I thought about them, the more I wondered what had happened later. My parents, school, and church told me to behave or things would go badly for me. But I wanted to know how their lives turned out. Did things go badly for them? As adults, did the arrest matter to them? What advice would they give to young people today about growing up?

I couldn't go back to sleep. When the sun rose, I knew I had to go back and buy the cards. I didn't know what I'd do with them, but I had to have them. At breakfast, I told my wife I wanted to go back to the flea market after Mass and buy the envelopes. She said, "I get it. That's what you had on your mind last night."

At Mass, the gospel reading told the parable of the rich young man. That's the one where a man asks what he has to do to go to heaven. The man is told to sell everything and follow along with the apostles, but he doesn't do it. The gospel says he went away sad, and the apostles hear the classic line about the "eye of the needle." When they ask about that, they hear another famous line. The one that says, "With God, all things are possible."

The priest at Mass gave his sermon to well-fed people in clean clothes, but I didn't hear him. The next thing I knew, my wife took my hand for the Our Father. My mind had drifted. Autopilot took me through the responses to the prayers and the standing, sitting, and kneeling of the Mass until just before Communion.

I've heard the story of the rich young man many times throughout my life, and I've used *Lectio Divina* to help me understand it. *Lectio Divina* is Latin for "divine reading." The idea is to use your imagination. Listen to words that ring out to you. Put yourself into the story as one of the characters. As an altar boy, I couldn't understand how the young man would give up his big chance to walk with the Lord. In the cynicism of my young manhood, I saw how few people even thought about God. As a young father, when my kids looked up from their bowls of spaghetti and bills came due, I reminded myself to trust that all things are possible.

But as an older man now, new questions have surfaced. They start with "What happened? The man walked away, but where did he go? What did he do with the rest of his life? The young man had been obeying the rules up until the time of his question. Doesn't that count for something? Did he forfeit the kingdom because he didn't sell everything and join up? Did he continue to follow the rules and regulations afterward, or did he say nothing matters anyway and abandon himself to nihilism? Is there any room for reconsideration? Could the young man come back later for a second chance? Does God come through in the end and show mercy, or is it all over? Does God send the rich young man to hell? In my mind, the story brought up more questions than it answered.

After Mass, questions about the rich young man dissipated, and I resumed thinking about the police cards. I drove back to the flea market, hoping the guy hadn't sold them, and went directly to his table. I didn't see him, and I didn't see the stack of envelopes either. I stood looking at the table where they had been and felt a loss. I worried that my hesitation had somehow taken away my chance at something. Then I saw the guy making his way to the table, and he most likely saw my look of frustration. He smiled and said, "Relax, here they are." He pulled a large yellow plastic grocery store bag out from under the table, and I felt a wave of relief. He passed me the bag, and I gave him a twenty and a ten.

Holding the bills in his hand, he said, "Thanks a lot," and asked me, "Are you going to get in touch with them?"

That stopped me. He'd asked the question I'd been asking myself.

"Yes," I answered.

"Good," he said. He nodded without further explanation, almost as if he knew how things would pan out.

I drove home with the yellow bag on the front seat next to me. I felt pensive and confused. Over the following weeks, I pored over the cards and photos. At one time, I thought I'd burn them. Now I read and reread them and couldn't get enough. I looked at the pictures and wondered about the kids. I considered how I'd get in touch with them as adults. What kind of approach would I use? I asked myself what I'd think if someone called me on the phone and wanted me to remember something that happened way back when I was fourteen or sixteen. It would be jarring. I'd get defensive. So I ruled that out. It would be unfair to show up on doorsteps, not to mention expensive and time-consuming.

I knew people use Facebook for this kind of thing, but I've never been able to catch on to Facebook. I settled on writing a letter. People are happy when they see their name handwritten on an envelope. You can delete an email, but a letter in the mailbox is different. You can toss a letter in the trash, but it's less likely. A letter would also give someone time to think. I didn't want to put anyone on the spot. I had no argument with these people. I wanted to ask them for their stories, the lessons, and feelings that stayed with them. It only made sense to ask politely.

Sending a letter brought the next question though. I didn't know how to find current addresses, and I didn't know anybody who did. That's when I called the lawyers. I figured they'd know research people. After asking them about finding addresses, I thought I'd ask for their legal opinion about my project. I'd run it past them. I should have guessed they'd immediately ask me why I wanted addresses for thirty people I didn't know. I explained about the fingerprint cards and my interest in them. This is when the project, still in the yellow bag, found a place on my bookshelf, where it stayed for three years. I don't know what I planned to do with the cards and photos, but I never got rid of them. Books and other memorabilia crowded the bag to the side, but I hadn't forgotten those kids.

As we get older, we encounter the problem of regret. As life comes to a close, people sometimes regret their mistakes. But more often than not, people regret what they did not do. They feel disappointed over lost opportunities or not saying something when they had the chance. One evening I looked at the yellow bag on the shelf. My project wouldn't ruin anybody. If some government official or a preacher got mad, so what? I'd just hand them their envelope, no harm, no foul. As time passed, I saw my regret over not doing the project as the more significant problem. *What's the risk?* I asked myself. *Our kids are grown, so they wouldn't be hurt, and I'm retired, so I don't have to worry about losing a career.* I kept returning to the fundamental question. Which would I regret more—disobeying good legal advice or not doing the project? I opened the bag and looked at the cards and photos again, but nothing had changed in the intervening years. I still had to reach these people.

I couldn't bother the lawyers again, so I typed "how to find people" into the computer. It surprised me to see finding people is such a huge business. Several ads for websites said their advanced technology could find anybody anytime. Many free sites advertised that they could reunite lost friends and reconcile family members. Maybe it wouldn't be as difficult as I thought. I typed in one of the names from the police cards. Nothing happened. No results. I assumed I'd entered something incorrectly and tried again. Nothing. I tried a different name, and again, nothing. I tried another website. This time the result said "Error." I tried a third site. This one said "Error 454." For a computer illiterate like myself, this wouldn't be easy.

The solution might be to hire someone who knows about these websites. I could find a young person or a college student who knows the internet. As I scrolled past site after site looking for an answer, the word "investigation" jumped out at me.

That's what I needed. An investigator would be able to find addresses. I typed "investigators" into the computer, which sent me in the right direction but landed me in an altogether different arena. One investigator screamed in bright colors and capital letters, "I WILL CATCH HIM, DELIVER PHOTOS, OR YOUR MONEY BACK!" Another one promised to "deliver evidence of her infidelities." I found one that said "Troxel will find them. No matter what!" The ad claimed access to state, professional, and legal records.

I called and got an answering machine. In my mind, I thought a receptionist at an office would take my call. I'd imagined it would be like calling Sam Spade in *The Maltese Falcon*. A "gal" named Effie would light a cigarette for her boss and tell him there was "a live one on the wire." The answering machine caught me off guard, but I left a message anyway.

A guy named Phil Troxel called about an hour later, and he did not sound like Humphrey Bogart. I explained my project and how I wanted to contact the teenagers now that they were adults. Phil Troxel assured me he would have no problem locating current addresses. He also said he'd throw in phone numbers and emails at no extra charge. He told me several news organizations used him for work on documentaries, and he usually charged $35 a name, but he'd give me a volume discount. He quoted $25 each and said it would take three days. Amazing. The information would cost $750, and this brought me happiness I felt in my nerves.

"Sure!" I said. I hadn't thought about it, but why not? I hadn't considered how much it would be worth until that moment, but it thrilled me to get an actual number. I would have agreed to more. The project had been on my mind for years, and $750 would make it possible.

"What's next?" I asked. "Do I bring you the cards?"

"Yes," Phil answered. "I work from home, so I'll meet you at a coffee shop. Bring half the fee. I'll take the cards, do the searches, and return them with current addresses. Then you pay the rest."

Again, my "film noir" image had the investigator working out of a second-story office downtown. I saw myself holding the envelopes and approaching a heavy wooden door with "Phillip Troxel" stenciled on frosted glass. The coffee shop sounded easier, and one of these days, along with learning about Facebook, I have to update my worldview.

"There's only one thing I ask," I added. "Please don't make copies of the records. I'm going to return them to the people. I want to say in good conscience that they have the only card and there are no copies."

"Sure," he answered. "There's no reason I'd need a copy."

We agreed to meet at a Starbucks the next day at 11:00 AM. I hung up the phone, elated.

I arrived on time. An early lunch crowd had taken most of the tables, and I didn't know how I'd recognize Phil Troxel, but as I opened the door, a barista called out, "Venti coffee for Phil, black, no sugar!" I didn't understand it then, but I do now. My guided tour had already begun.

I introduced myself to the guy who reached for the coffee. I told him I didn't know how I'd recognize him until I heard his name called. He smiled and said, "Amazing how these things work out."

I got a coffee while he picked a place, and we sat down. He had on tight jeans and a leather jacket. I judged him to be in his forties and possibly like the guys I wanted to meet. He had large brown eyes, dark hair pulled behind his ears, and a scruffy beard. I'll admit to being apprehensive as I handed over the yellow plastic bag and $375 in cash.

He put the cash in his pocket and hoisted the bag onto the table. He took out one of the envelopes, removed the card and photo, and scanned it while his expression remained passive. He replaced it in its envelope and put it back in the bag. He took out another envelope and again pulled out the card. He went through two more envelopes and considered the cards in each. "They're kids, all right," he said. "They might be youthful offenders, but these are just fingerprint cards, no charges."

"That's right," I answered. "That's why I think I can get away with it. Other than the fact they'd been arrested, I can't give information I don't have."

After a moment, I asked, "So will you be able to find them?"

"Sure," he answered. "There's plenty to go on here. I should have everything by the weekend."

Phil Troxel took a sip of his coffee. "You might be right," he said. "Just possessing the cards probably isn't a hanging offense. You don't want to sell their identities or social security numbers, and it all went down years ago. The cards say these arrests occurred from the late '70s through the '90s. And I think you're right about their ages too. From the birth dates, some of these kids would be in their late '40s or early '50s by now."

He paused to make another point. "The only thing is, the fact of an arrest is important. Sometimes, just saying someone had a problem with the police can work against them. It's tricky," he observed.

He looked at the bag and asked, "Are the other cards like the ones I saw?"

"Yes," I answered. "And they all have mug shot pictures too. Mostly young kids trying to be cool and wondering what will happen next. Only one of them is over eighteen."

Phil nodded. "A scary time for them," he added. He took another sip of his coffee, and I saw a slight grimace. He asked, "What do you expect they'll tell you if you get to talk with any of them?"

"I don't know," I answered. "They might not tell me anything. They could get mad and say 'screw you,' and they'd have every right, but I'll never know if I don't try."

Phil said, "I don't understand why you're so interested in the first place. You'll probably find they're no different from anyone else. All kids do something wrong, but these kids got caught. It sounds like you're trying to make a group out of them while there's no connection." In a movie trailer voice, he announced, "*The Caught 30. You got away with it. We didn't!*"

I laughed. "Maybe," I said. "Maybe that's all there is to it. Who knows?"

He looked up from his coffee cup and smiled. "Okay," he said. "Let's find out."

As we finished our coffee, I felt like I had to firm up the commitment. I said, "Thanks, Phil. I've been thinking about this project for years, and I'm glad to get it going."

He answered, "Sure, Tom, glad to help, but there are two things I should tell you right now. I've done this before, and I know what you'll run into."

"What?" I asked with trepidation.

"First," he said, "you're going to find out some of these people are dead. That's the way of the world, and I can also tell you right now, this won't be the end of it."

"What does that mean?" I asked.

"You're going to need more information," he answered. "The way these things usually work, one person leads to another, leads to another. You're going to be looking for more addresses or something like that. I want you to call me when you do."

I had to smile. Phil Troxel had a sales pitch, and that made me trust him. He wanted me to be a good customer, which meant he'd give me quality information.

"Sure," I said. "You've been a big help already. I'm glad I met you."

We drifted out into the parking lot with Phil carrying the yellow bag. He put it into the storage compartment of a motorcycle and said, "I'll call you in a few days. We'll meet here again."

"Sounds great," I agreed.

He started the bike and took off. I wondered if Phil Troxel had conned me. I'd given a guy on a motorcycle $375 and trusted him with a pack of police records that could get me in a lot of trouble. He could keep the money and turn me in. Maybe he'd keep the money and sell the social security numbers. I could only say that I wanted to believe he'd come up with thirty new addresses, but that's all I had. I wanted to believe.

Phil Troxel called Friday morning and didn't say more than necessary. "Same place this afternoon?" he asked. "Two o'clock?"

"Two o'clock is good," I answered.

I got there before he did, bought two coffees, and took a table where he would see me. He showed up on time and took a place on the other side of the table. By way of greeting, he said, "I've got what you're looking for."

"Any trouble?" I asked.

"None," he answered. He parked the yellow bag on the table. "But," he said, "I must tell you, seven of your people are dead."

"Okay," I said. "So that leaves twenty-three?"

"Right," he responded. "More dead than I'd guessed based on their ages, but that's how it is. As to their youthful offender status, the records are buried deep. If you want to know what these kids did, you'll have to ask them." He took a sip of the hot coffee. "Pure conjecture," he said, "but I wonder if whoever took the fingerprint cards also swiped the case files. It's funny. I don't think 'YO' or any other police records exist for these kids. The arrests came from Jamestown, a small town in upstate New York. Computer records had only started at that time, so without paper files, these kids got away with whatever they did. Whoever pulled their records gave them a clean slate. Also, several of them had their prints retaken when they applied for professional licenses over the years. That calls for fingerprints, but nothing related to criminality would come up without records."

Phil took another sip of his coffee and continued, "I know you want to keep this discreet. The addresses I gave you are mostly public offices and businesses. If I started asking for home addresses, I'd look like a stalker. You said you want to write letters, and that's probably okay. You never know who else is looking at your email. I recommend handwriting the address on the envelopes and marking it personal correspondence."

I reached into the yellow bag and opened one of the envelopes. I found a sheet of notebook paper where Phil had neatly printed an address.

"You handwrote the addresses?" I asked. "I thought you'd give me a typed list."

"Yeah," he said with a smile. "I got the idea you're old-school."

I nodded. I said, "Thanks, that's thoughtful," and I silently scolded myself for doubting him. While I worried he'd take off with the money, he'd gone out of his way to find the best way to communicate with me.

Phil told me each envelope contained at least one address, and he'd try again if they didn't get to the right person. I gave him the second $375, and as we made our way to the parking lot, he said, "Don't forget, call anytime."

"Thanks," I said. "I'll be in touch."

I started with cards and photos of twenty-nine teenagers and one adult arrested in the 1970s, '80s, and '90s. Seven died in the years since. I contacted the remaining twenty-three. Although the people involved have lived commendable lives, most asked me to keep their secret. I will. However, seven of them agreed to let me relate their stories. The retellings in this collection are from recordings, notes, and my memory of our conversations. They have been reviewed and approved by the subjects. Also, the son of one of the deceased sent me a letter which he has permitted me to include. Noteworthy is the fact that none of them asked for money.

An odd aspect arose as the project got underway. The people I interviewed pointed me toward a man who had a significant impact on their lives. When I looked into this man's life, I met his high school girlfriend. She helped me understand why I'd started the project in the first place.

CHAPTER 2

Patrick Williams: The Great Banquet

Once I had the current addresses, I planned to write a letter, send out a copy of the letter, and respond to anyone who answered. I'm embarrassed to remember that idea today. I would have failed. There could be no such mailing. I ran this idea past Phil Troxel, who advised me against it. I liked the guy, and in subsequent discussions, Phil said I had to approach the "caught thirty" one at a time. He cautioned me that my first job would be to win them over, and that came from demonstrating respect. If I didn't show respect, the exercise would go from intriguing to a waste of time.

He told me to take a step back, pick one name, and write to that person. If I made a mistake and said something wrong, I'd adjust for the next. I might lose one, but I wouldn't lose them all. I didn't know why at the time, but I picked Patrick Williams for my first try. Alongside the address for Patrick Williams, Phil noted, PhD superintendent of schools. Looking back on it now, I see I couldn't have started with a better guy. I sent him this letter:

Thomas Strongtree
Spring Valley, Ohio
Dr. Patrick Williams, PhD
Superintendent of Schools
Rochelle Park, NJ
Dear Dr. Williams,

My Name is Thomas Strongtree, and I am asking you to please share a part of your personal history with me.

Several years ago, I bought a pack of police records at a flea market. I felt drawn to the people they represent. The documents are photos and fingerprint cards with names and addresses of young people living in the Jamestown, NY, area during the 1970s, '80s, and '90s. I believe one of these records is yours.

They are not complete records. They contain no information concerning accusations or verdicts. I am writing to ask what you remember about the incident that brought you into contact with the police. I am wondering if your contact with the law at a young age had any lasting effect on your life, and what advice you would give to your younger self. I am not with the police. I am not a reporter. I have no affiliation with any institution. I am not asking for money, nor am I offering money.

Be assured I will maintain confidentiality and respect. Enclosed are my home address, phone number, and email address. Please get in touch however you feel most comfortable.

I would like to meet you in person. You set the time and place. I will return the original record card and photo to you when we meet. I have made no copies.

If you believe this police record does not concern you, please respond, alert me to my error, and I will search elsewhere.

For your attention, I express my gratitude.

Thomas Strongtree

I heard back from Dr. Williams a week later. He sent an email from his office.

To: Thomas Strongtree
From: Dr. Patrick Williams, PhD
Subject: Police records

I don't know who you are or what you are trying to do, but I will not be blackmailed or intimidated. Those records have been sealed and expunged. You have no right to access them for any reason. If you persist in this activity, I will notify the authorities.

A flush of embarrassment ran through me. My lawyer friend warned me about this. He told me, and now I told myself I had no business messing around with this information. I had to forget it. I tried, but it didn't work. I had to get out before the whole project came crashing down around me. And forget Phil Troxel and the money too. Lesson bought and lesson learned.

I replied to the email.

Reply to: Dr. Patrick Williams, PhD
Subject: Police records

Dr. Williams,

I understand and accept your refusal. I will not pursue the matter further.

However, it might be good that I bought the arrest cards rather than someone who would otherwise misuse your personal information. I have shared this card and photo with no one other than the investigator who found your address. In that light, please tell me how to proceed. I will destroy the card and photo, or, if you prefer, I will send them to you by registered mail at my expense.

I apologize for causing any anxiety.

I ask your forgiveness.

Thomas Strongtree

That's about all I could do. I'd disobeyed good legal advice, and if this Williams guy didn't come after me, I'd dodge the bullet. I didn't get an immediate reply from Dr. Williams. He might have ignored me, and that would have been fine, but I needed to figure out what to do with his record card. My nerves had almost settled when I saw he'd sent another email.

To: Thomas Strongtree
From: Patrick Williams
Subject: police records

Hey, Thomas,

I've been thinking a lot about this police thing. Yes, it's me.

I believe you meant no harm, but please, put yourself in my place for a minute. You'll understand my reluctance. A letter came out of the blue asking about the most embarrassing moment of my teenage years. It surprised me, but I've never kept anything about the arrest a secret. My family, friends, and employers are all well aware of it.

I consider it one of the worst days of my young life. I also see it as the day my life began.

You asked what I would tell my younger self. Ironically, I've built a career answering that question for the young people in my classrooms and for myself.

I'll be glad to meet with you if you're on the level. I'm still interested in how you got whatever you say you have. Finding it at a flea market seems a little far-fetched, but you can tell me about that when we meet.

I have this Friday off. I know that only leaves you a few days to get here, but that's the most convenient for me. School's out that day. I have meetings in the morning, but we'd have plenty of time in the afternoon. Let's meet at my office in the administration building. How about two o'clock? I'll link to the Rochelle Park Schools website for the address. If that's good, reply "okay." If that doesn't work, give me a few dates that would, and we'll work it out.

Regards,
Patrick Williams

That was all I needed. He added a link to the school system website. I replied "okay" and started packing. He wanted to meet on Friday, and the email arrived on Tuesday, but that didn't bother me. My excitement got me to New Jersey on time. My first guy, and it felt like he had a winning story. How did Patrick Williams, a young guy arrested in Jamestown, New York, become Dr. Patrick Williams, a school superintendent in New Jersey? He seemed friendly enough in the second email, certainly no criminal and probably not dangerous. I felt a kind of similarity.

I pulled into the parking lot of the Administration Building for Rochelle Park Schools ten minutes early on Friday. The place looked deserted, and I had no trouble finding a spot. I walked through the front doors and stopped by the building directory in the entryway. The names listed had titles that read "head of" or "assistant administrator of," but Patrick Williams had no title. It said, "Dr. Patrick Williams, PhD Room 5." To me, that means anyone looking for him knows who he is. I felt uncomfortable going any further, so I waited by the doors. He mentioned something about having a day off, and it sure felt that way. No lights in the building, and all the doors were closed. I didn't have long to wait. Dr. Williams arrived, driving a gray Lexus. I knew from his record card he'd be fifty-one years old, and a tall man of medium build jumped out of the car. He wore a crisp navy-blue suit, well-groomed salt-and-pepper hair, and black-framed glasses. I wouldn't be surprised if he told me he shined his shoes every morning. He walked directly toward me, gave me a huge smile, and shook my hand. He said, "You must be Thomas Strongtree."

"Yes," I answered as we shook hands. "Glad to meet you, Dr. Williams, and please call me Tom."

"Happy you could make it, Tom, and you, please call me Patrick," he said. "Let's go to my office where we can talk."

We walked down a corridor, and our footsteps echoed off the walls. From school days gone by, I felt correction all around me. If you don't know that feeling, I'm guessing you were a good kid who wanted to be in school. The harsh-sounding corridor of a school office building is last on the list of places I'd like to visit, but Patrick Williams's enthusiasm carried me on. He opened his office, turned on a light, and motioned me to a chair in front of his desk. While I sat in the chair, he hung his suit jacket on a coat tree and busied himself at a small sink. He switched on a coffee maker.

"I'll be able to offer you coffee in a minute," he said. "Any other time they have it made all the time around here, but everyone's off for after-test day. We have these quarterly exams now. The teachers get a Friday off now and then to compensate for the extra work. It's a fun little perk. Who doesn't like a Friday off?"

I said, "I appreciate you taking time out of your day off for me."

"Well, I don't know if I ever get a day off," he said. "But frankly, I'm interested in what you've uncovered."

19

I opened the leather backpack I'd started using as a briefcase. I took out the Manila envelope containing his record card and photo. After he found a place behind his large metal desk, I handed him the envelope and asked his permission to record our meeting.

"Sure," he said. "As long as we keep it to the old days."

"That's what I'm here for," I agreed.

He opened the envelope and took out the card and photo. "So," he said, "this is it." He looked at them for a long time. He moved his eyes from the image to the card and back several times. When he looked up, he said, "Yeah, that's me. That's what I looked like on my worst day."

He went quiet again for a full minute and returned to looking at the picture. When he looked up, I saw a smile in his eyes. He said, "Things took a turn that day."

He took off his glasses and put them on the desk in front of him. He said, "That coffee should be ready by now. Would you like some?"

"Thank you, that would be great, Doctor."

"Please call me Patrick. How do you take it?"

"Black is fine."

He brought two cups of coffee toward us, but this time he took a chair on the same side of the desk. He placed the cups with handles facing us, using the desk as a table. As he sat down, he reached for the card and photo. "How did you get this again?" he asked.

I went through the story and ended by saying I'd begun the contact phase of my project. "By the way, you're the first," I told him. "And I almost gave up when it didn't go well with you."

"Yeah," he said. "It did surprise me. I thought I'd heard the last of that over thirty-five years ago."

"I can imagine," I agreed. "So that's it. You responded, and here I am. Thank you so much for seeing me."

"Shoplifting," he said without preamble and dropped the word dramatically.

He waited a moment and continued, "Fourteen years old, and I got caught shoplifting on summer vacation. The card says July twenty-second, and that's right, two days before my mother's birthday. I remember the day like yesterday. It happened right before noon at a department store in Jamestown called The Big N. Another kid and I were out looking for trouble. We tried to walk out of the store wearing shirts from the men's department. A big ugly guy from the store stopped us and told us we had to come with him. He acted like a dick about the thing and took us to a grimy little office in the back. He made us sit on these dirty, worn-out plastic chairs and told us he saw us trying to steal the shirts. He said he'd already called the police."

Dr. William's casual and off-color description of the man's demeanor surprised me, but I came to see it as his man-to-man way of communicating.

"I'd never been so frightened," he continued. "A cop showed up and put us in the back of a police car. I looked around for the door handle, and the kid with me called me a fool. He said, 'Everybody knows you can't open the back of a police car.' I learned two things at once. I experienced how trapped animals feel, and I found out the kid with me had been arrested before when I asked him how he knew about the back of police cars.

"So the cop took us to the police station and made us sit in a waiting room where we could see the cells. He didn't put us in a cell, but we knew enough not to leave. Another cop at the desk called our parents.

"The police told my mother she had to come to get me from the station. They didn't let me talk to her. They just told her to come to the station. She drove down in the car, and I could see her hands shaking as the cop explained why he'd arrested me. We got in the car and didn't say a word all the way home. As we pulled onto the driveway, she said, 'We'll tell your father tonight.'

"I've replayed that day a million times in my mind. I had to wait all afternoon for my father to come home, and rage overtook me. I hated the world and didn't know why. I didn't need the shirt. I didn't even want a shirt. I wanted to do something risky. I wanted to do something wrong and get away with it. I'll admit this to you now. I'd gotten away with it before and got high on the rush.

"Talk about a teenager with an attitude." Patrick Williams continued, "At home, we lived with constant talk about college and success. My parents were all about making me into what other people wanted me to be. I had to answer test questions correctly in school to get good grades. Good grades would get me into college. A diploma would make me good enough for some business to hire me. Then I'd have to make my boss like me so he wouldn't fire me, and I'd have to make the customers like me too so they'd buy stuff. Making the sale became a way of life. I didn't want any part of it, and I couldn't see how anyone else would either.

"Well, my father got home, and when my mother told him, he turned livid. Not because I'd done anything wrong. He yelled at me about how he'd be embarrassed if anyone in town found out. During the rant, he came up with the idea that he wanted me to be a good person, but it didn't amount to more than moral wrapping paper. In the end, he couldn't help himself. He told me I'd better straighten up or I'd get arrested again. Then I'd have a criminal record, and no company would ever hire me. He told me if I screwed up again, he'd buy me a one-way ticket to Greenwich Village, where I could go live with all the other kids who hated their parents. We all went to bed that night exhausted."

I repeated Dr. Williams's statement as a question. "A one way ticket to Greenwich Village? What did he mean by that?"

"In his mind," Patrick explained, "Greenwich Village existed for no other reason than to rebel against everything he believed in. The threat meant he would cut me off and throw me out to starve. I have to tell you," Dr. Williams said with a laugh. "I thought about that night every time I paid for the bus or a plane ticket to get to Fordham or Columbia, where I went to college."

We both smiled, and he took a sip of his coffee. "So the store pressed charges," Patrick Williams continued. "They had a policy to prosecute all shoplifters, and my parents and I had to go to juvenile court. My father's big hands gripped the arms of his chair as he endured a guy in a robe pronouncing judgment on his son. The store policy also demanded restitution in all cases, which came to about fifteen bucks. I had to pay for that. The court charged $125 'court costs,' and my father paid that. I also got twenty hours of community service, which saved my life."

Patrick Williams took another sip of his coffee, and his countenance lightened. He said, "Jamestown had done some renovation at the City Hall. The building held the police department, the jail, the court, and offices for maintenance and administration. As part of the renovation, an old storeroom needed to be cleaned out. The police wanted to paint the walls and make space for some new desks. Racks of books and a few pieces of old furniture stood in the way. I had to help pack up and carry the old stuff out of the building for my community service. The police scheduled me to show up at 8:00 a.m. the following Monday at the police station the week before school started."

At this point, Patrick Williams froze in place. I thought something hit him. He reminded me of a TV show I saw once where a guy went still in the same way. In the show, blood leaked onto the guy's white shirt as he realized he'd just been shot. Williams sat without moving like that. I didn't know what to do.

I almost said something when he broke into a huge grin. He said, "'Kin' guy!" and shook his head back and forth, laughing to himself. He looked like he just got the punchline of a joke he'd heard a month ago.

He fixed a look at me and asked, "Did Foraker Macreavy have anything to do with this?"

"I'm sorry, Dr. Williams, I don't know who that is."

"Are you sure?" he asked. "His fingerprints are all over it."

"Forgive me," I answered. "I assumed they were your fingerprints, and, no, I've never heard of anyone named Foraker Macreavy."

Patrick Williams burst out laughing. He said, "No, I don't mean they're actually his fingerprints. They're mine, but come to think of it, that's the kind of play on words he'd use himself."

The superintendent took a long drink of his coffee and stared out the office window. For a moment, it looked like he might tear up.

"I'll tell you flat out," he said. "That guy changed my life, and I'll bet you, dollars to donuts, before this is over, you'll find out Macreavy had something to do with it."

"Please tell me why. Who is Macreavy?" I asked.

He looked at me and paused for a moment. "Okay," he said. "But it's a long story."

I returned his look. "I've come a long way," I said. "And it sounds like this is part of why I'm here."

"All right," he began. "The police scheduled me to report to this room at the city hall to move old books and furniture. They said a police officer would supervise and tell me what to do.

"I got there on time. My father made sure of that, and that's when I first met Officer Macreavy. I expected a policeman in uniform. Instead I got this tall good-looking guy wearing jeans and a T-shirt. He said he didn't have to wear his uniform that day because he'd be working with me doing the cleaning and moving.

"He seemed like a good guy, and he got to it immediately. He started with a stack of flattened cardboard boxes, opened out a few of them, and taped the bottoms. He explained he wanted to sort through the books before throwing them away. He told me if I saw anything I wanted, it was okay to take it. One by one, he threw the books into different boxes and gave me directions as we went along. Some of the boxes went to a truck he'd parked outside. Others went to a dumpster behind the building.

"That's how we spent most of the day. I took boxes either over to the truck or out to the dumpster. He also had me help him load up a few of the old bookcases and shelves into the truck. At noon he bought me a sub sandwich and a can of soda from Billing's Bakery near the City Hall. We sat on the truck's tailgate to eat our lunch, and Macreavy asked me what I liked to read. I told him I didn't read much, just what I had to for school. He asked if I'd seen anything interesting as we went through the old books that morning. I told him I didn't, but I hadn't been looking either. He told me he'd watch for something I might like.

"We went back to work, and by the end of the day, we'd just about cleared the room. He came up with a broom and had me sweep the floor while he talked with some of the other cops that came by. A few looked into the room and said I'd done a good job. One of the guys told me something I'll remember till my last day. He said, "'Kin' guy! Lucky for you to work with Macreavy today, kid.' It confused me, but the other cops laughed, and I let it pass.

"My mother said she would pick me up at four o'clock when the day ended, and Macreavy waited with me until she got there.

While we waited, he gave me a copy of *The Adventures of Sherlock Holmes* by Sir Arthur Conan Doyle. I still have it. On the inside, he'd written, 'To Patrick, Whatever remains, however improbable. Foraker Macreavy.'

"He asked me if I'd ever heard of Sherlock Holmes, and I told him I had.

"He asked me if I'd read any of the stories, and I said no. He told me I couldn't ask for much more on a hot August night than a good old Holmes story."

Patrick Williams looked at me with a smile and added, "I've found they're just as good on cold winter nights."

As I took a sip of my coffee, he resumed the story. "Macreavy said we had one more day for my community service. The next day, we'd unpack the truck. He told me to meet him again at eight o'clock at the police station the following morning. He'd take me in the truck to help unload the books and shelves. He told me that night I should read *The Adventure of the Speckled Band* from the book he gave me. He said however long I spent reading would count towards my community service. I read the story that night, and to this day, it's one of the best short stories I've ever read.

"I met up with Officer Macreavy in the morning, and we took the truck and the books to his house. As we drove along, he told me he'd read many of the books before, but he couldn't stand to throw them away. He said he didn't mind having extra copies around because he could give them away and not worry about getting them back. He asked me if I liked the story he told me to read. I told him I did, and he asked if I figured it out before the end. I said I didn't think anyone could have even guessed that, but that's what made Sherlock Holmes a great detective. He asked me how long I'd spent reading it, and I realized I didn't know. Somehow I'd lost track of time and didn't think to check on it. I didn't understand it then, but it's clear now. With that story, he taught me how to read, and he also taught me how to teach."

Patrick Williams finished his coffee and got up to make more. "Would you like another cup?" he asked.

"Yes, please," I answered.

He spoke to me over his shoulder as he worked the coffee maker and resumed the story. "Macreavy had this old place out on Lake Chautauqua. That's a lake near Jamestown. Have you ever heard of it?"

"I think I have," I answered. "Does it have anything to do with the Chautauqua Institution?"

"Yeah, that's it," he said. "Same lake, but Macreavy lived across from the institution and closer to Jamestown. The lake is twenty miles long, so there's a fair amount to it."

"Anyway, we pulled into his driveway off Old Route 17, one of those driveways you don't see unless you're looking for it. He had a mailbox and all. It's just that it didn't stand out. He bounced the truck down this long driveway to his house. The driveway ended at a boat-house that looked like a garage on the lake. Macreavy backed the truck up to the side door of his house. He flipped down the tailgate and picked up a box. He told me to grab another one and follow him. I followed along through this crazy old house full of antiques. It seemed like everything in the place came from a long time ago. He brought me a room filled with hundreds of books already and told me he called it his 'library of life.' First I helped him carry in the old shelves and cases and then he showed me where to stack the rest of the boxes. That's what we did for the next few hours. Macreavy said he'd sort everything later. He said it would be an excellent job for next January. I asked him about his house, and he told me most of the people nearby only live in their places during the summer, but he'd 'winterized' his place. He said he put in a new furnace, water heater, windows, and insulation so he could live there all year round. He said the driveway got interesting in the snow, but that's why he had a four-wheel drive.

"He asked me about the Holmes story again. I told him I liked it but asked why he wanted me to read it. He said he thought I'd like it, and it was a chance to meet with one of the greats. I didn't under-stand this at first, and Macreavy explained, 'You probably couldn't pick up the phone and talk to the president of the United States, the queen of England, or the quarterback of a team that won the Super Bowl last year. But you could talk with Arthur Conan Doyle.'

"I said, 'I didn't talk to him. I read a story he wrote.' Macreavy told me that's because I hadn't asked the question. When I asked him, 'What question?' He looked around at his room full of books. He said, 'Why did he write it? What did Conan Doyle, one of the greatest storytellers ever, find so important in life that he had to write about it?'

"Macreavy said the critical thing to understand about Holmes, Watson, and the criminals they fight is that they all came from one man's mind. Arthur Conan Doyle wanted to show how reason and emotion interact to fight evil. He said Conan Doyle wrote the story because his soul and spirit wanted to meet mine and show me how it's done.

"Macreavy looked for the experience in everything, and he taught me the trick to reading a book is to turn it into an experience. He said he never tried to learn anything. He set out to experience it. It's exhausting, but it's the way to live a whole life. He showed me how to connect with a book and collide with the characters, but it always went back to real people. He thought of reading as practice for the world. As a cop, he said he heard stories all day long that changed depending on who wanted what. He marveled at how different people recounted the same events and said he had to open his mind to understand what he heard.

"When I asked Macreavy where he came up with these ideas, he mentioned a few teachers in school but said he got most of it from his parents. He also said he had two uncles and an aunt who taught him to question everything about books and life. His family had died by then, but he said they taught him to always start with the question 'why.' I asked him how long he'd been with the police, and he had a funny answer. He said he wasn't sure. He said he'd started with the police, but they kept asking him to do things cops usually don't do, and he liked that. I said, 'Like watching kids on community service?'

"I got a laugh out of him, which made me feel good, but he said the things he had in mind had to do with serious stuff, and that's all he said. He didn't elaborate, and he changed the subject. Here's another line I remember. It got me through undergrad. Macreavy said he liked working with me on community service. He said, 'I think you're a good kid. You could be an interesting kid if you were better read.'"

Dr. Williams stopped to top off our coffee cups. He took a tentative sip, and I sipped mine as well. I sat quietly.

He put his cup down. "That's how I met Foraker Macreavy, and that's when I started reading," he said. "I also started looking at art and going to plays. Macreavy taught me I could read what someone wrote or look at a scene someone painted hundreds of years ago and communicate with them across time. I'd ask what they wanted to show me, what they found so important they had to write about it or paint it or sing about it.

"I saw Macreavy around town after that, and I'd go out of my way to say hello. He always remembered me and asked what I had going on. It felt genuine too, more than just friendly, and he never failed to ask what I'd been reading.

"School changed for me after that summer. I gave up worrying about grades, but the less I thought about them, the more they improved. Macreavy told me about that kind of stuff, too. He introduced me to the Zen paradox. That's when death comes before life, where you have to fall to rise, and how you can find freedom in confinement.

"Reading influenced my thinking process, but one event changed my perspective. It came on a Friday night that fall. My father and I ran into Macreavy at a high school football game. He'd taken a shift working as a security guard. We said hello to each other, and I introduced him to my father as the officer who supervised my community service. My father bragged to Macreavy about how I'd taken up reading and improved in school. He told Macreavy I got it together just in time to get into a decent college. He said, 'The last thing I want is my son to wind up a twenty-thousand-dollar-a-year-nothing like a teacher or a cop.'

"I could have died from embarrassment. I thought somehow my father didn't understand he shouldn't say that to a cop while the cop stood there in full uniform. For a moment, I thought Macreavy might not have heard him. He did, of course, and later in life, it occurred to me that it might have been my father's way of getting in a jab. The real irony came years later when we found out Macreavy had millions put aside even then."

"Wait, Patrick," I interrupted. "You say this Officer Macreavy had money?"

"Millions," he answered. "Family money. He gave it away little by little and paid for things to improve people's lives. Then he gave it all away in his will, and everybody got something. After he died and the house went up for auction, I went through his library. The funny part is many of the books we cleared out from the City Hall together that day ended up in a school library in Brooklyn.

"He gave me more than books though. As my high school years ended, he helped me find a direction. We had hamburgers a few times at a restaurant in Jamestown called Jenny's Lunch, and I asked him about what my father said at the football game. He came up with another classic line I'll never forget. He said, 'Your father isn't wrong, but he doesn't understand why he's right.' Macreavy said I should think of life as a fancy dinner, and I'd been invited. He said he knew dinners aren't fun all the time, but he told me a day would come when I'd want to share my soul and spirit, and I'd want people around to share them with. If I didn't accept the invitation, I'd be alone. Macreavy could be dramatic sometimes. He said, 'You're nothing if you don't have anyone to share with.'"

Dr. Williams paused and took a drink of his coffee. "I got such a charge out of that idea," he said. "I followed it into college. I said I didn't know what I wanted to do when I got there, but I did. I went into teaching.

"I went to Fordham, got a BA with a teaching certificate, and took a job at an elementary school in the Bronx. I read 'beat' poems out loud. I lived for those moments when I got to show poor kids famous paintings in museums and open their worlds. I stayed with teaching and went from job to job, looking for the kind of school where I wanted to work. I didn't find it, so I returned and got an administrator's certificate. I tried rebuilding a single school and making it go the way I thought it should. That worked until I ran into district rules. That's when I went back and got the PhD. But these days, I'm spending so much time dealing with political pressures I'm afraid I've lost contact with the kids. I remind myself of my father, and I've got to admit there are times when my career considerations hold the kids back. Now and then, though, something comes along that reminds me of why I got into it in the first place—something like you, Tom Strongtree, contacting me out of the blue."

He smiled and shook his head back and forth slightly. Then he repeated it. He drew in his breath, and as he let it out, he whispered, "'kin' guy..."

"What does that mean?" I asked. "That's the third time you've said that."

He answered with a laugh. "That's another thing I got from Macreavy," he said. "It's something he said, an expression that had a hundred meanings, and everybody who knew him wound up imitating it."

He said, "It started years before I knew him. Macreavy had a summer job working at Jamestown Finishes during his college years. Please excuse the vulgarity here. I'm sure it's nothing you haven't heard before. I'd rather not, but it's part of the expression. You'll see. Macreavy described Jamestown Finishes as an old-time factory that made industrial baking enamels. He told this story about a forklift operator named Blake who would drive around the factory all day complaining about, and I quote, 'the fucking guys around here.' He said that all day, every day about everything repeatedly.

"Well, Macreavy couldn't get over how this guy, Blake, could be so negative about everything so much of the time. He started mimicking Blake and mocking him to his face. Whenever he saw the forklift coming, he'd say, 'The fucking guys around here' to anyone nearby. The other guys got the joke, and they started saying it too. Every time Blake turned a corner on his forklift, he'd hear someone mocking him with his own words. The guys used the expression so many times they shortened it. They left words out and dropped the g. The phrase became 'fuckin' guys.' Then the women in the office civilized it by dropping the f. The phrase morphed into "kin' guys.' It became a term that bonded the group and united everyone against negativity. Blake finally got the message and had a serious talk with himself. The expression became a catchall for anything anyone did wrong, but with a twist. Mistakes became forgivable. If someone spilled some paint, the other guys around would just clean it up and say, 'kin' guy.' It would be even better if you said it with Blake's twangy Midwestern drawl and hung on the last 'eye' sound, as in 'kin' guyyyyyyyyy.' Tremendous. Macreavy turned a negative expression into a company chant and a signal that said all is forgiven. There aren't enough guys like that!"

Patrick Williams laughed aloud, and I couldn't help smiling with him. He said, "Macreavy told everyone that story, and he'd get everyone saying it. He only had one rule. You could never use it in anger." Patrick Williams sat for a moment with his coffee. "No offense brings anger," he said. "All is forgiven.

"Talk about forgiveness and different points of view. When I graduated with the doctorate, Macreavy sent me a 1905 first-edition copy of a collection of stories by O. Henry called *The Four Million*. He marked a story, 'The Gift of the Magi,' with a graduation card. I don't know where you stand on spiritual matters, Tom, but that story brought me back to God. Up to then, the church only confused me with ideas about faith I didn't understand and suffering I'd rather avoid. That story taught me how to be good." Patrick Williams sat quietly again. We'd come to the end of our coffee. He looked tired and distant.

"One last thing," I asked. "Why do you think this Foraker Macreavy had anything to do with the police cards?

"I can't say for sure," he answered. "But I'd bet on it. If you stay with your project, you'll hear more about old Officer Macreavy. He knew everybody in Jamestown."

Dr. Williams paused again. "Thank you, Tom," he said. "Even if you never hear about him again, telling you about Macreavy has helped me more than you know. It reminded me of a few things."

"I'm glad it did. I'm honored to have met you, Patrick. Thanks so much for meeting with me."

The superintendent of schools, Dr. Patrick Williams, PhD, showed me to the door. I'd completed my first interview, and it drained me. When I got to my hotel room that evening, I called Phil Troxel and left a message. I said, "Phil, this is Tom. Please see what you can find out about a policeman named Foraker Macreavy. He worked in Jamestown at about the same time as those kids. Thanks. I'll be in touch."

CHAPTER 3

Joyce Lundquist, Mrs. Joyce Earl: The Woman at the Well

Phil Troxel called after I'd returned from New Jersey and got right to the point. He said, "Coffee. Ten o'clock."

"Okay," I answered. We'd used few words, and the exchange made me feel like a badass. I might be learning to be a cool guy after all. I saw Phil getting off his motorcycle as I pulled into the lot. Cool guys arrive at the same time. Cool guys don't need to talk about where they'll sit. They find a place and deal. I bought two black coffees, walked them over, and put them down on the table along with two twenties, still not a word spoken. He smiled and took the cash, which told me he'd found something about Macreavy. "Thank you much," he said after taking a sip of the hot coffee. "Those addresses working out?"

"Yes," I answered. "You do nice work, my friend. What have you got for me today?"

"Well," Phil began, "talk about a strange dude. You know Foraker Macreavy is dead, right? He died in a bicycle accident almost twenty years ago. He's the last of the Macreavys and the Forakers too, for that matter. The Forakers are his mother's people. Both families go back as far as the colonies. He left millions when he died. A big chunk went to a medical clinic in Buffalo, New York, and he spread the rest of it around to various groups in Jamestown, New York, where the kids and fingerprint cards came from. That's his home-town. Some money went to renovating the family and juvenile court there, and he even left some to his old high school. He hardly left a footprint though—no articles in the paper, no boards of directors, nada. Sometimes super-rich guys keep a low profile because other-wise people ask them for money all the time. Guys like that know how to keep their money out of sight. After high school, he picked up a BA from Western Reserve in Cleveland and married a girl named Karen Carlo. She died young for some reason. The obit in her home-town paper didn't say, but my guess is drugs. After that, he went to the Police Academy in New York City. He worked in New York as a patrolman for three years until his parents died in a car accident. That's when he moved back to Jamestown. From then on, nothing happened, no move, no advancement, no promotion. He worked for the Jamestown Police Department for the rest of his life. He lived at his family's home in Chautauqua County, New York, until he died at age sixty-two. He had a law firm write a will, but they kept it under lock and key until after he died. That's when everyone found out about the money. A firm located in Seattle liquidated the estate. The house and everything in it sold at auction in three days." Phil took a long drink of coffee and let the story soak in. He asked, "Why do you want to know about this guy?"

"I'm not sure," I answered. "But one of the guys, one of the 'caught thirty,' thinks this Officer Macreavy had something to do with the cards and mug shots."

"Why?" asked Phil.

"He didn't know exactly, but he told me the more I talked to peo-ple about the records, the more I'd find out about Officer Macreavy."

Phil said, "I hope you don't find out about any rough stuff."

I answered, "Judging from the guy who told me about him, it didn't seem like that."

"Well, be careful," Phil advised. "Keep your foot near the brake."

"You don't have to say that twice," I agreed.

Phil got up from the table. He said, "That's it for now. I gotta run."

I saluted and said, "Thanks. Talk soon."

He finished his coffee on the way out and tossed the cup in the trash while I sat at the table, wondering who I'd contact next.

I decided I'd try one of the girls. Boys made up most of the list, but I wondered why a young girl would get arrested. When I got home, I picked up the envelope for Joyce Lundquist. Phil noted her married name as Mrs. Joyce Earl. He'd written "business" by her address, a funeral home in Chicago. I updated the letter I used to contact Patrick Williams, but I added,

> I am also interested to know if you are famil-
> iar with a police officer named Foraker Macreavy.

I wrote her address on the envelope and marked it "Personal Correspondence." Like Patrick Williams, Mrs. Joyce Earl sent her response by email, but unlike Patrick Williams, I don't think I made her angry. Maybe mentioning Macreavy's name made a difference.

> To: Thomas Strongtree
> From: Joyce Earl
> Subject: Your letter
>
> Hello, Mr. Strongtree,
>
> Yes, I remember that. I must have been six-
> teen at the time.
>
> Yes, I'm familiar with Officer Macreavy, the policeman in Jamestown who died and gave away all that money. I remember him personally because he supervised my community service. He treated me kindly and pointed me in the right direction.
>
> If you make it to Chicago, I'd be happy to speak with you. I work for the Kibler and Peters Funeral Homes. We can meet at the Bridgeport location.
>
> Please call to make an appointment.

Mrs. Earl had included a link to the website for the address. I called her, and we set an appointment for the following Wednesday afternoon. She explained she and her husband worked for a group of funeral homes, and the Bridgeport location would be the most convenient for her.

Bridgeport looked to be an upscale neighborhood in Chicago. I saw a mix of newer buildings between renovated older homes, and I had no trouble finding Kibler and Peters. Fresh paint made the house look clean and bright, and the grounds had been carefully maintained. A crisp hedge surrounded the clipped lawn. A receptionist led me to a comfortable room with a mahogany meeting table and matching chairs, most likely where families met to discuss funeral arrangements. The receptionist offered coffee and left to get some. I'd been in the room for no more than a few minutes when a pleasant-looking woman opened the door and greeted me with a warm smile and firm handshake. I knew from her card she'd be forty-eight years old.

"Hello, Mr. Strongtree," she said. "I'm Joyce Earl."

Mrs. Joyce Earl possessed the perfect demeanor for a funeral home. Without saying a word, her bright eyes and reassuring smile communicated "I know you've lost someone dear to you." The pocket of her charcoal-gray business suit jacket sported an embroidered Kibler and Peters corporate logo. She wore the jacket over a white blouse, a mid-length skirt, and black heels. She immediately shed the jacket and draped it over the back of one of the chairs. A pocket on her blouse carried the same embroidery.

I answered, "Glad to meet you, Mrs. Earl. Please, call me Tom."

"Okay, Tom," she agreed. "And you, please call me Joyce."

She gestured to a chair at the table and said, "Have a seat."

She repositioned a chair on the same side of the table. A moment later, the receptionist reentered, carrying a tray with coffee in a carafe and two cups. Joyce Earl thanked the receptionist, and while the two women poured and arranged the coffee, I dug in my backpack and took out the envelope with the card and photo. I assumed she would be anxious to see it. I handed it to her after the receptionist left and asked for permission to record our conversation on my phone. She nodded in agreement.

Joyce Earl opened the envelope and removed the card and photo. She looked at them for a long minute. Then she said, "He called it right. We don't know how beautiful we are at that age."

"Excuse me?" I asked.

She answered, "You know that Officer Macreavy you wanted to know about? He said we're all beautiful when we're young, and now I see what he meant."

"I think that's right," I agreed.

Joyce looked back at the picture and the card.

After another minute, I asked, "Do you mind telling me what the police arrested you for, Joyce?"

"Shoplifting," she said, stating a fact. "I'd taken a small cosmetics case from Bigelow's Department Store downtown."

For the moment, I wondered if the whole pack of records might be for kids caught shoplifting. Later I found this not to be the case.

"Yeah, the town had some policy that made swiping stuff a big deal." She said, "The police fingerprinted me, and they took a mug shot. I even had to go to court."

"What happened in court?" I asked.

"Well, even before my hearing, a lawyer told me I'd only have a juvenile record. He said they would seal it when I turned eighteen. Which brings up a question, Tom." She held the card toward me. "How did you get this again?"

"As I said in my letter, I bought it at a flea market," I answered. "And that's part of what I'm trying to find out. How could some random guy like me buy police records? I'm also beginning to wonder about Officer Macreavy. Do you think he might have held out the cards and photos?"

"Oh, I have no idea," she answered. "But I remember Officer Macreavy from the community service."

"You got community service for shoplifting?" I asked.

"Yes," she said.

Joyce Earl took a breath. "Okay, here's what happened," she said. "After they arrested me, I had to go to juvenile court. The judge scolded me, and the store made its point. They wanted everyone to know 'shoplifters will be prosecuted to the full extent of the law!' My

36

father had to pay $100 in court fees, and my folks didn't have $100 to waste on me at the time. It took months to get over it, and I felt terrible the whole time. I also had to do six hours of community service, picking up trash by the river."

"Picking up trash?" I asked.

"Yeah," she answered. "An environmental group concerned about litter along the Chadakoin put together volunteers and people assigned to community service to help with a cleanup."

"What's the Chadakoin?" I asked.

"You wrote in your letter that the records you found came from Jamestown," she said. "Jamestown is near Chautauqua Lake, and the Chadakoin River is the outlet for Chautauqua Lake. It's an Indian name. The river runs right through the middle of town. Jamestown started as a trading post on the Chadakoin, and when the factories came along, they used it for waterpower. Anyway, I had to spend six hours one Saturday with Officer Macreavy and a group of young people picking up junk along the riverbank. Macreavy said he and his family owed something to the river, and he hated seeing people throw trash into it.

"The group started talking and laughing as we got to know each other, and one of the other girls asked me why I had to be there. I told her about the makeup kit, and the girl asked me why I'd ever take a makeup kit. That sounded like an odd question. Did she mean it was okay to steal stuff but not makeup kits? I didn't know what to say, so I gave her a funny answer. I said, 'Because I wanted to look pretty.'

"That's when Macreavy chimed in. He said, 'Forget the makeup. You young people don't know how beautiful you are.'

"Everyone got quiet. We thought about this grown man being out on the river with a bunch of kids. One of the guys in the group must have known him from before, and he said, 'Hey, Officer Macreavy, no flirting with the prisoners!'

"Macreavy laughed at that. He said, 'First of all, none of you are prisoners. If you don't like what we're doing today, you can go home, and the city will think up something even more fun for next weekend. Second, if this young lady had to wait for one of you guys to say something nice, she'd be here until the river ran dry,' and everyone laughed. Macreavy turned out to be a good guy. He didn't mean anything weird about young people being beautiful. He meant it. He 'wore it on his sleeve,' as my father used to say.

"Later that day, I asked him, 'Do you think a river could ever run dry?'

"He said it wouldn't happen anytime soon, but it could. He talked about the sun's radiation and floods and deserts. He told me if I wanted to know about the local climate and water resources, I should get to know the people at the Chautauqua County Watershed Conservation Conservancy. He said they knew more about the lake than anybody."

Joyce Earl looked at me and said, "You might laugh, Tom, but that's what I did. That's why I said Macreavy sent me in the right direction. Until then, no one took me seriously enough to talk to me about 'watershed conservation.' Maybe they didn't think I'd under-stand 'conservancy,' but Officer Macreavy assumed I would. He spoke to me as an adult. I didn't know anybody else who cared about the river and that kind of thing, but his enthusiasm got me interested. I wanted to learn more about the river that ran through my town, so I went to the library and looked up the Watershed Conservation Conservancy.

"They had an office in Celeron. That's a town right where the lake meets the river. They took up the first floor of an old house and gave out information about the lake and the region around it. I went to the house and got to know some lady volunteers. They enjoyed having a high school girl around. We gave out water conservation brochures at local town picnics, and we had a table at the county fair. They always invited me to go along, and I went with them whenever I could. It got to be my activity. While other kids played sports or music, I went to meetings for local government and conservation groups. I learned about wastewater facilities around the lake and how the water department serviced the city. I felt like I belonged to some-thing meaningful.

"As high school ended, though, I felt lost. My parents told me I should get a job, but they didn't say what I should do. My friends didn't have much of an idea either. Then one of the ladies who worked for the water department said they had openings for young people to help in the office. I'd work part-time for the Jamestown Board of Public Utilities while attending Jamestown Community College. I could stay on and take the civil service exam, and I'd be the first to know if a full-time job opened up. That sounded like a great plan."

"Well, you're not working for the Utilities Department now," I observed. "What happened?"

"Ha!" Joyce said, "I'd been at the Utilities Office and going to school for about two years. I took business courses at the college and learned how the city did billing. Sometimes when the regular workers went out to lunch or had a day off, I'd answer phones and fill in. On one of those days, a guy walked in. He's frantic. He looked at the nameplate on my desk and said, 'Joyce, I have a problem. My water bill, my electric bill, and my gas bill all came on the same day. A spark caused an explosion and a flood. Now I want to know who will buy me a new mailbox!'

"I sat at my desk, looked him square in the face, and gave him my best deadpan. I said, 'I've heard that joke five times already this month, but I'll give you best delivery.' He acted disappointed like he couldn't believe I'd heard the joke before, and I told him he should take his best-delivery prize and go home happy. He stood by my desk and gave a speech accepting 'best delivery' like an academy award. Then I added, 'Best delivery this week.'

"He stopped the acceptance speech and looked at the floor. I thought I made him feel bad for a second, but then he got serious and said he actually did have a problem. I knew he felt better when he said he could tell, just from looking at me, that I might be the only person in Jamestown who could solve it. He made me smile. I couldn't help it. He told me he represented 'the Reverend Don Skinner's Refreshing Revival,' opening at the Clearfield Grace Church on Miller Hilltop Road in two days. The problem had to do with the water bill. The church said they paid it, but the water department said they hadn't and cut them off.

"He got excited again. He said, 'Now how is a revival supposed to revive people without water? How are we going to cook in the kitchen? How are we going to make coffee for all those people? Do you know what it's like when several hundred people are looking for a refreshing revival and don't get one? If we don't have water in the church, how can we even baptize the people, for Christ's sake?'

"I remember looking at him, and I'm sure my eyes opened wide. I said, 'Wait, what did you say? You can't say—' But he cut me off with a big toothy grin. He said, 'That's a double entendre. Except this time, it's different. Usually, the second meaning goes to the crude, but this time it goes to the good. Bet you haven't heard another one of those this week.'

"I asked him how long it took him to come up with that. He said he dreamed it up on the way over, and we had our first laugh together. About baptism, of all things. Who would have guessed? He explained he traveled with the revival show, and they did have a problem with the water over at the church. He said he had to get it straightened out or the show wouldn't go on. After his antics, I didn't know what to believe, so I looked into the church's account. Sure enough, it said the church owed $395. I told the funny man if he paid the bill, they'd have water for all the coffee they wanted to drink with plenty left for baptisms.

"He said he came prepared and took out a roll of twenties. He said he always got to the scene of the Reverend Don Skinner's Refreshing Revival a few days early. He called it 'advance work.' 'Make straight the way,' he said and looked at me to see if I picked up his Bible joke. 'Got it,' I acknowledged. He said he didn't have time to get involved in church politics. Somebody probably goofed up, but he had a cash budget to open the show on time whenever this kind of thing happened, and something always did. He proudly proclaimed that the Reverend Don Skinner never asked a church to repay him. When the show closed and the dust settled, everyone would be down the road dealing with the next catastrophe.

"With a grand flourish, he took a roll of cash out of his pocket, paid the entire amount with twenty twenty-dollar bills, and said, 'Joyce, my name is Austin Earl. Turn me on, baby!' I looked him straight in the eye, gave him half a smile, and said, 'I already have, Austin.' I got the best of him with that one. He gave me a slight bow and said, 'Touché.' I saw him start for the door but hesitate just before he reached it. He turned back and said, 'It would be great to see you at the revival,' and added, 'There's no admission, only a free-will offering to pay the utilities.' He took a pack of fliers out of his other pocket and gave me one. He said he'd look for me and meet me after.

"I'll tell you, in those days, I had no shortage of company when I wanted it, but Austin made me laugh, and he came from the world outside of Jamestown. I got the water turned on at the Clearfield Church and made up my mind I'd go to the revival. The flier said it started at seven thirty in the evening. That gave me enough time to get home from the water department, have something to eat, and change out of my work clothes. At first I didn't know what to wear to a revival, but I kept a plain blue dress that I'd wear now and then, nothing too short or too long. I just wanted to blend in, see the show, and have a few laughs after with Austin.

"I got home, made a sandwich, and changed quickly. I threw on the dress and added a pair of black shoes with heels to make me look dressed up. I thought I wouldn't need a coat that evening, but I just took along a white sweater. I brushed my hair, grabbed my shoulder bag, and shot out the door. I drove over to the church feeling excited. The parking lot had almost run out of space, and I remember thinking, *Good turnout. Good for you, Reverend Don Skinner, and good for you, Austin!* The Revival put a Psalm on a banner by the church door so that everybody could see it from the parking lot. I still say it all the time. Would you like to hear it?"

"Yes," I answered. "Please."

Joyce recited, "Honor His name with Hallelujahs, you who seek God. Live a happy life! Keep your eyes on God, watch for his works. Be alert for signs of his presence. Remember the world, wonders he made, miracles and verdicts he's rendered." Joyce paused after she finished. She said, "Austin told me he put that banner up before every show."

She continued. "As I walked up to the church, I could hear a band playing inside. I went in and sat off to the side. I started looking around for Austin, and I laughed when I saw him playing bass in the band. It didn't sound like church music either, more like a rock group. They wore these crazy costumes too, matching high-waisted blue and yellow striped suits with white collars and puffy pants. Red piping trimmed the sleeves of their jackets, and they wore black berets. I found out later they were supposed to be Swiss Guards like at the Vatican, and they looked great. You could tell the guys wanted to be there. They had smiles on their faces and got everyone in the church smiling too. You couldn't help it.

"The band stopped, and a deep voice came over the speakers. The voice asked us to please rise for prayer, and we all stood up. The voice asked God to bless our meeting and announced the entrance of the Reverend Don Skinner. The band started again, and Reverend Don came in from the back of the church, dressed in a dark suit. He took long strides and walked up to the altar. The band quieted down, and the reverend directed us to sit again.

"He put his hands on the sides of the pulpit and lifted his voice over the people. He said, 'Ladies and gentlemen, there's been a mix-up in our program for this evening. We should have made this clear in our advertisements. Tonight's revival is for sinners only. If any of you haven't sinned, you're supposed to come to the meeting tomorrow night.' I heard some nervous laughter around the church. Real laughter broke out when a man in front started to get up, and the woman sitting next to him pulled him down by the sleeve.

"Then the Reverend Don Skinner did something else I don't think anyone expected. I heard him do it many times in the years that followed, and it always choked me up. He said, 'I've asked the band to play a song I think you'll like. It's one of my favorites. Listen to this song, and ask yourself, "Who's talking? Is it a man talking to a woman or a woman talking to a man? Is it a parent talking to a child or a child talking to a parent? Is it someone talking to God, or is it God talking to that someone? If you listen carefully, you'll hear it's all of us talking to each other and to God, and God talking to all of us. It's all happening at the same time, and each of us understands every word. That's the mystery. That's grace. That's the glory of soul and spirit." The guitar player stepped forward to sing, and the Reverend Don Skinner sat in a chair. The band played a version of Psalm 139, and as often as I've heard it, I never get tired of it. I walked down the aisle to that song when we got married."

Once again, Joyce recited from memory, "You've searched me, and you know me. When I sit and when I stand. You know me from far away. Know the way I find my way, I know you stand behind me. Your hand is on my shoulder. Where did all of this come from? It's more than I'll ever know."

Joyce sat quietly for a moment and took a sip of her coffee. "When the music stopped," she said, "no one made a sound, and the Reverend Don Skinner retook his position at the pulpit. He said, 'Something happened this week that doesn't usually happen when preparing for our Refreshing Revival. We found out the water department turned off the water here at the church.'

"This made me nervous," she said. "I didn't know what he had in mind. The Reverend Don Skinner assured us the situation had been resolved, but he said that got him 'to thinkin' 'bout water.' He said, 'Water is all around us. It's in every cell of our bodies, even in the air we breathe. It's on rooftops when it rains and in wash buckets when we mop the kitchen floor. Even if we say we don't want it, we can't live without it.' The Reverend Don Skinner asked us to imagine what a person would look like if they hadn't had water for a few days. He said, 'Grace is the living water that brings glory to God and meaning to our lives, even when we think we don't need it, or don't want it, or think we've done something wrong and don't deserve it.'

"The reverend asked us to remember a time when we stood by the kitchen sink on a hot summer afternoon and filled a tall glass with cold clear water. He asked us to remember how good we felt when we drank that water. He told us we could have that feeling forever by accepting the living water of grace. He brought up the idea that water could take all forms—hard ice, steam jets, clouds in the sky, heavy humidity, lakes, rivers, or glaciers ten thousand feet deep and ten thousand years old."

Joyce smiled at me and said, "Tom, the reverend had moved into my neighborhood, and I couldn't get enough of it."

Her eyes opened wide at the memory of the evening, and she continued, "Then the reverend said, 'Now I actually do have two different messages for you folks tonight. The first is for all of you who don't believe in God. I'm not gonna argue with you. I'm not a man who claims to have all kinds of fancy reasons and proofs for God. I've found the more I argue, the more people pull away. No, I'm a man of God, and I'm telling you God exists. It's that simple. God created us, and when he did, he gave us all a piece of Himself. We call that our soul. He also gave us a spirit. That's what we call our will to do whatever we want. When those pieces come together and line up, there's a spark, and we call that spark the Holy Spirit. Now listen, friends, it's the Holy Spirit that guides us. Let's not make it so darn complicated. Any more than that is beyond us. Yes, there is a God, and now I'm also gonna tell you how to talk to Him. Yes, talk to him. That's what us preachers with the big floppy Bibles and all them every-week church-goers call "prayer." Say this. Say, "God, I'm not sure about you, but my wife, or my husband, or my friend brought me to the Reverend Don Skinner's Refreshing Revival, and the Reverend Don Skinner said you've been tryin' to talk to me for a while now. Please give it another try." Then sit down, shut up, and listen. God will find a way to talk to you and only you. It will be in a way or a language only you can understand. He will say something to you that no one else has ever said. Ninety-nine times out of a hundred, it'll have something to do with the people you live with or work with, but you'll know it when you hear it. Now when that happens, and I say "when" because I know it will happen, ask God, "What do you want me to do today?" He'll tell you, and the two of you take it from there.'

"The Reverend Don Skinner paused and looked over the people looking back at him in rapt silence. 'Now I have a message for all of you who'd tell me you're believers. Harsh judgment is what separates us. Watch your contempt. And CYA. That stands for challenge your assumptions.' He told us the big mistake comes when people think they're doing God a favor or lending God a helping hand. The Reverend had a great line, and he tossed it out over the crowd. He said, 'Don't tell God what He has to do. You just do what he told you to do.' Then he landed it. He said, 'Come hell or high water!'

"He finished by asking us to stand and pray. The reverend told us prayer is simple. He said all we had to do is think about God, and

God Himself would help us come up with something to say. He said, 'God gave us a glorious gift, the gift of life and grace. All we have to do is drink it in.' The Reverend Don Skinner said, 'Lord, thank you for bringing us together tonight to share the evening with you and with each other. Help us find our way and deliver us from our loneliness.'"

Joyce said, "Some of the people from the Revival went up and down the isles giving away prayer cards. Reverend Don said, 'Reach out and take a card. Put it in your silverware drawer or someplace where you'll see it again every day.'"

Joyce said, "The card had the same Psalm 105 from the parking lot printed next to a pencil sketch of an eye."

Joyce Earl recited again, "Honor His name with Hallelujahs, you who seek God. Live a happy life! Keep your eyes on God, watch for his works. Be alert for signs of his presence. Remember the world, wonders he made, miracles and verdicts he's rendered."

She said, "While they gave out the prayer cards, the band picked up their instruments. The reverend ended his message by shouting, 'Glory be to God, and glory be to the Holy Spirit that lives between us!' The band broke into an old Beatles song and had us up on our feet singing to everyone around us.

"The Reverend Don Skinner put on a great show. I took a place at the altar call and promised to search my heart and live the life God wanted. I put a twenty in the collection and thought about how Austin would probably give it away next week so the revival could open at another church. I thought that wouldn't be so bad. The refreshing revival ended, and I sat waiting for him as the crowd cleared out. When I saw him, I jumped up and hugged him.

"'Wow!' I said. 'You didn't tell me you were in the band. What a great show!' He said he had a great time playing the music. They got paid for carrying the amplifiers.

"We took my car and went out for ice cream. We sat in a booth, and Austin regaled me with stories from the road with the Refreshing Revival. He hadn't changed from his band costume, and I kept thinking he could be the modern-day boy who ran away with the circus. We must have looked like a crazy couple trying to make each other laugh.

"Around eleven, I told Austin I had to get home. The revival crew had an RV parked near the church, and I told him I'd drop him off there. We got in my car, and I started it. I had my foot on the brake and shifted into reverse to back out of the parking spot. I put my hand on the seat behind his head and looked over my shoulder. I saw him looking at me, and the next thing I knew, he kissed me. I didn't want the car to start moving, so I kept my foot jammed on the brake, but I also didn't want to stop kissing him long enough to shift into park, so I managed the lever with my left hand. Ridiculous!"

Joyce broke from her story. She said, "Tom, I'm glad Austin isn't here now. Whenever we tell our story, he takes over and gets everybody laughing. I admit he's better at it than I am, but the problem is then I don't get to tell my side of it."

Joyce leaned away from the table slightly. She crossed her legs and took a sip of her coffee. She smiled at me and said, "It's my turn this time, and I'll tell you how I saw it."

"Okay," I said.

"So I got the car in park," she said, "and I finally broke away from him. I asked him if he wanted to come to my apartment, and he said yes. We drove to my place, where I lived in the upper half of a two-story house on McKinley Street. I took him by the hand and led him up the stairs. I took my hand back to turn the key in the lock, letting him into the kitchen. He looked around, took off the blazer from his costume, and hung it on the back of one of the chairs in my kitchen. I don't know why, but he left the beret on. I took off my sweater and hung it on another chair.

"He reached for me and kissed me again. We both started working on the blue dress. I stepped out of it with my shoes and tossed it on my sweater. When I changed earlier, I didn't think I'd need to wear showy underwear to go to a revival, but my everyday things didn't matter to Austin. The thirsty man drank me in. He kissed me hard. He had his left hand on my bottom while his right arm held me to him. At other times when I found myself in a situation like this, I had a thing I did. I reached around his back and embraced him. I held my breasts to his chest and pressed all of myself against all of him. I leaned in and whispered in his ear. I said, 'There's something I want to ask you, and it's important to me.'

"'Okay,' he answered back. In as pleasant a voice as I could manage, I asked, 'Will you please wear a condom?' He froze. He hit the pause button and backed away. I said, 'I'm sorry, but I don't know you, and you don't know me. Please, let's be safe. If you don't have one, I do. They're in a drawer in the bathroom.' Austin released me and slowly sat on the chair where he'd left his blazer. He looked at me and said, 'Please sit down, Joyce.'

"I took the other chair, and Austin said he couldn't go through with it. He said it wasn't about the condom. He said when I told him I wanted to ask him something important, it came to him in a flash. He said he'd been spending his life maintaining separation. It thrilled him when I told him I wanted to ask him something important. He thought it would be about someplace I wanted to go or something I wanted to do. He thought 'important' meant an idea. He wanted to hear about something we could do together, not something that would keep us apart. He said he wanted to imagine me sitting at my desk in the water department. He said it's like in the sixty-third Psalm when the guy says 'see your face before me as I lay in my bed.'

"I knew what he meant. I could have said the same thing, but it scared me, so I deflected. 'Great!' I said. 'Now that we've put away the condoms, lets everybody take out our Bibles.' Austin didn't say anything—no snappy comeback this time. He said he wanted me to be important to him, and he wanted to be important to me."

Joyce chuckled. She said, "Well, God got the laugh that time. He put us together at my kitchen table—me in a big white bra and granny panties, and him in a clown suit. He looked like an over-grown organ grinder monkey with the beret, and we're talking about the meaning of 'important.' I offered sex, and he told me he'd rather care about me. I started laughing uncontrollably. I threw up my arms, opened my hands, and shouted, 'Okay, I'll marry you!'

"We both looked at each other. Neither of us could believe what I'd said. It just came out, and we sat looking at each other, stunned. Austin said, 'Really? You mean it?' That's how it started, Tom, and we've been married for almost twenty years now."

Joyce and I smiled at each other. I raised my coffee cup to salute.

Joyce said, "I didn't believe it at first, and, no, we didn't do anything that night. I put my dress and shoes on and drove him to the church. I thought Austin might wake up in the morning and regret the whole night, or maybe I would, but we didn't. The Revival had another show the following night, and I went to see it again. By the time I got there, the band and the whole crew knew about it. They couldn't stop congratulating us, but the Refreshing Revival packed up and left the next day. Austin promised it would all work out.

"He called from outside of Boston, where the Revival had its next show, then from Philadelphia. Two weeks later, a letter showed up in my mailbox. It went like that for two years. He got to see the country, and I finished school. Now and then we'd meet up, and we both put money aside. He wrote fabulous letters. I still have them. They're in a box, and I hope the kids save them after we're gone."

"You have kids?" I asked.

"Yes," she said. "A girl and a boy. Our daughter is looking at colleges now, and our son is starting high school."

"And how did you get to Chicago?" I asked her.

"Well," Joyce said, "a day came when the Reverend Don Skinner decided to retire. He'd been on the road for most of his life and found a farmhouse in North Carolina where he and his wife decided to 'set up their last tent.' Over the years, people often asked the Reverend to preach at funerals, and Austin saw the funeral business as an opportunity. He said we could find life in death. He connected with Kibler and Peters at the right time. It's a national group, and they were expanding into Chicago. They sent him to a school for embalming and mortuary science as long as he promised to work for the company for five years. He signed the agreement two days before the revival put on its last show. Austin moved his suitcase to a small apartment in Chicago and began to see funeral work as a calling. The skill in the funeral business is showing respect while arranging details during hard times. It's about looking for the joy in remembering a person's life, and that's Austin through and through. I moved into his crazy old apartment, and we finally got to be together all the time. We had a small wedding where we walked from our apartment to the church. The Reverend Don Skinner married us and then we walked to a restaurant where we had a reception. Some of his old friends from the revival came. His mother came from Minnesota, and my parents and friends from Jamestown came. A few people at Austin's new job said they wouldn't miss it, and just like that, we'd started our new life. Kibler and Peters also needed someone with the business and computer skills I'd learned at the water department, so they hired me as well. I work at the main office, keeping track of six different funeral homes in the Chicago area.

"That's about it, Tom," she said. "Pretty boring after that, but it's great here. We found a safe place to raise our kids, but anything you want is here in Chicago. Austin's happy, and after all these years, he now has an encyclopedic knowledge of hundreds of deaths and funeral jokes. I tell him he's got a knock-'em-dead delivery, and after he's had a few beers at a barbecue, he 'kills.' I've got to say, Tom, there's no one better at nailing a coffin joke."

Joyce got me going. She kept up the rapid-fire, and I started laughing. I could imagine how much fun Austin and Joyce would be at a backyard barbecue.

Joyce let up and tipped her coffee cup to finish the last of it. She said, "Austin can get everyone laughing so hard they stop eating and talking to each other. Everyone stands around the grill laughing, and whoever's hosting the party won't know what to do. They ask me to get him to slow down. It's embarrassing, and I have to tell him to let everyone catch their breath.

"I never heard Austin complain about leaving the road. It ran its course. He does good work here. He understands and truly helps people say goodbye. When the service is over, everyone feels like getting on with life, and that's how it should be."

A young man in a gray suit like hers knocked on the door to the meeting room. He stuck his head in, and Joyce said, "Duty calls, Tom. I'm going to have to break off for now."

"Joyce," I said. "I can't tell you how enjoyable meeting you has been—what a fabulous story.

Joyce Lundquist, now Mrs. Joyce Earl, waved the fingerprint card and photo toward me and laughed. She said, "Now that I look back on it, I suppose I'm glad I got caught taking that makeup kit. I can't wait to show this to Austin tonight."

I had an idea as I got back to my car. I searched on my phone for the song she told me about. The music began, and I turned onto the street to drive home. I thought about young people and how beautiful they are.

CHAPTER 4

Lee Pridemore: The Prodigal Son

After returning from Chicago, I went back to the stack for another envelope. I've described the cards and photos as having to do with teenagers from Jamestown, New York. However, one of the cards didn't fit either detail, which intrigued me. The card for Lee Pridemore had him as twenty-four years old at the time of his arrest. His photo showed sunken eyes and a vacant stare. The stringy hair that hung down to the collar of his T-shirt and his dirty beard didn't look like a fashion choice. The second detail that didn't fit interested me even more. His card came from New Orleans, Louisiana.

When I checked for Lee Pridemore's current address, I saw Phil Troxel had written "deceased" next to his name. At first, I thought I'd have to pick another envelope and move on, but then I had an idea. Next to Lee's name, Phil had written "Ron Pridemore, older brother," with a Jamestown address. That told me Lee might have something to do with Jamestown after all. I wrote to Ron Pridemore and asked to meet with him about his younger brother. While trying to word the letter appropriately, I almost forgot to ask about Macreavy. I did, though, and sure enough, he figured into this story also.

I dropped the letter in the mail, but a response took a long time. I didn't hear back for close to eight months. After a few weeks, I assumed there wouldn't be a response, so I went on and had three other successful interviews. However, none of those permitted me to record our conversations, nor would they allow me to retell their stories. I have given my word, and I will not.

Checking the mailbox one day, I found a letter with a return address from Pridemore Homes, Jamestown, New York. I couldn't wait to open it. The envelope contained an eighteen-page typed letter. I looked at it quickly and realized it had to do with Lee Pridemore, but I didn't read it immediately. I refolded it and put it back in the envelope. I wanted to give it my full attention that night after supper. My wife made pork chops and green beans that evening, and I had a large cup of coffee for dessert. After we finished, I took the letter out of its envelope again and began to read.

Alex Pridemore
Jamestown, NY
Dear Mr. Strongtree,

My name is Alex Pridemore. I am responding to the letter you sent my uncle, Ron, concerning his brother, Lee. Unfortunately, Ron is not able to respond. Perhaps you are unaware that Fenton Manor, where you sent your letter to Ron, is a nursing home here in Jamestown. Ron is a patient in the dementia unit, and the disease has progressed to the stage where he is unresponsive. Fenton Manor passed your letter on to me.

As the last family member living locally, I make it a point to see him at least once a week. Sometimes I wonder why, but I visit anyway. My grandfather would have wanted it that way. Initially, I planned to send a brief note telling what I knew of Lee's contact with the law, but the more I wrote, the more I remembered. I wrote and rewrote my recollections several times to get the sequences right. This letter is the result. No doubt, it's more than you're interested in, but remembering the events of our lives and coming to terms with them in writing has been a healing and redemptive experience for me.

After World War II, my grandfather, Jason Pridemore, started a construction company, Pridemore Homes. (You can take pride in a Pridemore Home!) My grandfather may have been the happiest man I ever met. He went through life with the joy of a man who couldn't believe his good luck. During those years, everyone in America wanted to settle down and buy a house, so his building business took off. He might have been in the right spot at the right time, but he worked for his success, which didn't give him much time to socialize. He married late, but he got a good one. I owe so much of my life to my grandfather and grandmother. At the end of the baby boom, the couple had two sons, and I can't tell you how much he wanted to be with those boys. Even if he'd been at a job site all day, he tried to be home for dinner most nights. And he got to their baseball games, too, even if he had to return to the office to do paperwork until midnight.

His sons, Ron and Lee, grew up with hammers and saws in their hands. While my grandfather and his crew built the houses, the boys always had jobs to do, even when they were small. They became excellent craftsmen in their own right, which pleased my grandfather to no end. Ron, the older brother, could frame a house dead plum using a circular saw, a hammer, and a four-foot level. He measured everything, and when he'd finished, the house wouldn't be off by more than a sixteenth of an inch from one side to the other. Lee, the younger brother, specialized in trim. For him, good carpentry meant more than solid construction. He believed Pridemore homes had to look beautiful too. Lee could make kitchen cabinets feel light, clean, and comfortable. His hardwood floors never squeaked, and somehow he could match grain so well that his built-in bookcases looked like they grew from a tree. He knew almost everything about moldings, tray ceilings, picture windows, staircases, and fireplace mantles. The brothers had high expectations, but they differed in how they achieved their tremendous level of quality. Ron demanded it. Lee coaxed it.

The father and the two sons made a formidable team. They each took different parts of the business. My grandfather sold the ideas, Ron supervised the construction, and Lee finished the projects. I've restored and renovated some of their work from over fifty years ago. They built fine homes, and I smile every time I uncover one of the creative solutions they found to solve a construction problem they encountered.

Things changed after Lee turned 21. This is where it starts to get fuzzy. I've pieced the story together over the years, but the reports don't differ radically, so I feel sure enough in my understanding to draw an outline. Lee started drinking. I couldn't say when, but everyone thought it started after he turned 18. He'd have a few beers with the guys on the construction crews at the end of the day. I don't know this for a fact, but my guess is one night, one of the guys offered him something else. I don't know what drug. He never told me, but that night, or whenever it was, he took his first step down a long hard road.

The story sounds like it might have come from a magazine article. Lee deteriorated over two or three years. He couldn't stay up with the work. The family tried to keep it a secret, but they lost jobs because of him. They tried everything to help him, but none of it worked. Lee turned into a destructive tornado in the center of the family and the business.

A harrowing night came when a problem showed up at a repair site. One of the first places my grandfather built right after the war needed new gutters and downspouts. Because of their copper content, the old ones had scrap value. Whatever money they brought as scrap would go into new aluminum replacements. The homeowner called my grandfather and complained about guys working late and making so much noise taking the old gutters off the house. My grandfather knew no one should be at the place that late, so he drove over to have a look. He found someone had stripped the copper from the home.

The next day, he called the roofers, the exterior trim carpenters, the painters, and the other trades who may have taken the old copper. No one knew anything about it. When my grandfather called the scrapyard, they said they had taken the gutters in that morning. When my grandfather told the yard the gutters were stolen property, the yard said they made a Polaroid of every significant transaction and called the police. My grandfather met the police at the scrapyard to look at the picture.

His heart broke into dozens of pieces as he looked at that picture. Lee had turned his back on his family and burned the business for 200 dollars salvage. When my grandfather and Ron checked the office, they found the petty cash missing, and the company safe cleared out also. Pridemore Homes often used cash to get the best prices on materials, and when they checked with the bank, they found Lee had taken 1000 dollars earlier that morning.

A detective from Jamestown tracked Lee as far as Colorado, and the police in Denver said they'd pick him up if they could find him. A few days later, they called and said they found his truck abandoned, but no sign of Lee. That's the last they heard of him for three years.

No one knew what happened to Lee, and the world didn't see him as a lost son or a lost brother. The detective described it as an unfortunate but all too regular event. He put the whole incident into a single sentence. He said, "Another guy gets into drugs and steals a pocket full of dollars."

The detective also said that the theft might help in Lee's case. Typically, searching for a missing person over 21 is low priority, especially if drugs are involved, but he figured Lee would likely get in trouble again. That would trip an outstanding warrant. My grandfather and grandmother worried about their son every minute of those years.

Lee had gone to New Orleans and used his carpentry skills to stay out of sight. He worked day labor and slept at drug houses. He'd stay drunk and stoned for as long as his money held. When it ran out, he'd hang around job sites and talk about building houses until someone listened to him. They'd reckon he knew something about construction, hire him, and pay him under the table. He'd show up long enough to get paid, and then he'd be gone again. Sometime during those years, he met Deshauna, my mother.

Because I've never been diagnosed with any significant mental defect, I believe my mother stayed away from drugs as long as she carried me.

After I came along, though, she dropped me off with her mother, my Grandma Lola. After that, my mother picked up the drugs again, and I never got to know her. She'd come around looking for money now and then, but she and Grandma Lola had terrible fights. I remember once Grandma Lola yelled at her, "Why don't you send him up to your big-deal, white man in New York City?" By four or five, I figured out 'him' meant me.

Sometimes Grandma Lola had boyfriends, but she never had a job. I stayed on a cot in a room off the kitchen and couldn't come out when a boyfriend came to the house. Grandma Lola and I shared cans of food. Sometimes she brought pizza and loaves of old bread from a place down the street. I think she may have received assistance or food stamps because now and then, she'd come home with cereal and a quart of milk. I also remember blocks of cheese. She died a month after my seventh birthday.

I'm sure there's more, but that's all I remember of those days. I never went to school and can't account for the time. I recall a day in February when a man came to the house looking for me. I remember February because one of the other kids laughed at how I pronounced it. I recognized the man because he'd been to the house before. He told me my Grandma Lola died at her friend's house, and my mother had died a year before that. He said I had to live with my father and told me to pack my things. I had two sweatshirts. I had one on and put the other in a plastic bag. When he asked me if that's all I had, I said, "yes." I remember he looked down at me and shook his head.

I asked him if I had to go to New York City to live with my father. He explained that whenever anyone said New York to Grandma Lola, she thought they meant New York City. The man said before my mother died, she told him my father had not come from New York City. He came from the other side of the state. The man seemed sure of himself, so I went along, but it confused me. I didn't know anything about states and cities at the time. The man drove me to his house and told me to wait in the car. Sitting there alone, I felt as frightened as I ever have. I cried. The man came out of his house carrying a jacket. He tossed it into the car, and it landed on my lap. He told me I should take it, and I still have it. He said it's cold in New York, and I'd need it. The jacket's extra-large. I could wrap it around me like a blanket, which is what I did in the coming days. It's a souvenir team jacket from the New Orleans Saints. Years later, I had it pressed and preserved. I want to be buried in that jacket. I want to wrap the saints around me on my final journey too.

The man must have seen me crying, but he didn't let on. He said things would be better with my father. The man took me to the bus station. He told the lady through a window at the ticket counter that he wanted a one-way ticket to Jamestown, New York. The lady explained that the trip would involve taking several different buses. She typed up the tickets and put them together with a staple. The man paid the lady with a roll of bills he took out of his pocket. Then he took two twenties and gave them to me. He sat with me on the plastic chairs at the depot while we waited for the bus.

We sat long enough for the man to buy me a hamburger and give me some instructions. He told me I had to keep the money and the tickets in my pocket. He even checked for a hole where they might fall through. He said whenever the bus came into a station, I had to ask the driver to take me to the right bus. If the bus stop had a coffee shop, I should ask for a hamburger or a sandwich and pay with one of the bills. When they gave me the change back, I should keep that for a hamburger at the next stop. He told me to stay on the bus, I should never let the bus leave without me, and I shouldn't go with anybody who said they could get me to Jamestown sooner. He also gave me a piece of paper with a note on it to put in my pocket with the money. He told me when I got to Jamestown, I should ask someone at the bus station how to get to the police department. When I got to the police, I should give them the note. I couldn't read it then, but I still have it. I held on to it the way I kept the Saints Jacket.

When the bus came, the man showed me how to find a seat and left. I had the ticket, the money, and the note. I put them deep into my pocket. I knew I couldn't lose them. The sun went down, and the bus rolled. After a few hours, the loneliness and vibrations of the bus put me to sleep.

I don't know how many days and nights it took. Sometimes the driver would say I had to change buses. Sometimes he'd tell me to stay in my seat, and I'd sleep again. One time a lady sat with me on the bus. She told me everyone called her Blondie because of her white hair, and she liked that better than her real name, Angela. She said we'd have time for hamburgers when we stopped. I paid with one of the twenties and told her I'd buy her a hamburger too. She said hamburgers were good, but she didn't need to eat. She said she only wanted to make sure I had one.

I'd been riding the bus for a few days when the snow started. I knew about snowflakes, but the snow outside the bus made the world look like nothing I'd ever seen. When I got off the bus, it stuck to my shoes and the legs of my pants. It melted when I got back on, and my feet felt cold and wet. I pulled the jacket around me as tight as I could.

Finally, the bus pulled into a station, and the driver said, "This is your stop, kid." I dug past the coins left over from the twenties and found the paper with the note. It must have been first thing in the morning because I can remember cold sunlight along with the snow, and I asked a woman at the station how I could find the police. She looked at me like she didn't understand me. She probably couldn't make out my Creole. She said something, and I didn't understand her. Some words she used sounded familiar, but I couldn't get them. I showed her the paper the man had given me. It said,

My name is Alex Pridemore.

My mother is Deshauna Decroix from New Orleans.

She died a year ago.

Lee Pridemore is my father.

The woman drew in her breath as she read it. She called another woman at the station, and the two of them read the note together several times. All these years later, I'm smiling at what these Jamestown women must have thought about this little Black kid showing up at their bus station early on a February morning in the middle of a snowstorm with a note claiming to be Lee Pridemore's son. The women looked at each other, and they looked at me. They both started talking at the same time, and I kept repeating the word "police." The first woman ran to get her coat and must have told the other woman she was taking me to the police station. I say she "must have" because that's what she did.

The woman took me by the hand and led me out into the snow. I got scared all over again. I remember ice and cold cutting into my face. I know now the woman led me down Prendergast Avenue and over a block onto Second Street. She brought me into the warmth and the bright fluorescent lights of the Jamestown Police Department. She gave my note to a policeman sitting at a desk, and everyone had another long look at me.

A policeman gave me a donut, and I ate it in three bites. He gave me another one and got busy on the phone. He spoke to someone, and I heard him say my name. He looked over at me and listened for a while longer. Then I heard him say "okay," and he hung up.

That's when I first met Foraker Macreavy. He walked in through the doors of the police station and took off his coat. He walked directly toward me, shook my hand, and said, "Glad to meet you, Alex. I'm Officer Macreavy." He sat down at another desk and started making calls. He must have talked to a few different people because I remember him talking and hanging up and talking and hanging up again several times. I heard him say my name on each one of the calls. When he finished on the phone, he got up from his chair, came over to me, and this time he said,

"Okay. Let's go." I remember he smiled at me, and I felt I could trust him.

We walked through the snow to his police car. When we got into the car, he said, "I got in touch with your people, Alex. We're going to meet your dad and your grandfather and grandmother." He spoke slowly, and I got most of it.

The snow hadn't let up, and we drove over streets that looked like pictures in magazines I'd seen at the drugstore. We stopped in front of a house, where an older white man stood out front. He'd been shoveling the snow to make a path and came running towards the car. Officer Macreavy came around and opened the car door for me. The man called out, "Welcome, Alex!"

He and Macreavy took my hands. They led me along the walk and up the porch steps. We stood on the porch while the man reached for the door, but a white woman pulled it open from inside before he got it. She wore jeans and an oversized sweater. She had a kind expression with bright eyes and kept looking at me like she wanted to see all of me at once. A younger white man came around from behind her. The woman smiled and moved aside. She said, "Alex, this man is your father." The man fell to his knees and pulled me to him. He held me for a long time until the older man and woman reached for me. We all walked to the kitchen while Macreavy stood in the doorway. The two men and the woman sat in chairs, and I stood between them. They kept looking at me and holding me one after the other.

Officer Macreavy spoke up. "So what are ya gonna do?" he asked.

The older man answered without hesitation. He said, "We're gonna thank God!"

The younger man, my father, said he'd go to the store to buy me some clothes. The older man said he wanted to bring some steaks up from the freezer. The woman said she'd start cleaning me up and motioned for me to follow her to the bathroom. Everything looked neat and clean. I saw reflections on the floors. I'd never seen the inside of a house look this shiny, which frightened me.

The woman filled the bathtub and told me to take my clothes off. She pointed to the toilet and raised an eyebrow. Somehow I understood this as her asking me if I needed to go. She put her hand in the bath water, feeling the temperature. She shut off the water, pointed to a towel and a robe hanging on the wall, and left the bathroom. It may have been the first time I'd ever had a hot bath in a clean bathroom with a whole bar of white soap. I sat in the tub and felt warm again. I even tried to rub the soap on my skin. The woman spoke to me through the door. She told me to dry myself with the towel and put on the robe she'd left. The robe must have been hers or the older man's because it hung past my feet.

The woman sat me on a chair in the kitchen. Now and then, she'd smile and hug me. I realize this could have been the first time I felt cared for. I had to learn to accept it. It took a while, but the Pridemores would have it no other way. The younger man came back with two bags of clothing. He'd gone to the Big N Discount Store and filled a cart with clothing for me. He brought back two shirts, two pairs of pants, a pack of underwear, socks, and what turned out to be my first pair of work boots. He also brought me a coat, a knit hat, and a pair of winter gloves.

They overwhelmed me. I'd never experienced anything like this and didn't know what to think. The older man cooked the steaks, and the woman boiled potatoes and green beans. They ate with knives and forks. They tried to show me how, but it took weeks to learn. I ate some of what they put on my plate, and then the woman gave me a glass of milk and a piece of chocolate cake. The snow stopped, and golden light covered the houses by late afternoon. I couldn't keep my eyes open. The woman took me to a room and showed me a bed. She said my father slept in the same bed as a boy. That's how I came to Jamestown, but I hadn't yet met Uncle Ron.

It took me years to piece the New Orleans story together, and here's how I understand it. One night while he lived there, my father went back to one of the jobs where he'd talked his way into working as a carpenter. He stole a power miter saw, a compressor, and three nail guns. He'd met a guy with a car, and they thought they had a sure thing. But when they tried to sell the tools at a local pawnshop, it didn't go as well as they thought it would. Unlike my grandfather, the contractor in New Orleans had lost tools before and knew where they'd end up. He called pawnbrokers around town, and my father and the guy with the car walked right into an arrest. The New Orleans Police Department checked for outstanding warrants and reported the arrest to Jamestown. At this time, Officer Macreavy had just started working with the Jamestown Department. He knew the Pridemore family from growing up in town and offered to drive his car to New Orleans and return the prisoner. My grandfather rode with him. I'd been conceived shortly before my father's three years on the run ended with his arrest, and Deshauna Decroix never told him about me.

Before knowing Macreavy had left to pick him up, my father, Lee, called his father, my grandfather, from the police station. My father told me about it years later. He said he wanted to admit to his father that he knew he'd put the family and the business into a horrible situation. He wanted to tell my grandfather he'd work as a carpenter, repay the family, and sweat out the drugs and alcohol on the job site.

Macreavy and my grandfather brought my father back to Jamestown, but they didn't bring him home. Macreavy knew better. This is where his professional understanding helped. He checked my father into the Jamestown General Hospital's alcohol and drug rehab unit. My father lived there for the next ten months, slowly returned to his senses, and returned to working full-time.

I don't know the particulars of the legal situation, but it must have been straightened out. The contractor in New Orleans got his tools back, and I suspect Macreavy gave him some money to drop the charges. The responsibility for the original theft went to my grandfather's business. The business covered the losses, and my grandfather didn't press charges, so in that way, he gave his son a second chance.

After my dramatic entrance at the bus station, I began life in Jamestown. To start with, I stayed with my grandparents, but for the first few months, I had trouble accepting their attention. I acted out, but they made sure I didn't get away with anything. They expected the best from me, and I came to understand I disappointed them when I brought on their disapproval. They corrected me if I hid food or stole coins from the change jar. After a while, I realized I didn't have to worry about food or money, but I did have to keep my room clean. I had to respect everyone and learn how to read and write. My grandmother took care of that. For years she taught special-needs kids, and I benefited from her lifetime of experience. She didn't send me to school right away. I had to catch up first. She taught me to read, basic arithmetic, and how to tell time.

For a brief moment in the 1960s, Robert Kennedy represented New York State in the United States Senate. He had Jamestown declared part of Appalachia, which brought money to the town. Jamestown used the money to build a first-class library. After she taught me the basics at the kitchen table, my grandmother took me to the library every day. She told me that intelligent people learn at the library, and I could be wise someday if I never let myself stop learning.

After a few months, my father made room for me at his house. We woke up every day at six o'clock and had breakfast together. After my father went to work at one of the construction sites, my grandmother would arrive to take me to the library. We spent hours there every morning reading, writing, and working numbers. At noon we'd meet my grandfather downtown and go to lunch, where I learned about business. My grandparents had an excellent way of explaining things. My grandfather said, "There are dollar bills and Bills who spend the dollars." His way of remembering customers are people with names. Another time my grandmother said, "The most important part of living is the people you are living with."

While my father and grandparents taught me how to get along, my uncle Ron taught me what I needed to know about resentment. After I landed in Jamestown, my father's older brother, Ron, kept his distance. As an adult, I understand how I embarrassed him, and he harbored a grudge against me. Ron knew how much his younger brother had cost their father, which bothered him.

Uncle Ron couldn't find a way past the rules. He lived by blueprints, and as I said earlier, he measured everything. Ron believed people are forever in danger of making a mistake. This is not entirely negative and untrue. Ron felt by sticking to rules, we come closer to achieving our full potential. I believe this. There is value here. I want to reach my potential, and I try to follow the rules. I'm watchful, but I know I get confused and make mistakes. I also know my existence came from when my father didn't follow the rules.

Uncle Ron believed in retribution. He thought if you don't have to pay for your mistakes, you'll make the same mistakes again. This may be true, but I'm not sure what Uncle Ron wanted my grandfather to do about my father's mistakes after the fact. He never said it, but he made it clear, nonetheless. Spending money at a rehab clinic wasn't it, although I found out much later that Macreavy helped defray some of the cost, when Ron saw this little mixed-race kid show up, I reminded him of everything Lee had done wrong, and Ron couldn't stomach how my grandfather gave me a place at the table. He didn't acknowledge me at Sunday dinners. He ignored me through years of family gatherings and never asked me to work at one of his job sites. At Christmas, he'd give me a five-dollar bill in an envelope. None of it concerned me at the time, though. My father paid enough attention to me for himself and his brother, and I had enough to deal with without worrying about Uncle Ron.

During my first year in Jamestown, my grandmother took charge. After our morning lessons at the library and lunch downtown with my grandfather, she and Macreavy got in touch with the hospitals in New Orleans. They had my mother's name, my father's name, and the approximate year of my birth. They found me in the records and got a copy of my birth certificate. They brought me up to date with vaccinations and set me up for full participation in town life.

My grandmother brought intensity to my lessons, and that made them difficult. My mind rebelled at reading and writing, but my grandmother expected me to learn. She wouldn't let up. She made it like breathing, no option. It turned into a battle of wills, and I'll be forever grateful she won. During the summer of that first year, my grandmother declared I would be ready for the second grade by fall. The other kids my age had third grade in their sights, and I probably should have started in the first, but she thought I would be uncomfortable with kids so much younger. I had to reach to make it in the second grade, but the Pridemores expected me to get it, and I did. School went well, and I owe it to my grandmother, who started me right.

Aside from my grandmother's lessons, my father sensed I saw myself as different. Even as blood relatives, he thought all the White people around me might make me uncomfortable. He mentioned this to Officer Macreavy once, and that's when old Macreavy took me for a haircut. He knew the Black barbershop would be an excellent place to introduce me to the Black people in town. On the first day of school, some of the Black kids came over to me. They wanted to meet the new kid they'd heard about and made room for me at the lunch table. I got along with the White kids and the Black kids in Jamestown, and I'm still in touch with some of those guys today.

Growing up in the Pridemore family meant constant contact through dinners, business meetings, and get-togethers, not to mention day after day at the job sites. I started working for Pridemore Homes the following summer. I went to job sites with my father, and he started me off picking up loose nails. I had to make sure not a single one found its way into anyone's foot. I began with that and kept learning.

After a few years back in town, my father met a woman named Mary Ellen who had a free spirit that matched his own. The three of us lived as a family, and it worked. Uncle Ron met Rachel, a dark-haired beauty from Texas who agreed to relocate to Jamestown. She came complete with beauty-pageant poise and a Texas drawl that knocked us over. She took over the social scene in Jamestown, and the couple stayed in constant rotation at weddings, shows, graduations, and holiday festivals. It's a wonder they had time to have their three children, two boys and a girl.

We had great years drenched in sunshine. My grandparents sat at the head of a blessed and beautiful family. The brothers kept the business going despite their underlying differences, and I got along well with my cousins. Like almost all small-town kids everywhere, we started every conversation with, "I can't wait to move away from this place."

In time, though, clouds blew across the sun. My father and Mary Ellen thanked God for every day they had together, maybe because they understood their days wouldn't last. The chronic medical conditions they picked up during their younger years of wandering and addiction took them out early. Mary Ellen made it to 45, and my father lasted to 47. It is a great joy in my life that my father and Mary Ellen lived long enough for me to introduce them to my partner, Jeffrey, and to know they gave us their blessing. One of my fondest memories is of a warm Labor Day afternoon. Along with my father and Mary Ellen, Jeffrey and I sat barbecuing ribs with Macreavy and his girlfriend out at Macreavy's place on the lake. The summer had ended, and a new season had us full of hope.

My cousins took off for college one by one. Of course, they went to top-shelf, name-brand institutions you've heard of, and they did well. Yes, we all said we couldn't wait to leave town, but it surprised me to some extent that none of them even thought about coming back. They wanted no part of Jamestown or Pridemore Homes. Then, after their last college graduation, Rachel asked Ron for a divorce. She said she'd raised the kids and put up with Ron long enough. She'd met a divorced man during an event at the Chautauqua Institution. He'd retired as a manager for an industrial pump manufacturer in Cleveland. The divorce devastated Uncle Ron.

As a teenager, I'd been working for my father for several years when Macreavy asked him to restore a beautiful old cherry staircase at his place. My father sent me along with the older guys and asked them to introduce me to the art of restoration. The work had to be done by the Fourth of July because Macreavy said he had a friend coming to visit and wanted it finished by then. My father said we should spare no expense, and those old guys did fantastic work. They worked through several weekends and showed me what they were doing. They got me excited about old houses, and I eventually went to school for restoration architecture and design.

My grandfather died a peaceful death, and my grandmother held on for a year after him, but she missed him every moment of it. Around that time, Jeffrey and I had been looking for a place of our own. Before my grandfather died, he suggested we move in to care for my grandmother and get to work restoring the old home, which needed some overdue attention by that time. So that's what we did.

I mentioned my father died young, a few years before my grandfather, but things began to slip for Uncle Ron as he got older. I had to spend more and more time at the office and act like an owner. I'm sure you've heard stories like this before. At first, I noticed small things, missed deadlines, or lost inspection requests. Then Ron forgot the names of customers. One day he couldn't remember the name of a contractor who'd been laying tile in Pridemore Homes for thirty years. With each misstep, I jumped in and smoothed things over. The worst came when we showed up to closing one day without a certificate of occupancy. After that, I paid more attention to the new construction end of the company. I kept things afloat, but barely, and we squeaked by until we ran into a real downturn. We hit six months when we didn't sell a single new home. Sometimes people who can't afford a new home decide they can live with the old one if they add a room or fix up the basement. Pridemore Homes switched to remodeling full-time.

I met Jeffrey at school. He has an innate understanding of balance in design and a fabulous sense of color. He'd help me solve restoration problems daily, and I relied on him more and more. When Uncle Ron couldn't make it to the office, I tried to do it all myself. Jeffrey saw me getting swamped, and he came in to help cover while I got out to manage the work sites. Gradually Jeffery spent more time in the office than I did, talking to clients and selling projects. We got good at teamwork, and then we got better. That's how two gay Black guys became the premier design-build renovators of historic homes in Western New York. Pridemore Homes (Take Pride).

Unfortunately, things continued to slide for Uncle Ron. Doctors called it early-onset Alzheimer's. His children, my cousins, had careers and lived far away from Jamestown. Two of them had their own kids and would rather not think about their father. Uncle Ron couldn't live on his own any longer, and I hired a caretaker to come in. When dementia took hold and got worse, he fell into violent fits of anger, and we had to do something. I called his oldest son, Lawrence. He said problems with Uncle Ron couldn't come at a worse time, and he proposed a deal. He would arrange for me to have legal power of attorney for the business and power of attorney for Uncle Ron's health care. I would have access to Uncle Ron's insurance information, and I could set up any nursing home arrangement that would benefit him and be convenient for me. He would divide any extra expenses with his brother and sister. He as much as said, "Don't bother us about our father." Lawrence told me Uncle Ron had nothing to leave in his will. He'd spent it all, and I knew he'd been dipping into the business for years. In exchange for my attention to his father's needs, Lawrence offered Uncle Ron's home and the company. Lawrence told me if it weren't for Jeffrey and me, Pridemore Homes would be long gone. He said, "Keep it. Take it, and do it right the way I know you will. None of us need the money or the headaches."

He said Jeffery and I could sell Ron's home and keep whatever we got for it. We could continue to live at my grandparents' place, and he'd help me attain the full title. But one question still puzzled me. Even though I'd been keeping the business going for years, I never understood the ownership. The final piece concerned how my grandfather left the company when he died. Official correspondence about taxes, insurance, and that kind of thing came addressed to Ron. I just wrote checks and took care of it, but I had to know it all if I were to run it for good. Lawrence said my grandfather wanted to divide everything equally between his two sons, but since my father had died my grandfather wanted to leave part of the business to me. That angered Ron. He thought the company should be left entirely to him. He never forgot the pain and anxiety my father caused with his disappearance. Lawrence also admitted that Uncle Ron felt embarrassed by me. He told me how his father would stomp around their house yelling about "that stupid Lee" and how he would never accept "the little Black bastard." Ron demanded my grandfather leave the whole business to him, and my grandfather didn't have the energy to fight him. Lawrence put it to me bluntly. He said he couldn't care less about his father or Pridemore Homes and didn't want any part of either one. He told me his brother and sister were also glad to be out from under their old man. They never felt good enough around their father. They spoke with their mother in Cleveland all the time, but they'd lost heart with their father.

So, that's the arrangement. My cousins opened a long-term care policy for their father because they knew the day would come for good old Uncle Ron. That takes care of the dementia unit at Fenton Manor, and I send Lawrence and his brother and sister any bills that aren't covered. Jeffery and I sold Uncle Ron's house, and we'll keep Pridemore Homes. Lawrence promised to make sure it goes to me when Uncle Ron dies. Lawrence said his brother and sister came up with this plan when they first noticed their father's problems. Since he'd been failing for a few years by that point, it occurred to me that some of their generosity might have something to do with guilt, and maybe not.

Nonetheless, I saw the whole thing as tremendous good fortune. I called the other two cousins to ensure they agreed with the deal. They said yes, offered congratulations, and told me they'd put it in writing. Lawrence signed over full Power of Attorney, and everything is going according to plan. Jeffrey and I rolled arrangements for Uncle Ron into our daily lives and moved him to a room in the dementia unit at Fenton Manor. I stop in to see him once a week. I feel no animosity. I learned about forgiveness a long time ago from my grandparents.

I'm glad you got in touch, Mr. Strongtree. Writing this letter has helped me process feelings I've struggled with for years. Thank you for your attention. My father started a snowball rolling down a long hill when he tore those gutters off that house, and I'm not sorry he did.

My best to you, those you have forgiven, and those who have forgiven you.

Thanks and Respect,
Alex Pridemore

I wrote to Alex and expressed my heartfelt gratitude to him for answering my inquiry. He said it helped him review the events of Lee's life and his own. I'm glad about that, and I wanted him to know his story taught me something about forgiveness too, something I needed to know. For me, the parable of the prodigal son is another one looking for an ending. Did the brothers learn to get along after the prodigal came home? And how did the father divide the farm when he died?

I found Lee Pridemore's envelope with the card and photo. I put it into an oversized envelope with my letter back to Alex. I signed it "thanks and respect" the way he had. I took it to the post office and sent it certified mail to Mr. Alex Pridemore, care of Pridemore Homes, Jamestown, New York. I marked it "personal correspondence."

CHAPTER 5

Rubin Gubbio: Calming the Storm at Sea

As I looked over the photos and fingerprint cards, deciding who to approach next, one of the guys, Rubin Gubbio, puzzled me. He wore a sports coat over a turtleneck sweater, and the camera caught a smirk on his face. Assuming the police took the photo soon after they arrested him, I'd think he would look more frightened. I could even understand a blank expression, but I didn't get the *Mona Lisa* act. I updated my letter and sent it. His response came back to me in a handwritten note three weeks later.

> Rubin Gubbio
> Albany, NY
> Dear Mr. Strongtree,
>
> Thanks for getting in touch. Wow! What a blast from the past! You got the right man, and yes, I knew Macreavy, but I wonder if anyone ever understood that guy.
> I'll meet you anytime if you're good with the trip from Ohio. Call the day before, and I'll schedule a long lunch. I get away with a lot after

everything that happened. A few hours in the afternoon should be okay.

By the way, I know you said you're not a reporter, but you'll have the scoop if you're looking to bring my "youthful misadventures" into the whole thing.

I'm looking forward to meeting you.

Thanks for using the USPS,
Rubin Gubbio

I read over the reply a few times. Rubin Gubbio must be referring to something he thought I knew or should know. He'd enclosed his card, and the extra-large type announced him as the assistant postmaster of a post office in Albany, New York. I called the next day, we spoke for a few minutes, and arranged to meet the following week. I almost hung up before I thought to ask him, "Tell me, Rubin, what did you mean when you mentioned 'everything that happened'?"

"The shooting," he answered. "Or the 'almost shooting.'"

I told him I didn't know anything about it, and he said that didn't surprise him because nothing had happened. He said no one would know anything about it except a reporter wrote it up in the local paper as a human-interest story, which got him a trip to Washington. He said everything else after that happened behind the scenes, and he'd fill me in when he saw me.

I went online. The newspaper in Albany is called the *Albany Union*. I went to their website and searched "Rubin Gubbio." A story came up of how he stopped a post office shooting. The paper used the word *interrupted* because the shooting had begun. The report said Rubin stopped a gunman named Lance Lupo before he killed or injured anyone. The article explained that Lupo, thirty-eight, a twelve-year employee of the post office, reported at his usual time, went to his locker, and came out into the central part of the building with a handgun. He saw a group of employees and opened fire, but he missed hitting anyone. The sound of gunshots rang out, and panic swept through the building. The employees scattered. Some dropped to the floor, and others ran for cover. Lupo followed a group of them that ran down a hallway. Rubin Gubbio approached the shooter in that hallway. Employees in the building say Rubin, unarmed, walked steadily toward the man, fixed his gaze, and whispered, "Be quiet." As the man held the gun, Rubin put his hand over it and took it away. He then had the man sit with him on the floor until the police arrived. The paper said the police arrested the man "without further incident." At the time the article ran, Lance Lupo had been referred to the New York State Office of Mental Health, Division of Forensic Services.

No wonder Rubin Gubbio could take a long lunch. I couldn't wait to meet this guy, and I felt fortunate he'd agree to see me, let alone have a long lunch together.

When I arrived five minutes early for our meeting, he greeted me with a firm handshake and said, "I'm hungry. Where have you been?"

I answered, "Sorry, Rubin, am I late?"

"No," he said. "You're not, but I'm glad to hear you're not afraid to apologize. Except you shouldn't apologize if you don't have anything to apologize for."

I laughed. I said, "Okay, Rubin Gubbio, I apologize for apologizing,"

He laughed at that, and before he let go of my hand, he briefly touched my arm with his left hand. Rubin Gubbio, a tall handsome man in his early fifties dressed in a gray suit with a post office blue tie, looked me in the eye. He flashed the same smile I'd seen in his police photo, except now I thought it might be self-deprecating— what a character. In the time it took to greet me, he'd put me on the defensive, disarmed me, and confused me all at once.

He announced to another employee at the counter, "We're going to lunch." Turning to me, he said, "Since you're buyin', we'll go to a nice place."

"Fine by me," I said. "I wouldn't have it any other way."

He offered to drive, and we took his Cadillac to a downtown club-style city restaurant in an older part of Albany. A woman hostess in a tuxedo uniform beamed at him as we walked through the door.

She smiled and practically ran to greet him. "Good afternoon, Mr. Gubbio," she said. "Please come this way."

The hostess escorted us to a corner table on the far side of the dining room, miles away from the kitchen. Another waitress arrived with menus and the same bright expression and fawning attitude.

She asked, "What can I get for you, Mr. Gubbio?"

Rubin made a show of looking off into the distance before he answered. "How about one of these fabulous corned beef sandwiches you make here? I can't remember what you call them."

"You mean our Reuben on rye?" she asked with a smile.

"Yes, that's it!" he said, "I'd like one of those. How about you, Tom? I can't recommend their Reuben highly enough."

"Fabulous," I answered." I'll have a Reuben deluxe," and I added, "with a cup of coffee, please."

Rubin wouldn't be outdone. He said, "Make it two café Americanos, Kathy."

Since they all knew him and he knew them, I figured he must be a regular. I also figured he'd be wondering about the police records. While we waited for our lunch order, I reached into my backpack and handed him his envelope. "This is it," I said.

He smiled and reached for it. "Yes," he said. "What have we got here?"

He opened the envelope and laid the card and the photo on the table. As the others had, he looked at it for a long time.

I said, "This is the only copy that I know of. It doesn't say anything about what you did, and it doesn't say anything about a verdict. It's yours. You don't have to tell me anything, but I am curious. Also, if you wouldn't mind, I'd like to record your thoughts and observations."

He looked up at me. "Oh, sure," he said. "I don't mind the recorder. They wrote about everything in the news, but I'll tell you where it came from. Man, what a night. Fifteen years old, and I'd just stepped out the side door of a house I robbed when good old Officer Macreavy pulled up in his patrol car and parked in the driveway. He got out, walked around to the passenger side, and opened the back door. I walked over, sat down, and said, 'Take me in.' Officer

Macreavy put his hand on the door and asked me if I hadn't forgotten something."

"What did you forget, Rubin?" I asked.

"I reached into my pants pocket and pulled out the money," he said. "I don't know how much. I never got a chance to count it, but I remember twenties with a few tens. I handed him what could have been my biggest score. Macreavy walked up to the house and knocked on the door. When the people came out, he handed them the money, turned around, and walked back to the car. Giving back the evidence against me might have been as illegal as anything I did, but you'd have to know Macreavy."

Kathy, the waitress, showed up with our coffees. Rubin quickly tucked the card and the photo back into the envelope and put it on the chair next to him. As soon as she left, I held my hands up. "Stop!" I said. "Rubin, I'm lost. You're going to have to explain this to me. What house? What money? And how did Macreavy happen to be there?"

"Yeah, you're right," Rubin agreed. "It needs some explanation, but seeing a picture of myself at that age brought it all back. You asked, so I told you."

"Please," I said. "Tell me again, slowly, Rubin. I'm interested."

"Okay," he said. "Here's what happened. Nosing around a video store, I found this old TV show from the sixties called *It Takes a Thief.* The show is about this James Bond kind of guy named Alexander Mundy and how he would break into places and steal stuff. Of course, TV morality had him doing it for the right reasons, but Alexander Mundy's personality took the spotlight for me. I thought about Alexander Mundy all the time. I talked about the show with my friends so often they didn't want to hear it anymore. I watched every episode, and because I had them on VHS tape, I could watch them again and again. The more I watched, the more I'd see things I hadn't noticed before. I asked myself, over and over, 'How does Alexander Mundy get away with it?' I decided to try to steal something myself.

"Alexander Mundy looked good in sixties fashions, and I tried to dress the way he did. He also had some excellent burglary tools but didn't go anywhere without his secret weapons—preparation and confidence. Alexander Mundy would think first and plan what to do. He'd observe the rhythm of places and work out ways to mesh in. He'd devise ingenious plans and then he'd put his plans into action. But in every caper, something unexpected happened. Alexander Mundy would have to improvise. He'd almost get caught in every show, but his confidence would save him. I knew, and Alexander Mundy knew, he'd find a way. At the end of every adventure, he'd sit on the balcony of a seaside resort or at a table having drinks with a beautiful woman. He'd resolve everything by handing over the jewels or the money or the secret papers and finish with a sly comment." Rubin Gubbio looked at me and said, "Tom, I wanted to be that guy. I wanted to be Alexander Mundy."

Rubin told me he looked for an opportunity to steal something, and he gave it a lot of thought. He tried shoplifting a few times, but it didn't tax his confidence. To him, items on a shelf in a store didn't have enough value. He wanted the excitement of danger. He said, "I don't know where it came from, but a scheme popped into my mind. Most houses in Jamestown had the kitchen in the back and the living room in the front. I watched people come home from work every night and have supper. After they washed the dishes, they'd go into the living room and watch TV. Most kitchens had a section of the countertop where the people would put their mail and important papers. If they had any cash for whatever reason, they'd also put it there too.

"It rarely gets hot in Jamestown, and hardly anyone had air-conditioning in those days," Rubin continued. "On summer nights, people left their back doors open. The screen door would keep the bugs out, but it also let me hear everything happening in the house. Once the TV went on, people wanted to stay away from the kitchen.

"I'd walk up and down the streets looking for a promising situation. I could see people watching TV in their living rooms through their front windows. If I found a likely setup, I'd walk around to the side or back of the house and stand by the kitchen screen door. I'd listen for the TV. When the commercials finished, I figured the people would be in the living room watching a show. That gave me a few minutes to walk into the kitchen. I'd turn on my 'calm and confident,' locate where they put their important stuff, and see if they'd left any cash.

"It didn't work," Rubin admitted. "I walked in and out of nine or ten kitchens, but I only found money in two of them—total haul, fifteen dollars, a ten, and five singles. I could have made off with more, but jewelry scared me. Sometimes the women in the houses took off their diamond rings and left them by the sink when they washed the dishes, but I didn't want to get caught trying to sell diamonds. What's funny is I congratulated myself for deciding the risk wasn't worth the chance I'd get caught. Alexander Mundy could have gotten away with it, but not me. I told myself I needed more experience."

Rubin's eyes sparkled, and he said, "I thought my two 'scores' got the police involved, but Macreavy laughed when I asked him what put him onto me. He told me somebody complained about a weird kid wearing a black turtleneck and sports coat walking around the neighborhood looking in windows. He drove to where the complaint came from, parked his cruiser, and waited. He saw me sneaking around wearing the sports coat in the middle of July, and it didn't take him long to complete the picture. He pulled up just as I came out of the house."

Kathy, our waitress, arrived with lunch, and I let Rubin's retelling rest between us while she placed the sandwich plates in front of us. Rubin took a break from the story while we focused on the tremendous, overstuffed sandwiches. I liked this guy. This confident and relaxed man began as an awkward, goofy teenager trying to imitate a TV hero.

"Did he put you in jail? I asked.

"Who, Macreavy?" Rubin asked. "No, he talked it over with another policeman, and they decided they'd call my parents instead."

"So your parents came and got you?" I asked.

"It turned into a bad scene, "Rubin said. I heard my father say, 'Yes, sir, officer, sir,' and realized how humiliated he must have felt. My parents brought me home, and I went to my room. They sat in the kitchen for hours in stunned silence. As I got older, I realized I'd confused them more than anything else.

"The charge could have been breaking and entering," Rubin said, "but Macreavy didn't report the money he caught me with, and before that, I hadn't gotten away with much, so he called it 'mischief.' The prosecutor treated me as a youthful offender. Still, I'd broken the law, and the judge didn't want people thinking the police let kids walk in and out of their kitchens while they watched TV. I admitted my guilt, and I got off easy. The judge put me on probation and community service. I found out later he could have sent me to juvenile detention, but Macreavy told the prosecutors and the judge he thought I had come to a turning point. He said incarceration would only teach me to be a better criminal, and he offered to look after me. Macreavy became my new cool guy. He'd put together a campaign to clean up the trash along the river, and I had to help for three Saturdays."

Rubin finished his Reuben sandwich and upended his cup of Americano. "No question," he said, "Macreavy got me to understand things about the world and myself that I live by to this day."

I finished my coffee, and Kathy, the waitress, came over asking if we'd like more.

"We certainly would," Rubin answered. "Two more café Americanos, please, Kathy. I'm just getting started."

I smiled in agreement. "Yes," I said. "I'd like another."

Rubin continued. He said, "After the river, Macreavy took me to the shooting range."

"Guns?" I asked.

"Yes, guns," he said, punching the word.

"Macreavy told me he had a sailboat, and he rode bicycles a lot. He asked if I wanted to come along with him, but that didn't interest me. Guns and bullets did. Macreavy told me about a Rod and Gun Club program for people who wanted to learn about shooting. The club had a range in the country and used .22 caliber target rifles.

"These people weren't messing around," Rubin observed. "We shot real bullets, and the Rod and Gun instructors ensured everyone always paid attention. They made us repeat their motto, 'Stay focused or go home.'

"I liked it," Rubin said. "In my mind, I thought of it as 'secret agent school.' The class went for six sessions, and I went to every one of them. The night before the final test, I met with Macreavy at Jenny's Lunch, a little restaurant by the police station."

I thought to myself that this must be the same place Patrick Williams had mentioned.

Rubin said, "Macreavy asked me what I'd learned in the classes. He had me recalling lessons and anticipating questions. He taught me how to study, and it made sense. Macreavy reinforced what I'd learned from Alexander Mundy. Preparation is the path to cool. I passed the test, and he took me to another shooting range a few days later. At this place, we used handguns."

Rubin said, "Nothing loose and carefree there either. Macreavy watched and checked every shot." He paused and continued, "I don't have to tell you, Tom. Macreavy went out of his way and did me a huge favor, more than I knew at the time."

Rubin surprised me when he said, "I never owned a gun or shot at the range after that. I guess I got it out of my system, but I used what I'd learned at the range for taking tests in school. I'd study and shoot at the questions like targets. I saw grades as hits or misses, and my schoolwork improved." Rubin smiled.

"Bravo!" I said.

"That's what got me into college," he said. "I went to SUNY Albany."

"What's SUNY?" I asked.

"State University of New York," he answered. "Because I started doing better in school, I even qualified for tuition assistance. I took accounting in college because Macreavy said I should. I finished the program to get the degree, but I'd already decided I didn't want to be an accountant. Macreavy said accounting taught me things I didn't know I'd learned. It's funny. Every time I talked to that guy, he'd say something like that. Something I'd never heard or thought of before.

"As school ended, I didn't know what to do, and a week before finals, I saw a note on a bulletin board that said the post office in Albany wanted recent college grads. I applied, and they took me." Rubin said, "Just that simple."

I laughed. I said, "So you wound up walking around neighborhoods like old times?"

Rubin laughed, "That's about the size of it. After four years of college, I ended up walking around neighborhoods looking at houses, the same as before. I only did delivery for about a year though. I had a degree and kept an eye out for jobs in the system. An entry-level management job opened up, and I jumped at it.

"Brutal work," he said. "You wouldn't think so. How hard could it be? It's the post office, right? But in those days, they gave the workers ridiculous amounts of mind-numbing work and never enough time to get it done. Even if a worker managed to finish on time, another mountain of mail waited around the corner. The workers complained, but the post office wouldn't listen. You probably remember those post office shootings back in the '90s. I understand why they happened. As a young manager, one of the older guys told me how to be a boss at the post office. He said, 'Just whip the dogs harder.'"

Our coffee showed up, and once again, Rubin paused to smile and chat with our waitress. When she left, he said, "A couple of years out of school, I found myself managing men and women decades older. I had only the vaguest idea of how to get things done and too much to do. The workers would talk to me like I could do something about it, but it frustrated me to see how little anyone could do. The postal system pounded the life out of everyone. It opened up underfunded every morning and limped along the edge day after day. If people could find a new job, they'd quit and leave critical operations staffed with new employees, which made things worse. People who couldn't find a new job feared losing their post office job in a climate of high unemployment. Ironically, the job at the post office promised it would never end. People hung on until they gave out.

"My department didn't do well. I missed quotas, but I kept my cool. I knew enough to understand the problem, so it didn't bother me personally. The management told me they wanted my department to go faster, and I'd agree. I'd change something to make it look like I'd addressed a problem, but I knew it wouldn't work. I also knew no one would fire me. Management threatened to fire people constantly, but one of the guys told me, 'To get fired around here, you'd have to set one.'"

Rubin took a sip of his Americano and continued. I could hear the rasp of exasperation in his voice. "The biggest problems I had at the post office," he said, "came when directors tried to manage around me. One regional manager started arguments between my workers. Sometimes when people are mad at each other, they compete to see who works harder or faster. They think they'll win the argument by winning the workday. It's a management trick. It works once in a while but not every day.

"On the other hand, if people like and trust each other, they tend to work better, not always, but often enough. People who get along develop creative ways to get things done. Some people want to work in a highly competitive environment, so it's not for everybody. But in the long run, there's no percentage breeding animosity."

Rubin took another moment for his café Americano, and I saw an opening. "So," I said, "tell me about Lance Lupo."

"A firecracker in the middle of a dynamite factory," Rubin responded. He paused and said, "Lance Lupo had been with the post office for years and never had any trouble. Then one of the other workers who knew him outside of work heard things had fallen apart for the guy. His daughter got involved with drugs. She went to live with a guy on the other side of the city, and if she came home at all, she'd be asking for money. His son lost his job and moved back home, and his second wife decided she'd had enough and took up with a guy she met at the Masonic Lodge. Then his first wife, who never remarried, came down with a mental illness that put her into a psychiatric ward.

"Lance started missing his 'dailies.' That's work scheduled to be completed in a day. I called him into the office, and, of course, Lance said he had everything under control. Lance probably thought I'd reprimand him, and no one likes to be accused of incompetence, especially from a college-boy manager. I thought the guy might want to unload some of it, but he didn't tell me anything. I heard more stories about Lance and his home life from the other workers, and from what they told me, it kept getting worse. I called him into the office a few more times. I'd ask him about fishing, cars, or anything else that might get him talking. After a while, I got the idea Lance liked being called in. It meant he could sit in a quiet place for a few minutes, away from the mayhem of his life. It didn't solve anything though. The work kept piling up, and the guys who worked with him complained about him because their department attracted criticism. They accused him of causing the issues in his life rather than having them. I tried to give the guy a break, but he made me look bad because my bosses thought I couldn't do the job when I couldn't manage Lance. They said they'd 'handle the problem' if I couldn't. In our building environment at that time, everyone focused their frustrations on Lance Lupo, and the poor guy took it in the gut. It knocked the wind out of him, and that's shameful. The mess at the post office involved much more than problems coming from one guy."

As evidence of the enormous problems for the US Postal System in those days, Rubin pointed to the massive overhaul the system went through in the years that followed. I'll pick up the story where Rubin recounted the day of the shooting.

"I'd already started working at my desk that morning," he said. "And I've talked to therapists and psychologists, trying to understand what Lance might have been thinking when he came in that day. I didn't even know he owned a gun, but the way I've come to see it, shooting the gun got Lance on top of the uncontrolled frustration, irritation, and anger in his life. The post office, his family, and the world kept kicking and punching him. His life's hot metal frying pan rested on a glowing burner, and the water had boiled off. Disrespect blasted him in the face. His anger blossomed into violent despair, and he couldn't shout loud enough to be heard over the chaos. He needed something louder. I heard the shots and recognized them as gunshots from the days on the range with Macreavy.

"I saw some employees running past my office, and someone shouted, 'It's Lupo. He's got a gun!'" Rubin laughed and said, "I hadn't thought of Alexander Mundy for years, but the old 'cool guy' came back to me. A plan clicked in my mind. I grabbed a file folder from my desk and took off walking. I told myself, 'Just another day, walking a report to another department.' I walked in the direction of the shots, and the moment I saw Lance with the gun, everything got quiet. I'd done the preparation. I'd listened to the guy and given him a quiet place to sit when no one else would. I believed he'd trust me, and I acted like it. I walked toward him as if I hadn't heard the shots. I held the folder in my left hand and glanced at him the way you might when you pass someone in a hallway. I caught his eyes. I felt fear creeping in, but my mind returned to the safety classes at the Rod and Gun. As I got closer to Lance, the evenings I'd spent with Macreavy came back. I saw the gun, and I let my face register concern. I reached for his hand the same way Macreavy had when he saw me carrying a gun with my finger on the trigger. I said the same thing Macreavy said back then, but I didn't mean to tell Lance what to do. I spoke to the gun. I said, 'Be quiet.' I put my hand over the gun and took it away."

Again, Rubin flashed that same smile I'd seen in his police photo. He said, "Everybody thought I spoke to the man, but I spoke to the violence. I didn't want to confuse the issue, so I let them believe what they wanted.

"I had Lance sit on the floor with me. We leaned our backs on the wall. I put the gun on the floor and slid it into the hallway. I knew somebody in the post office would call the police, and I figured the best thing would be to sit there and wait. We talked and waited. I don't remember what we talked about, except that none of it made any sense. I tried to get Lance ready for the show.

"We heard the police enter the building. They came roaring in, pointing their guns at us, and four policemen ordered us to plant ourselves face-first on the floor. I knew if we came close to the gun, the police might take it the wrong way and kill us immediately. While we both stretched on the floor, I tried to get Lance as far away from the gun as possible. He didn't try for it again, and inch by inch, the police made their way closer until they handcuffed both of us. It took hours at the station. Fortunately, some of the workers at the post office saw everything and told the police what had happened."

I said, "Rubin, that's a wild story." We'd come to the end of our second Americano, and I asked him, "What did Macreavy say? I'm assuming you talked to him about it."

"Oh yeah," Rubin answered. "He heard about it at the police station in Jamestown the day it happened. He called me later that night when I got home and congratulated me. The cops who brought Lance and me in said I'd taken a huge risk, but Macreavy understood how it happened. I saw him again when I went home to visit my folks, and we had a huge laugh about it together."

"What did your folks say?" I asked.

"They didn't know what to say," he answered. "My mother had been worried about post office shootings since I took the job, and my father got plenty of slaps on the back from the guys at work. That's about it."

Rubin Gubbio said they summoned him to Washington to meet with the national directors at the Post Office Department, and he held his own with them too. He said, "I took full advantage of the situation. I got an expensive suit and did my best Alexander Mundy impersonation. I told them they had a problem. I said, 'Ask anyone, anywhere in America, what "going postal" means.' They finally got the message. They eased the pace and let the workers solve some of their own problems. The reorganization allowed managers to show more empathy.

"Look," Rubin said. "The post office is messed up. It's got problems that might never get straightened out, but have you noticed you don't hear about post office shootings anymore? I haven't heard 'go postal' in years. It won't be long, and you'll have to explain it to young kids. Granddads will tell their grandkids 'that's what people used to say back in the "olden days."'"

I'd noticed his wedding band before, and since he mentioned kids, I asked Rubin if he had any. "Yes," he said. "We've been married for fifteen years and have three boys." Then he anticipated my next question. "And, no, it all happened before I got married, and I don't know if I would have walked up to Lance Lupo the way I did if my sons were around at the time. That's another thing I learned from Macreavy. There is no answer since it didn't happen now, it happened then. It happened the way it did. If you want to talk about other facts and different outcomes, consider this—the notoriety attracted the woman who became my wife. Without Lance Lupo, she wouldn't have looked at me twice. I might have married someone not nearly as great as she's been."

On the way home after visiting Rubin Gubbio, I thought about the storms that rage in isolation and loneliness. Rubin Gubbio reached into a swirl of violence and fear and came out with a handful of calm and understanding. We drank coffee and ate sandwiches together. He trusted me enough to show me a piece of his most vulnerable young self. He trusted I'd respect his story the way he'd respected Lance Lupo's humanity. I needed to meet Rubin Gubbio. He reminded me of things I didn't know I'd learned. He told me Macreavy went out of his way for him, he went out of his way for Lance Lupo, and the gun went quiet.

CHAPTER 6

Chauncey Cook USAF
The Faith of the Centurion

This time I picked an envelope at random. The first thing I noticed about Chauncey Cook is that he's a Black man. When I looked for his current address, it surprised me that he lived practically around the corner in the next town over, Beavercreek, Ohio. I wouldn't have far to travel. His card put him at fifteen years old at the time of his arrest, which meant he'd be fifty now. I sent him a letter and got an email back a week later.

> To: Thomas Strongtree
> From: Chauncey Cook USAF ret.
> Subject: your letter
>
> Good day, Sir:
>
> Sounds interesting. I remember a scrape early on.
> I'm retired now, but I teach auto shop, so I'm free most days I want to be.
> How about Wednesday or Thursday of next week? You decide, morning or afternoon.

Yes, I knew Foraker Macreavy. He saved my
daughter's life, and before that, he saved mine.
Reply to this email.

Regards,
Chauncey Cook

At this point, I had no doubt Patrick Williams's prediction had
been correct. Foraker Macreavy would have something to do with every
one of the "caught thirty." I responded, and unlike my other trips, the
drive to Beavercreek only took twenty minutes. Chauncey Cook lives
in a neighborhood of modern two-story homes with well-kept lawns
and medium-sized trees. I parked on the street so I wouldn't block
the driveway. Sharp landscaping surrounds his house, and I guessed
Chauncey Cook might be in engineering. The Beavercreek area is near
Wright Patterson Air Force Base in Ohio. I've heard that the suburbs
around Wright Patterson have the highest density of engineers per
capita globally. From what I've seen of the area, that wouldn't surprise
me. Everything is crisp, well-ordered, and clean.

A tall handsome Black man opened the door and greeted me
warmly. He had short gray hair, wire-rim glasses, and wore a polo
shirt tucked into blue dress slacks. Some middle-aged guys tuck in
their shirt tails to show they haven't put on extra weight over the
years. It's more subtle than wearing a sleeveless undershirt, and way
more effective. He shook my hand and smiled. "You must be Thomas
Strongtree," he said. "Come on in. I've been waiting for you."

He brought me through the living room into his home office
and study. Four oversized red leather chairs, a walnut desk with a
computer screen, and a bookshelf holding a TV took up most of the
room. Three bookcases across from his desk held hundreds of hard-
covers. I only scanned the titles, but the words "serious collection"
came to mind.

He said, "Have a seat, Thomas," and waved a hand toward one
of the leather chairs. "Welcome to my home. Can I get you a cup of
coffee? I brewed some for lunch, and I made extra. I hope you'll have
some with me."

"I sure will," I answered. "And I'll take it however you take yours. But please call me Tom, and tell me, how do I refer to you, sir? Do you have a rank?"

"I use a little cream in mine," he said. "And please call me Chauncey. I'm retired from the Air Force now."

I said, "Cream would be great then, Chauncey."

By the time I got to Chauncey Cook, I'd interviewed about half the "caught thirty." Along with stories about Macreavy, every one of the people I'd met drank coffee and delighted in the habit. While Chauncey left the room for the coffee, I went into my backpack and took out his Manila envelope. In the meantime, while I waited for him to return, I took another glance at his bookshelf. Engineering and technical textbooks took up a good part of it, with some medical, but the most prominent section concerned civil war history. Off to one side, I couldn't help noticing the complete *Sherlock Holmes*.

Chauncey returned to the room, placed a cup of coffee on the table next to my chair, and settled himself into a matching leather chair across from me. I started right away. He'd been welcoming and friendly, but I didn't want to try his patience. "Well," I began, "here is the envelope with the fingerprint card and the photo I wrote to you about, and, as I think I mentioned, it's the only copy I know of." I handed the envelope to him. He took a look inside and removed the card and photo. Like the others, he also looked at the picture for a long time. I explained that my visit came from my own curiosity and asked for permission to record his recollections. Chauncey agreed, but I sensed some hesitation as he sat forward in his chair. He laughed and said, "Some stunt for a fifteen-year-old. I'm a little embarrassed. One heck of a day though!"

"So that's you?" I asked.

"Oh yeah," he answered. "Or who I wanted to be."

I didn't say anything. Chauncey sat still for close to a minute. I could see his eyes moving back and forth from the card to the photo in silence. When his face relaxed, his eyes showed some amusement. He said, "Yeah, quite a day," and asked, "How did you get this again?"

I explained as I had to the others, and I said, "I want to know how a brush with the law at a young age may have affected your life."

I paused. "That's how it started anyway, and I've heard some amazing stories along the way. This Macreavy guy seems to have been a real character there in Jamestown." I put some respect in my tone and added, "I understand he passed away almost twenty years ago."

"Yeah," Chauncey agreed. "Bicycle accident." After a pause, he said, "Well, I suppose you want to know what I did."

"It's entirely up to you," I answered. "Tell me as much or as little as you want. I'm curious about your young life and the law, but I'm not a reporter. I'm only interested in how you see it."

"Well," Chauncey Cook stated, "I got arrested for stealing a car. It could have been grand theft auto, but it didn't go that far." He knew that sounded dramatic, and he let it ring.

I echoed his tone. "So!" I said. "A real badass."

He laughed and agreed. He said, "Yeah, real bad, and a real ass."

We both laughed. He took a sip of his coffee and held the cup in his hand. He said, "My father and his brother, my uncle, fixed cars on Washington Street in Jamestown. Along came one beautiful Saturday in March. The snow had started to melt, and everybody had a touch of spring fever. As a young guy, I worked cleaning up and helping at the shop. On this particular Saturday, a friend of my father's brought in his classic 1956 Buick Roadmaster Sedan for an oil change. Beast of a thing, black with chrome trim, a huge V8, four ports, and I kept repeating the name in my head. They called it the 'Roadmaster.' I wanted to be the 'Roadmaster.' I don't know how I thought I'd get away with it, but I got the idea for a high time that afternoon. I probably don't have to tell you, Mr. Strongtree, it involved a girl."

"Springtime, a car, and a girl. Sounds like fun already, Chauncey," I said. "But please call me Tom."

"Okay, Tom," he said. "I knew this girl from the neighborhood. When my dad and uncle left the shop for lunch, they wanted me to watch the place and answer the phone. Instead, I got in the Roadmaster and drove it to the girl's house. I parked in front, knocked on her door, and asked if she would like to go out to lunch with me. She saw this gigantic black car shining in the noonday sun and said, 'Sure.'

"I didn't have much money, but I had enough for Arby's, down the street from the shop. I thought I'd have enough time to go there, bring her to lunch, and get back to the shop before anyone missed me.

"Well, our lunch started great. The girl laughed at all my jokes, and I kept her smiling as we enjoyed our roast beef sandwiches. She got quiet all of a sudden as two cops walked in. They asked about the Roadmaster parked outside, and I told them I could answer any questions they had about it. The next thing I knew, they slapped the cuffs on me."

"How did it all happen so fast?" I asked.

"It came after a string of accidental sightings. As we sat eating our lunch at Arby's," Chauncey said, "the guy who owned the Roadmaster passed by. With his classic car sidelined in the shop, he had his regular car out doing errands. The Roadmaster stuck out from all the other vehicles in Arby's parking lot. The guy looked in to see if my father had taken it to lunch. When he didn't see my father at any of the tables, he went to the repair shop. My father and uncle had returned by then, and the guy told them he saw the car down the street at Arby's. They couldn't figure out what had happened, and at that moment, a cop car drove past, and they flagged it down.

"I got in big trouble. I stole the car, true enough, but no harm done. My father got crazy mad at me. The girl had to walk home, and the guy who owned the Roadmaster got a free oil change, tune-up, and tire rotation. The police had to follow procedure though. They couldn't just let a car thief go because of a misunderstanding. Well, they might have, but no one wanted to cut me any slack that day.

"I went to juvenile court, my father appeared with me, and I had to explain what happened. The judge sat quietly and listened through the whole story. Now that I remember it, he may have held back a smile. Still, he came up with a sentence for me. The ticket for driving without a license cost $80, the court fees came to $125, and I had to serve eighteen hours of community service. The police department had nine vehicles, and I had to spend two hours washing the outside and vacuuming the inside of each one of them. I started the next day after school, and I went to the police garage every day and on Saturdays until I'd cleaned every car. My father paid the ticket and the fees. After I finished the service work, he told me I had to work at the garage again until I'd repaid him in full.

"Funny how these things go," Chauncey said. "The cops at the garage made it easier than I thought. I got to know some of them, and they all knew my story. They teased me about it, but they let up when I showed I could take a ribbing. That's when I met Officer Macreavy. He talked about getting his sailboat ready for a race on Seneca Lake that summer. He needed someone to wire lights on his boat trailer so he could haul it over there. I told him I knew how to do that. I'd splice them into the directional signals. It wouldn't take more than an hour if I had the lights.

"He told me to buy a good set of lights and said he'd bring me to his place on the lake where he kept the boat and the trailer. I'd do the job, and he'd bring me back to town, but I had to ask my father if I could go. He said he'd pay whatever the job usually costs plus $50 for the house call service. I checked with my father, and the next time I saw him, I reported to Macreavy that the whole thing would cost $95. The first Saturday after my community service, he took me to his place, and I wired the lights onto his trailer.

"While I worked on the lights, Macreavy hung around and made me a cup of coffee. We were into April by then, still a little cold, and the coffee warmed me up. More than that, though, he made me feel like a real mechanic. He told me I did something for him that he didn't know how to do himself, and he said he always paid top dollar when someone did it right."

I took a sip of my coffee then. I could see that recalling this feeling meant something to Chauncey, and I wanted to share it with him.

"I asked him about his sailboat," Chauncey continued. "Macreavy told me his Uncle Henry built it back in 1932. That impressed me. A guy made his own boat. He said his uncle used a special kind of wood from trees that grow near Jamestown. The wood is called Jamestown rock-hard maple. The wood is rock-hard because of the long winters in Jamestown. A tree doesn't grow in the winter, and if a tree doesn't grow much over the summer year to year, the annual rings are closer together, affecting the wood's density. I told him I knew about cars and trucks but nothing about boats or wood. He laughed at that and said he planned to use his truck to take the boat to a regatta in July. He said he'd arranged for his sailing club to hold it at Seneca Lake in the middle of the state to make it easy for people to get to. I'd never heard the word 'regatta,' and I asked him what it meant. He laughed again and said it's a fancy name for a sailboat race.

"I guess I've always been a bit of a wise guy, and I said, '*Regatta* sounds like a White-people word.' He looked at me and said, 'Don't let yourself get tied down, Chauncey.' But he didn't dwell on it. He told me more about the boat and sailboat racing and asked if I'd be his crew at the regatta. He explained that meant I'd be his partner on the boat for the race. He said his usual partner wouldn't be able to make it, and he needed to find someone else. He told me it would be a three-day deal. The day before the race, we'd haul the boat to Seneca Lake and set it up. The next day we'd race the regatta, go to the clam bake that night, and come home the day after that. He gave me a brochure to show my parents and get permission. He said he'd pay for the trip so it wouldn't cost anything, and I'd have my own room at a resort hotel, but my parents had to write a note saying I could go with him.

"He told me I had to learn to sail if I decided to go. He'd show me how, but we'd have to practice. He said I'd have to work the jib sail and learn why it's important to the boat and the race. We'd be a team and work together like a well-oiled machine. I didn't know what to tell him about being on a team with him and sailing a boat on a lake I'd never heard of, so I said I'd take the brochure home and think about it. But he told me not to think too long. He said he asked me as his first choice but he'd find someone else and start practicing with them if I couldn't.

"I told my father and mother about the regatta when I got home. I explained about the sailboat and how Officer Macreavy wanted me to 'crew' for him. I went over the details and acted like I knew everything about it. I kept talking and talking because my parents didn't say anything. They got real quiet. Eventually, I ran out of things to say, and they still hadn't said a word. My father and mother looked at each other. I know now about the conversation they had with their eyes. When my father spoke, he said, 'You know they'll all be rich White people there?'

"'Probably,' I answered. 'But Officer Macreavy asked me to go, and he wouldn't ask me if he thought there'd be trouble. And he's a policeman,' I added. My parents still didn't say anything. Their eyes danced as they looked at each other. My father spoke again. He said, 'There will be men who don't want you there.' I answered, 'Officer Macreavy wants me there.' My mother finally spoke up. She said, 'Oh, let him go. Officer Macreavy knows what he's doing, and he'll watch out. It's time the boy got out into the world and found out about things anyway. He's darn near a man now that he's driving girls around to lunch and all.'

"My father smiled and said, 'You're not off the hook for the ticket and the court costs. You have to go to school, and you've got to work at the shop. Do you think you can do that and practice for the regatta too?' I answered, 'Yes, sir. I'll make it happen.'"

Chauncey said, "I can still remember it. My parents howled with laughter at that one. They laughed and laughed. They held each other in the kitchen, and my mom started to cry. I didn't know why. I couldn't tell what I'd said to make them laugh like that. I didn't know a man and a woman could experience that kind of joy over their child until I experienced it with my wife years later."

Chauncey continued, "I found Macreavy at the police station. I told him my parents said it was okay and I wanted to do it. Macreavy told me the lake had thawed but we had to work on the boat before putting it in the water. He called it 'dry dock.' We made a plan for me to go out to his place two Saturdays from then. That would give me time to put in some work for my father.

"Macreavy had this cool garage right on the lake, concrete floor on one side and water on the other. He could open a door and sail the boat out onto the lake. He called it his boathouse. The boathouse held this beautiful wooden sailboat called a Snipe. He told me his Uncle Henry named it *LISPENARD*, after a street he wanted to remember in New York City, where he'd worked in the 1920s. He showed me where his uncle had written the name in script on the transom—that's the back of the boat. He started teaching me by calling the parts of the boat by their proper names. Macreavy told me when he first moved back to the lake, he sanded every square inch of it and refinished the whole thing with marine varnish. We hauled the boat on its trailer out of the barn, washed it down, and waxed it until it glowed.

"We opened the sails and spread them out on the lawn. He explained how sometimes the wind pushes the sails directly, and sometimes it pushes them indirectly. We spent an hour looking over both sails and checking all the ropes, called 'lines' on a boat. Then we rolled the boat back into the boathouse garage, and Macreavy said we were ready for lunch and some 'classroom' work.

"We went into his house and sat at a round oak table in his kitchen. He made ham and cheese sandwiches and put on a pot of coffee. While we waited for the coffee, we ate the sandwiches, and he began to tell me things I had to know about what he called the 'theory of sailing.' He took a piece of paper and drew pencil diagrams of boats, sails, and wind directions. He also listed ten sailing terms I had to know. 'There's a lot to learn,' he said. 'But I have confidence in you. You're going to do well.' I didn't know what I'd gotten myself into, but he seemed pretty sure of himself. I still have that paper. That's it over on the wall. I found it at my folks' house a few years ago and had it framed."

I got up from my chair and took a look. I saw remarkably well-rendered pencil sketches of sailboats with arrows showing the wind and water. On the lower left of the paper, I saw the list of sailing terms neatly numbered one through ten. "Amazing," I said. "Everything you need to know about sailing, all on one side of a piece of paper."

"That's about all you need to start," Chauncey said. "The rest is feel."

I sat back in the chair. "We met the following Saturday again," Chauncey continued. "And this time, we put the boat in the water. Macreavy had an extra life jacket and said I should bring a hat and sunglasses the next time.

"I got a kick out of it. We stayed on the water for about an hour, and Macreavy kept tightening lines and adjusting things. He made the boat go this way and that, toward his house and away from it. He tried to teach me a little about sailing but said he didn't expect me to learn everything immediately. For the first day, he just wanted me to feel the wind and the sun, and the water. That's all."

Chauncey checked our cups and decided we needed refills. He left for the kitchen, and this time he returned with the coffee pot and a carton of half-and-half.

Chauncey settled into his chair again and said, "As you can guess, Macreavy taught me a lot about life. Some kids learn from sports. My father and uncle learned from cars, and I learned from sailing. You can't sail directly into the wind. You have to sail a zigzag line. It's that simple, but that doesn't mean it's easy. It's called tacking. That's the skill. That's the art, and each time the boat tacks, the sails have to be held just so. Macreavy taught me sailboat races and life are won by how we tack." Chauncey Cook let the observation he learned as a young man hang in the room. The two of us sat in companionable silence.

As I looked around his study, I noticed his bookcase again. "I see you've done a lot of reading about the Civil War," I observed.

"Oh yeah," he answered, "Macreavy got me into that too. One time after we got back from sailing practice, we sat in his kitchen having sandwiches and coffee. I told him my parents had asked me about the rich White people at the regatta. Macreavy didn't answer immediately. I thought I'd said something that made him mad, and I regretted it. I liked this guy. I didn't want to say anything against him, and we ate our sandwiches without talking.

"When we finished, he said, 'Come to the library, Chauncey. I want to show you something.'

"He had a room in his house filled with books, and he pulled a chair over and had me sit at a desk. He took down a big book with a thick leather cover and placed it on the desk. He opened it to page after page of old-fashioned handwriting, and Macreavy said, 'Let me explain something about rich White people. Sometimes when a child is born into a wealthy family, they give the kid the mother's family name as a first name. My name is Foraker Macreavy from my mother, Martha Foraker, and my father, Frank Macreavy. Both families had

100

money, making me one of the rich White people. I don't deny it, but there's more to the story.'"

Chauncey said, "The big book he showed me contained Civil War rosters, and Macreavy opened to a page marked with a Union ribbon. He showed me the names of three brothers listed in perfect handwriting—John Macreavy, William Macreavy, and Sean Macreavy. When the Civil War broke out," Chauncey said, "the three Macreavy brothers went to fight. Only nineteen, eighteen, and sixteen, they joined the 165th New York Infantry and left home to preserve the Union and end slavery. The two older brothers died. The oldest brother at the Siege of Port Hudson and the middle brother at the Battle of Vermillion. The youngest, Macreavy's great-great-grandfather several generations back, came home from the war without his right arm."

Chauncey said, "I looked at that book, and those guys became real men for me. I'd heard about the Civil War, and I knew some of my family were slaves way back, but when I saw those names, I realized men from around Jamestown fought in that war, and some of Macreavy's family died in it."

Chauncey looked at his collection of Civil War histories, drank some of his coffee, and continued. He said, "But Macreavy hadn't finished. He told me how rifles shot round balls instead of bullets back in the Civil War. If a rifle ball hit you in the arm or the leg, it would explode the limb. Gangrene infection might settle in and kill you. A man could live without an arm or a leg, so they'd cut off the damaged part to stop the infection from spreading. I've done a lot of reading about this, Tom. You can't imagine how painful it must have been, and blood flowed in torrents. When a battle ended during the Civil War, wounded men lay all around the battlefields. The creeks and rivers nearby ran red with blood. Macreavy said this is where his mother's side of the family came in. Several generations back, another of his great-great-grandfathers, Arthur Foraker, served as a surgeon in the 165th New York Infantry, Medical. After a battle, Northern doctors begged their way onto the battlefields and tended to the wounded. Macreavy's great-great-grandfather went with those surgeons and brought his sister, Clara, to serve as a nurse. That's the only way women could get onto the battlefields in those days. They couldn't join the fighting, but they could care for the wounded. They got together their own army and called it the Red Cross. In 1909, Jane Delano organized it into the Red Cross Nursing Service, but it started in the 1860s to help wounded soldiers in the Civil War.

"The scene after a battle back then must have been a vision of hell. The air filled with the smell of gunpowder and death. You'd hear wounded men crying and moaning in pain. The surgeons set up tables made from planks of rotten wood and barrels they found in burned-out barns nearby. They laid the planks on the barrels and got to work in blistering heat or freezing rain. Sometimes frostbite locked their hands. Other soldiers hauled the wounded men to these makeshift tables. Sometimes they had basic morphine back at the hospitals, but they had no sterilization or anesthetics on the battle-field. To beat gangrene, they had to cut soon and fast. Best to get it over with or, in the following weeks, the infection would bring a horrible death, slow and sure. The surgeons went from one wounded man to the next, trying to do as many amputations as they could in the least amount of time."

Chauncey said, "I don't think I could bear it. A nurse would throw herself on a wounded soldier and hold him with every bit of her strength. The soldier would hold the nurse like the last woman on earth. At that moment, she became his mother, his sister, or the girl he remembered from home. The frightened young men—boys, really—held the nurses' embrace in a fevered mix of anger, fear, and lust. They crushed her bones or tore at her clothing and raked her skin. The nurse offered no resistance granting the wounded man a moment of solace and distraction. A nurse gave her body that way. As she held the soldier, other men strapped him down. She spoke softly into his ear and tried to keep him calm until the surgeons arrived with the saw. Most of the soldiers passed out from the pain.

"After the amputation, the nurse and the other soldiers tied a tourniquet into place. They wrapped the wound with a bandage they made out of the uniforms of soldiers who'd died. They loosened the straps and removed the soldier from the table. The nurse picked up the cut-off section of limb. She carried it to a cart or a pit and threw it in on top of dozens more. The soldiers, surgeons, and nurses worked until exhaustion dropped them to the ground. They had to get as much done as possible before an ambulance train collected them, along with the wounded and the dead, to bring them back across Union lines.

"Macreavy said his great-great-grandfather Foraker saved a lot of soldiers who fought to make men free and save the Union. He helped them the only way they knew how back then. He kept them alive, but they lived with missing arms or legs for the rest of their days. The doctor returned after the war and added manufacturing to his medical practice. When the industrial revolution kicked in, he made money and built a summer cottage about a mile up the lake from the Macreavy place. He married and had a family, but his sister, Clara, never recovered emotionally and psychologically. He always made a place for her, and she stayed with his family for the rest of her life. Years after the war, people said they heard her scream across the lake one summer night. A family legend recounted one horrific psychotic attack when she threw off her nightgown and ran from her room down to the lake. The family saw her scarred body where the men in the war had clawed her skin. She threw herself into the water, trying to wash the blood away."

Chauncey looked over at me. He said, "When Macreavy finished telling me this, he said, 'People have paid a dear price so everyone can live free in America. Now, I've invited you to participate in a sporting event with me. You have to believe that you have every right to be there. People spent their lives, their blood, and their well-being so we could sail a boat together. Let's do that.' I answered, 'Yes, sir.' I paged through the book he showed me and saw row after row of men's names. Macreavy made his point. I rested my hand on the book and said, 'It's a deal.' After he died, I made sure the book went to the Fenton Historical Society in Jamestown."

Chauncey glanced at the bookcase and then over at me again. "About the middle of June," he said, changing the subject, "Macreavy decided we were ready for our first race. It would start across the lake at the CLYC—that's the Chautauqua Lake Yacht Club—but Macreavy assured me the other boats would be like ours. There wouldn't be any yachts there. We'd sail across from his place to the club, do the race, and sail home." Chauncey laughed and said, "When race day came, I told him, 'Just tell me when to tack.' I'd learned that much.

"When we got close to the Yacht Club on the other side of the lake, Macreavy said we had to sail past the starting barge to enter the race. Guys with clipboards checked us in, and one of the guys asked about me. The wind had our sails luffing, and Macreavy shouted over the noise. He said, 'His name is Chauncey. He's my crew. He's good, and we're gonna sail the hell out of Seneca Lake this summer!' The guy shouted back, 'Bet you will, Macreavy! Glad to meet you, Chauncey. Keep your eyes open, young man. You're sailing with the best!' I took a lot of encouragement from that. Then the man asked Maceavy something I didn't understand at the time. He shouted, 'Where's Nel?' Macreavy answered 'DC' in the same loud voice, and the man on the barge pursed his lips and nodded his head.

"About ten other boats like ours shifted around and passed close to each other. Macreavy explained that floating barrels with flags sticking out of them had been anchored to the bottom of the lake, and they set off the racecourse. One of the guys on the barge fired a shotgun, and Macreavy told me the race had started. I didn't understand anything about sailboat racing, but Macreavy told me what to do, and I did it as fast as possible. I only dropped my line twice. We sailed around for about an hour and a half, and a guy shot off the gun again.

"I asked Macreavy why they shot the gun this time, and he said, 'That tells the rest of the boats that someone crossed the finish line. We did it, Chauncey! We won! You're a great crew!' It seemed easy, but I discovered how difficult it could be in the coming months. I had a lot to learn. On the way back across the lake to his house, he asked me if I could swim. I told him I'd never tried it, but I thought the life jacket would hold me up if I fell in the water. He said he wanted me to 'try it' anyway. He said if we had an accident, he wanted me to know how to swim.

"The following week, I got a swimming lesson at the end of Macreavy's dock. June hadn't ended, and Western New York State isn't hot until July and August. The lake water stays cold through most of the summer, and I couldn't believe I had to learn to swim in an ice bath. I had on the same blue jean shorts and T-shirt I wore on the boat. Macreavy told me to walk back down a ladder he'd bolted to the side of the dock. I slowly stepped down into the water. With teeth chattering, I got down to where my shorts got wet, and Macreavy told me to jump in. I did, and I panicked. My head went under. I flailed my arms and gulped for air. My eyes must have been bulging out of my head. I tried to scream, and my mouth filled up with water. Man, that scared me. I heard Macreavy yelling, 'Chauncey, put your feet down. You can touch the bottom there.'"

Chauncey Cook paused and looked at me. "Tom," he said, "that turned out to be one of the most important lessons of my life. So many times, when I got in too deep, I stopped and put my feet down. But Macreavy didn't plan this. He told me he thought I knew I could stand there. I got mad at him then, but I'm glad it happened that way. I never forgot the lesson. After he showed me I could stand on the bottom, he taught me how to put my head underwater and float on my back. He even showed me a little about moving my arms and kicking my feet. After the lesson, he brought me inside to warm up. He gave me a towel to dry off and went into his library. He came out with a book and handed it to me. He said sailing, floating, and swimming taught him about forces. He said some forces could push and help us, and other forces could kill us. He said he wanted me to read a book that would help me understand."

Chauncey got up from his chair and walked over to his bookcase. He reached for a book with a worn-out cover. He said, "This is the book he gave me that day." Chauncey held the cover open and handed me *The Souls of Black Folk* by W. E. B Du Bois. The inscription read, "To Chauncey Cook, My crew and partner in understanding the forces. Thanks and Respect, Foraker Macreavy."

Chauncey said, "I didn't get most of it at first, but Macreavy told me to reread it. I found out later he'd given me a first-edition copy of the book. I've gone back to it over the years and got something new every time. It brought Donna into my life too.

"Who's Donna?" I asked.

"My wife," he answered.

I said, "Please, Chauncey, I have to hear about that. How did your wife come from a book?"

"Okay," he said. "But let me finish about the sailing first. We went to more races on Chautauqua Lake, and I got the hang of it. After a while, the tactics made sense, and I saw how Macreavy used the wind. That's not easy to do, but the hard part is the wind isn't the same all the time. The thing is, Macreavy understood this. He could balance the sky, the water, and the wind on the head of a pin. He matched his mind with the forces of creation and sailed his boat right into the middle of them every chance he could. He could sail that boat in heavy air and on nothing more than a puff." Chauncey Cook looked down, shaking his head. He said, "'Kin' guy!"

I'd heard about the origin of "'kin' guy," and when Chauncey used it, I assumed he'd picked it up from Macreavy, but I didn't call attention to it.

He said, "We took the boat to Seneca Lake and sailed in the New York State Snipe Invitational. We got the bronze medal." Chauncey pointed to a framed medal and ribbon hanging on his wall. "That's the one right there," he said. "We got third place. We stayed at a resort hotel, ate at a restaurant there, and the Snipe fleet had a giant clam bake the night after the race. Let me tell you about kindness and a great group of people. They might have been confused about having a Black kid on one of the boats that finished in the money, but most everybody knew Macreavy. He introduced me as his crew, and I'm sure that made a difference. He said, 'Take your place, Chauncey,' and I knew what he meant.

"On the drive home, he made this speech about how third place is the best. He said he always aimed for first, but joy came from third. He asked me how I felt about getting third place, and I told him I felt great about it. I didn't know if we'd place at all. He said, 'That's what happiness feels like, Chauncey.' He broke into a huge smile and told me I should always remember that feeling. He laughed and said, 'Ha! Our trailer lights are on. We sailed the best we could, and we're rollin' along, happy and lovin' life!'

"What a great summer," Chauncey mused. "I learned big lessons doing that regatta with Macreavy, and I thanked him for it many times over the years." Chauncey took a good-sized swallow of his coffee. "So is that what you wanted to hear, Tom?" he asked.

"Absolutely," I answered. "That's exactly what I wanted to hear. I'm more than impressed with guys like you and Macreavy, but how did the book lead you to Donna?"

"Oh yeah,' he said. "If you're interested."

"Please," I said. "I want to know how W. E. B. Du Bois got you the girl."

He laughed. "Okay," he said. "After high school, I knew I wanted to do something to make my life mean something. The Macreavy boys carried Springfield muskets onto the battlefield when they were young. They fought with the New York 165th and put their lives on the line to stop slavery and defend the Union. I thought about air, wind, and forces, and I got the idea to start with what I knew about car mechanics and go into the Air Force to learn about jet engines. I had no idea how difficult it would be, but I told myself I'd put my feet down and stand up any time I got in over my head. Sometimes I had to start swimming, but you'd be surprised how often that's all I had to do.

"I signed up, and after Air Force boot camp, they sent me to Sheppard Air Force Base near Wichita Falls, Texas. That's where I went to school with the big boys. That's also where I met Donna.

"One night, out to the bars with the guys in my group, we met up with some local girls. A beautiful girl named Donna Clark happened to be home on break from college. She told me she wanted to become a lawyer. I thought she might be out of my league, but I turned on the charm. I told her about sailing in regattas in New York. I didn't let on that Western New York is nine hours away from New York City and nothing like it. I let her imagine me as a big-time guy sailing with my buddies at yacht clubs and hanging out at clambakes. I played the 'smart card' too. I quoted things I'd read from W. E. B. Du Bois. I got her phone number, and we started talking on the phone. I'd meet up with her whenever she came home from college.

"This went on for a year, and then one afternoon over at her house, she got quiet. She said she had difficulty seeing us together for a long time. She had a problem with me being a mechanic.

"I felt hurt and rejected. I didn't know what to do, but then it came to me. Macreavy had shown me how to handle something like this years ago. He'd let drama tell the story, so I told her I wanted to show her something.

"I took Donna over to Sheppard and out onto the flight line. By that time, I had clearances, so I brought her close to the runway. I gave her goggles and hearing protection, took her hand, and brought her closer. We watched an F-15 takeoff. The massive engines fired in a roar of thrust and shot the plane to heaven. When the sound died and the ground stopped shaking, I told Donna, 'You just saw and heard and felt one of the most powerful and sophisticated machines ever invented by humankind. I'm studying to be on the team that tears those engines apart, repairs them, and puts them back together better than new. I'm doing that because that's what I can do to help defend this country where a Black kid can sail in a regatta, and a Black girl can study to become a lawyer.' I told her that's my idea of 'mechanic.'"

Chauncey Cook looked pleased with himself. "I think I made my point," he said. "Three years later, she graduated from law school. We got married, and our baby Shantell came into our lives a year later."

"Wow, Chauncey," I exclaimed. "What a play! You got the girl, and she got her very own military gentleman."

"Yeah," he agreed. "We had it good. I qualified as an Air Force mechanic, and we traveled the world. Donna found work wherever the Air Force stationed me. We had careers, money, nice houses, and new cars. We had it all with our beautiful little girl, Shantell, which brings me to another Macreavy story if you want to hear it."

"Chauncey, I have to hear it now. Didn't you write something about how Macreavy saved your daughter?"

"Okay," he said. "As a little girl, Shantell happened to see Condoleezza Rice on television. The senate had her on the hot seat answering questions about George W., but I don't think Shantell understood anything about that. She saw a strong, confident Black woman speaking with authority and holding her own as she answered questions from a bunch of White men. Condoleezza Rice became Shantell's role model. We even started calling her 'Little Condi.'

"Shantell read everything she could about Condoleezza Rice and found out she held a national rank in figure skating. Once Little

Condi heard that she wanted to try figure skating too, and we encouraged it. We're back now, and that comes after many other places, but at that time, I happened to be stationed here at Wright-Patt. We looked like one more suburban family waking up early to get to the ice rink. I felt that happiness I'd learned about with Macreavy, and everything looked great until Shantell had an accident.

"She got pretty good at skating. She could skate backward, do jumps, and even had a partner for junior ice dancing events, which is not bad for a twelve-year-old. One day she jumped up in the air, and her body froze. They say she went up spinning and came down in a heap on the ice. She couldn't move, and someone called 911. They took her away on a board and brought her to the trauma center at the Miami Valley Hospital. Donna called me at work from the rink, and I met her at the hospital. We waited. We didn't know what had happened. No one told us anything because they didn't know what to say, and no one wanted to deliver bad news. After a long time, a doctor asked us to come to a meeting room. He told us Shantel fell on the ice because she had a tumor either in the brain or somewhere near it, which caused a loss of balance. She hit the ice hard, and the fall injured her spine and broke her right arm.

"The doctor told us they had Shantell in line for scans, and they had a consult set up with the neurosurgery department to determine the next steps. He said he would keep us updated and asked us to stay close. He thought we might have to give consent for surgery, and they wanted to be able to get to us right away.

"When I heard the words tumor and brain and spine, I kept thinking about my little girl and how she wanted to be graceful and elegant like Condoleezza Rice. I went blank, and Donna went into legal mode. She took notes and told me to be quiet.

"I told myself to stop flailing and put my feet down, but I couldn't find the bottom this time. While Donna spoke with a woman behind a desk, I wandered down the hallway. I felt like a boy again and wanted to talk to Officer Macreavy. I wanted to ask him what to do. Cell phones had recently come on the scene, and I'd started using one. I called the Jamestown Police Department and asked for Officer Macreavy. They said they'd reach him and have him call back. The phone rang five minutes later.

"I told him about Shantell and Condoleezza Rice and ice skating, and I shocked myself all over again when I used the words tumor, brain, and spine. I told him I tried to put my feet down, and he knew what I meant. I didn't have to explain it. He remembered. Macreavy said, 'Let me think.'

"He didn't say anything, but I could hear him there, so I waited. Then he said, 'Okay, here's what you're going to do. I want you to call Nelson Bell.' He gave me a phone number and said, 'Mention my name. Tell her I told you to call. We don't have a lot of time. That's why I'm telling you to call her directly. Also, I think you're better at selling the idea right now.'

"'Wait!' I said. 'Is Nelson Bell a man or a woman?'

"'She's a woman,' he answered. "Remember I told you once how sometimes people name their kids after their mother's family name? Well, her mother is from the Nelson family, fabulous people. She goes by Nel Bell. Just address her as Dr. Bell. She's a PhD.'

"'Okay,' I said. 'And what's the idea I'm supposed to be selling?'

"Macreavy said, 'We don't have time for me to lay it out right now. Make sure you mention my name and tell her you're calling for your daughter, Shantell. Use her name too, Shantell, and tell Dr. Bell how she wanted to be like Condoleezza Rice. Now get off the phone. Don't waste any more time with me. Call her now. I'll be in touch with her later to see what's happening.'

"That's what I did, Tom. I dialed the number he gave me, and the woman herself answered. I remember her cheerful voice, and I started talking immediately. I said, 'Hello, Dr. Bell. My name is Chauncey Cook, and Foraker Macreavy told me to call you."

"'He did, did he?' she responded. I could hear amusement in her voice, but I kept going.

"'Yes, ma'am,' I said. 'My daughter, Shantell, is twelve years old and badly injured.'

"I told her about Condoleezza Rice and the ice skating. I used the words tumor, brain, spine, and broken bones. I told her I talked to Officer Macreavy, and he told me to speak to her."

Dr. Bell asked me, "Where is your girl?"

"When I told her Miami Valley Hospital in Dayton, Ohio, she said, 'But I'm across the country.'

"I didn't know how to answer this, so I said, 'Ma'am, I'm calling because Officer Macreavy told me you would help my daughter. That's all I know.'

"She said, 'Hold on, Chauncey,' and then I heard nothing. I didn't know what to do. I thought we might have been disconnected, but I held on because she asked me to.

"As I hung on the phone, it occurred to me I didn't know any woman named Nelson Bell, and I didn't know why Macreavy would want me to call her. I could only say that I knew he wouldn't steer me wrong.

"After a minute, I heard her come back on the line, and she asked, 'How do you know Mac anyway?'

"I answered, 'From sailing on Lake Chautauqua.'

"'Really?' she asked.

"I answered, 'Yes, ma'am, I crewed for him one summer years ago.'"

Chauncey took a drink of his coffee and said, "I didn't think of it at the time, but her next question might have been a security check. I found out later Dr. Nel Bell is smarter than the average bear. She asked me, 'Which boat did you guys sail?' I told her I didn't know he had more than one. 'We sailed the boat his uncle built.' She acted like she didn't believe me, and I got impatient. I told her, 'We sailed the *LISPENARD*, the one his uncle Henry built in 1932,' but I couldn't figure out why she wanted to talk about sailboats.

"She said, 'Okay, hold on. Let me try once more.' And Dr. Bell's line went quiet again. This time I did think we'd been disconnected. Then she came back, and I heard, 'Chauncey, I'm trying to make a call on another line. Stay with me.' I waited for about two minutes. Again, no sound. Again, I thought I'd lost her, but she came back, checking on me this time. She said, 'Are you still there? I'm trying to get in touch with someone, and he may want to talk to you. Stay with me.'"

Chauncey said, "I waited and waited. I held for five minutes or more, and again, I wondered why. The next time she returned, she said, 'Thanks for your patience, Chauncey. This may take a while.' I told her, 'Dr. Bell, ma'am, I'm in the military. I know how things go. Officer Macreavy told me to call you. I trust him, and I trust you. You know where we are. Give the orders and do what you can. If you can help, I know you will. Thank you for listening to me and for everything you are trying to do. I'm going to sign off now, get back to my wife, and let you do whatever you're going to do to help my daughter.'

"'That's right,' she said. 'You're a good man, Chauncey Cook. Go back to your wife, and I'll do what I can from here.' She recited the words Shantell, Miami Valley Hospital, and Dayton, Ohio, back to me as if she were checking them and memorizing them simultaneously."

Chauncey drained the last of his coffee. He stopped talking momentarily, filled his cup again from the pot he'd brought in, and topped mine off as well. He looked at me with a strained expression on his face.

He said, "I went back to the meeting room and sat down with Donna. She looked worried, and I didn't say a word. I held her hand, and we sat silently for an hour while our daughter lay in some ICU bed somewhere. A doctor finally came and told us to go home for the night. He said they'd stabilized Shantell, and nothing could happen for a few hours. He said we should go home and sleep because the next day would take all our energy.

"We went home, but we didn't sleep much. We got back to the waiting room by eight o'clock the next morning. About a half hour later, a tall man in a gray suit came into the waiting room and sat in the chair next to us. He held his glasses in his hand and introduced himself as the hospital administrator. He addressed us as 'Sergeant' and 'Mrs. Cook.' He said he couldn't tell us anything about Shantell. However, overnight, the hospital received notice of a surgical team en route. He pledged the doctors at his hospital would do everything they could to assist.

"He paused for a moment and spoke again. He said, 'The team coming is well-known in the field. People always say they have the best doctors, but this group specializes in difficult cases. They are as good as it gets. There are none better.' He looked back and forth at the two of us. Then he said, 'But I have to ask you, how do you know Dr. Johnson?'

"I'll tell you, Tom," Chauncey said. "I realized this administrator's question had to do with why a Black family rated good-as-it-gets attention. It confused me too, but then it dawned on me that Macreavy and the woman I talked to might be behind it. The administrator had put me off, but he had my little girl in his hospital, so I didn't want to start an argument with him. I didn't want to get too familiar with this guy either, so I gave him the facts without explanation. I said, 'A guy named Macreavy told me to call Nelson Bell.'

"The administrator and my wife both looked at me with puzzled expressions. My wife remembered me telling her about the summer I'd had with Macreavy, so his name sounded familiar, but after a moment, she asked me, 'Who is Nelson Bell?' At the same moment, the administrator asked, 'Did you actually talk to her?' When he said 'her,' that told me he knew the name Nelson referred to a woman. How he asked me the question told me he knew something I didn't. I learned more about her later.

"As I said, I didn't want to get into anything with this guy then, so I answered his question as simply as possible. I said yes, and I didn't say anything more. He must have seen how distraught we looked, and he didn't want to badger me anymore, so he let it drop. He said, 'Okay, let's pray for the best.' He held out a folder and asked us to sign a consent form. Donna looked it over, and we signed. The administrator said, 'Dr. Johnson and his team have been in contact with our staff already. They indicated they would be here just before noon. They gave us preparation orders two hours ago, so we'll be able to begin working with them the moment they arrive.'

"When the administrator left, Donna had a hundred questions for me. I hadn't told her about the call to Macreavy or this Nelson Bell because I didn't know what to say. It all sounded like smoke, and I didn't want to get Donna's hopes up. I could only say that I believed in Macreavy, which might sound crazy to her.

"At about quarter to eleven, a nurse found us in the waiting room and asked us to come to the meeting room again. She said Dr.

Johnson and his team had landed at Dayton International Airport. The CareFlight helicopter had them en route to the hospital. At eleven o'clock, they let us see Shantell for a few minutes. But the nurses said she couldn't eat, they didn't want her moving around, and they sent us back to the waiting room." Chauncey got a faraway look in his eyes. He shook his head slightly and said, "Tom, you won't believe what happened next.

"A set of double doors opened, and four people walked into the waiting area shoulder to shoulder. They looked right at me, and something told me to stand up, but Donna stayed in her chair. What a crazy-looking group. Two men, two women, and they didn't look anything like a medical team. A tall good-looking Black man in his midforties stood to one side of the group. He wore a gray suit with a dark red tie and bright oxblood leather shoes the same shade as the tie. He said nothing. A tall thin woman with a perfect cream-colored complexion and a shock of red hair stood on the opposite side. She wore a black leather motorcycle jacket over a white blouse and a blue jean skirt. She stepped forward and walked toward us in chunky black shoes. She shook Donna's hand first and then mine.

"She said, 'My name is Marion Gately. I am Dr. Johnson's operating room nurse. I'll speak for all of us to save time.' With her hand raised toward the tall Black man, Nurse Gately said, 'This is Dr. Calvin Johnson. To his left is Mr. Andrew James. Mr. James is Dr. Johnson's physician's assistant.'"

Chauncey said, "This Andrew James could have been yuppy, exhibit one. He had on a white shirt with no tie, faded jeans, and black leather shoes, but over that, he wore a silk sports coat that looked like it came from the Himalayas someplace. Next, Nurse Gately introduced a younger nurse named Maura Widell as the 'technology specialist.' She wore a gray sweatsuit and running shoes, had short dyed-black hair, and a black and white yin-yang tattoo on the side of her neck.

"Nurse Gately said, 'We got the call last night. We've reviewed the images and know what we're looking at. We'll do everything we can to help Shantell. Do you have any questions?'

"Everything got quiet, and we all looked at each other. Then Donna rose to her feet and walked over to Dr. Johnson. She looked into his eyes. She put her hand on his sleeve, and neither moved the slightest bit. The rest of us stood looking at the two of them. Dr. Johnson spoke to her in a deep voice. He said, 'It's going to be okay, Donna. You are a good mother. You are a good wife and a good lawyer. Thank you for believing in us.'"

Chauncey said, "At first, it surprised me that this Dr. Johnson knew her name and that she was a lawyer, but thinking back on it, the team had exchanged information with the hospital. A smart guy like Dr. Johnson would have added the girl's parents to his mental file. He saw in Donna's eyes that she needed personal contact and affirmation, so he called her by name. The guy had a brilliant mind, but he had more than that. He understood people. That's how you get to be the best in the world."

Chauncey took a moment for another sip of coffee and continued, "So then this nurse with the red hair said, 'Sergeant Cook, Mrs. Cook, we need to scrub in. We want to meet Shantell.' She turned around and opened the meeting room door. The administrator had been waiting and led them to wherever they had to go next. Our meeting only took a few minutes, and we didn't see them again for twelve hours.

"We thought the waiting room doors might open anytime during that whole day. The hours dragged until we could hardly stand it. A few minutes before midnight, Nurse Gately and the assistant, Andrew James, emerged through the doors. This time they wore operating room scrubs. They'd flown in overnight and spent the last twelve hours in surgery, but they looked at us with bright eyes and smiles.

"Nurse Gately said, 'A good day. We think she's going to be okay. The tumor hadn't made it to her brain—total encapsulation. Dr. Johnson and Mr. James here think we got it all. All four of us and the doctors at this hospital are betting tests will say it's benign, but no one will say so until the lab signs off. Some spine damage, no doubt about that. I don't think there will be much ice skating in her future, but the nerves held on. Walking will come back to 80 percent, but I'll warn you now it's going to be a long recovery. I don't know how long. Everybody's different, but she's young, so let's expect the best.

The arm breaking could have been a good thing. It may have kept her head from hitting the ice. She might have suffered a mild concussion, but that's better than a severe concussion. See if anyone at the ice rink happened to have a camera going. That would tell. They set the arm here yesterday. Good job, and it will heal the way broken arms usually do. That's it. Do you have any questions?'

"Donna and I sat in stunned silence. Donna started to cry with relief, and the nurse took her hands in both of hers. We stood, and I said, 'I can't thank you enough.' Mr. James said, 'That's quite all right, sir.' He turned to the nurse, and in a mock movie voice, he said, 'Nurse Gately, I think our work here is done.' The two of them turned to leave when something occurred to me. I said, 'I do have one question.' They both stopped to look at me. I asked, 'Who is Nelson Bell?' Mr. James answered with a question of his own. 'Sergeant Cook,' he asked, 'have you ever heard of Bayard Rustin?' I told him I'd heard of him as Martin Luther King's political buddy.

"'Well,' Mr. James said, 'it has more to do with Daddy King, Martin's father. Daddy King knew of a young man at Ebenezer Baptist named Calvin Johnson, who had recently graduated from Morehouse. Daddy King thought Calvin would make a good doctor, so he talked to Bayard Rustin about him. Mr. Rustin knew everybody back then and got in touch with Dennis Nelson, who helped Calvin get into Columbia Physicians and Surgeons. Dennis Nelson also supported Calvin all the way through. Dennis Nelson is Nelson Bell's uncle, her mother's brother. Dr. Johnson met Nel Bell a few times when he visited her Uncle Dennis at their home in Jamestown, where I believe you are from, sir. Nel Bell called Dr. Johnson last night, and we made our way here today.'

"Andrew James paused, and, with a smile, he added, 'Oh, and by the way, the next time you see her, tell Shantell that Condoleezza Rice also plays piano and speaks fluent Russian.' We saw Shantel the following day, the first day of years of recovery, but thank God. She did recover."

Chauncey Cook looked into his coffee cup. He'd been taking sips throughout his story, emptying it again. He said, "I don't know how much more I can tell you, Tom. We didn't have any more big adventures after that. Shantell is looking at graduate schools now. She wants to study neuroscience, of all things. I wonder where she got that. I retired from the force and have a second career teaching auto mechanics here at Sinclair Community College. Donna and I are still together, and lately, she's been trying to figure out how to retire too.

"I do remember one other thing about Macreavy though. A few weeks after the surgery, I thought about the bill. I hadn't received anything from the hospital. I knew we had insurance, but I didn't know how much brain surgery would be covered. I thought I'd have to go into hock for the rest of my life, so I called the hospital. A woman in the billing department asked me to hold because the administrator wanted to talk to me. I waited while they tracked him down. I thought about the time I'd met him before, and the waiting also reminded me of waiting for Nelson Bell.

"When he came on the line, he said, 'I'm sorry, Sergeant Cook, I thought you knew, or I would have called you immediately. A Mr. Foraker Macreavy covered the bill. He wired a million dollars to the hospital on the day of Shantell's surgery. We never did get a bill from Dr. Johnson or his team. Possibly Mr. Macreavy paid them as well. We're checking into that. In the meantime, to be on the safe side, we put Mr. Macreavy's donation aside to cover Dr. Johnson's bill if he sends one.'

Chauncey Cook shook his head slightly the way I'd seen him do it before. He said, "'Kin' guy!"

We'd come to the end of the interview. We'd finished our coffee, and I thanked this proud and impressive man for a fascinating afternoon. On my way out, I paused at the front door. With a touch of irony, I asked, "So you'd say your brush with the law had a positive effect on your life?"

"Oh yeah," he agreed. "If that guy had taken his Roadmaster to some other place for an oil change, things would have been different."

I didn't have a long drive home this time to think about what I'd learned, but I didn't need a lot of time. Chauncey and Macreavy had used intellect, compassion, and connections to tack into the forces that blew around them. They crewed together, and, as Chauncey said, they finished in the money.

117

CHAPTER 7

Francis Patel: The Good Samaritan

The pandemic of 2020 hit out of nowhere, and everybody had to go into lockdown. Fortunately, by that time, I had interviewed almost all of the "caught thirty." The imposed time off posed significant problems, but my wife and I saw it as a gift. We finally had the time we wanted. She spent days in her art studio, while I wrote up my meetings.

After vaccinations became available, I decided to try another interview. I spread out the remaining fingerprint cards and photos on our dining room table. This time a young boy named Francis Patel drew my attention. He looked like he may have come from India or had Indian parents. He hung his head, his eyes focused to the right of the camera, and his hair flopped to the side. His collar hung askew with the top three buttons of a dress shirt undone. He could be a college guy at the end of a stormy night, but that would be unlikely. The arrest card had his age as fifteen.

Phil Troxel listed Francis Patel's current address in a town called Geneva, New York. I looked for it on a map and found out Geneva is a resort destination in the middle of the state, built around the Finger Lakes. Next to the address, Phil had written "Walworth Resort, Owner."

I reviewed my inquiry letter, which I'd written before the pandemic. I checked to see if I'd written anything that could be considered insensitive to what he and his hotel may have suffered during the lockdown. I dropped the letter in the mail and wondered if he'd kept the business going through the tumult. A reply came by email.

> To: Mr. Thomas Strongtree
> From: Walworth Resort
> Subject: Your letter
> Hello, Mr. Strongtree,
>
> Thank you for your interest and concern. Yes, I remember an incident in my youth. I'm not proud of it, but I'll meet with you if you want to discuss it in exchange for the card and photo. Please get in touch with me at the hotel the next time you are in the area.
> I'm sorry, but I am unfamiliar with Officer Macreavy. He became famous around Jamestown after he died and left all that money, but I did not know him.
>
> Regards,
> Frank Patel

He attached a link to his resort's website, which looked like a great place. I dialed the number and asked for Mr. Francis Patel. The person who answered the phone asked for my name. I told her, and Francis Patel came to the phone less than a minute later. He sounded out of breath as if he'd run for the call.

"Hello, Mr. Strongtree. I take it you received my email. How can I be of assistance?"

The man must have answered the phone a thousand times as a hotel owner, but somehow he sounded genuine. I told him I'd like to reserve a room for two nights and drive over to meet with him.

Francis Patel told me his resort "met or surpassed all local and federal protocols to ensure exceptional cleanliness." He said he had openings Tuesday and Wednesday nights of the following week, which told me he'd made it through the worst of the pandemic.

"We're on!" I said, "Do you want me to reserve the room online?"

"No need, Mr. Strongtree," he answered. "I'll write you in."

"Well, thank you, Mr. Patel," I said. "And, please, call me Tom."

"It will be an honor to meet you, Tom," he said. "And you, please call me Frank."

I made my way into Western New York, and after a few hours on the New York State Thruway, I saw signs for the Finger Lakes region. A billboard for the Walworth Resort advertised "Fine Traditional Indian Dining."

I checked in at the desk and arrived late to the dining room on the evening of the Tuesday we'd discussed. Frank Patel, a well-dressed man of athletic build in a gray business suit, greeted me with a smile and a slight bow. He treated me as an honored guest and had the chef prepare a late dinner. We didn't say a word about the card and photo, but as he got up from the table, he mentioned he'd be available in his office after nine the following morning. I took that to be the time for our appointment.

The following morning, I had a full Walworth Resort breakfast and made sure I'd finished by nine. As the hour approached, I sat at my table and made myself available. I'd seen Frank Patel that morning. He'd greeted me, this time dressed in a blue suit, but didn't stop to chat. He'd also welcomed other guests while delivering instructions to the service staff. I assumed he'd meet with me when he could, and I didn't want to get in his way. About a quarter after nine, Frank stepped into the dining room and indicated I should follow him with a brief hand gesture. I brought my coffee along as he led me to his office.

He had a pleasant office, nothing ornate—a desk with a computer, four file cabinets, framed photos of religious temples in India, and a three-by-eight worktable covered with a tablecloth against the wall. A few upholstered straight-back chairs were tucked underneath it. He pulled one out and offered it to me.

"I see you brought your coffee with you," he said. He picked up the phone and called for a coffee service to be delivered. "So you'll be able to add to your cup any time you wish, Mr. Strongtree, and I'll have some with you."

I smiled and said, "That would be great, but again, please call me Tom."

"Certainly, Tom," he said. "Welcome to Walworth."

Frank avoided his desk and took one of the other chairs at the table with me. He sat and crossed his legs. As I had with the others, I got right to the point. I reached into my backpack and handed Frank Patel the envelope with the fingerprint card and photo. "This is the only copy," I said. "There are no others that I know of." I let him open the envelope and remove the contents. He looked at them in silence. I gave him a few moments and said, "I would like you to tell me about that time. You don't have to, but I'm interested to know if contact with the law at a young age affected your life. Also, with your permission, I'd like to record your thoughts and what you remember."

I placed my iPhone on the table, and he glanced at it briefly.

"Sure," he said. "And thank you for bringing me these. I don't mind telling you about it, but I'm trying to remember how it all started."

We sat without a word, and I let him take his time. When he spoke, he said, "Andrea Lange. Her parents' house."

I repeated the name with a question. "Andrea Lange. A girl you knew?"

"Yes," he said. "She had a party at her house. The summer between ninth and tenth grade when I started high school. It turned out to be a joke."

"How do you mean a joke?" I asked him.

"It's part of the immigrant experience, Tom. Let me explain. My parents are from India, but my brother Steve and I were born here. Our parents gave us American names, but they wanted to raise us as if we lived in India, and they constantly complained about the lazy American kids. My brother and I walked the line between my parents and the kids at school.

"The word went around about a party at Andrea Lange's house. Her parents were going out of town for the weekend. She asked me to come, and I heard she only invited the cool kids. I thought I'd made it. I thought I'd been accepted. My older brother didn't know about it, which made it even better. I'd be the cool brother. I talked with the other kids about drinking beer at the party and playing spin the bottle with the girls. I couldn't wait to get there.

"Twenty-five or thirty kids showed up at the house, everybody running around and cranking up the music as loud as it would go. Her parents had this old vinyl record player, and we all jumped on the floor hard enough to get the needle to skip. One guy brought beer he'd taken from a grocery store. Another kid got into his father's bar cart and brought a bottle. One of the fun games turned out to be "Let's get the Indian kid drunk." I had three big glasses of whiskey and a can of beer. I wanted to be a cool American kid, and the other kids kept cheering me on.

"The next thing I knew, a policeman shook me and told me I had to wake up. I'd thrown up the whiskey all over Andrea Lange's living room carpet and passed out. I found out later we'd made so much noise the neighbors called the cops. A police car pulled up in front of the house, and all the kids scattered."

I had a hunch and asked Frank to see the fingerprint card again. I hadn't thought to look before, but now I saw it. A pencil note in the lower left-hand margin read, "Arr Off—For Mac."

"Officer Macreavy took you in," I told him.

"Really?" Frank asked. "How do you know?"

"I don't really, but I think that's what this abbreviation means. Arresting Officer—Foraker Macreavy. Maybe another policeman picked you up and passed you off to Macreavy, but I doubt it. The card also says the police released you to your parents. How did that go?"

"Not good," Frank said. "And we all had to go to court the following week. They charged me with nuisance behavior and underage drinking. The judge took one look at my parents scowling at me and figured he didn't have to sentence me to any more than that. He recommended my parents offer to have the carpet cleaned or replaced, but that's it."

A waiter knocked on Frank's office door and wheeled in a coffee service. Frank gestured to me, and I topped off my cup. "Thank you," I said. "You have great coffee here."

"We only serve the best, and I'm glad you enjoy it," Frank said.

He poured a cup for himself and continued, "You can imagine how the rest of the summer went. My parents found all sorts of jobs for me around the hotel we owned, and by the end of August, I couldn't wait to start high school. But when I got there, no one would talk to me. I saw some of the kids from the party that night, but none would have anything to do with me. I found my classes and tried to talk to some kids I'd known from junior high who hadn't been to the party, but they wouldn't speak to me either. Finally, someone told me the kids thought I got everyone in trouble at the party because I got sick. They might have come around if I'd let a little time pass, but it got worse. At lunch that first day, I sat at an empty table by myself. My brother had a different lunch period, so I couldn't even sit with him. This fat girl came over and sat at the table. She pulled a bag of potato chips and a can of orange soda out of her backpack. Wow, she looked terrible. No chance any other kids would sit at the table with me now. She had acne all over her face, and thin dirty hair she tried to pull into a ponytail. She had these torn-up blue jeans and an old long-sleeved sweatshirt that looked too warm for September. What I remember most is she clomped around in oversized work boots. They must have been three sizes too big. I found out later she had no other shoes. On top of all this, she smelled terrible.

"This girl sat across from me in the middle of the table. We didn't talk to each other. Next, this guy comes over and sits next to me. He says, 'My name Emile. I Syria.' I tried to smile and broke out my last bit of good cheer. I said, 'Glad to meet you, Emile. I'm Frank.' The girl looked over and said, 'My name is Connie.' Emile added these phrases, 'glad to meet you' and 'my name is' to the other half dozen words he'd learned. The kid landed in Jamestown from Syria three days before school started, and he couldn't speak English. The exchange student program placed him with a family in town, registered him at the high school, and unofficially signed him up for total immersion. Even though we didn't speak Arabic, Connie and I tried to talk to him a little. I'm not sure he spoke Arabic either, but that's what it sounded like.

"One day turned into two, and a few days turned into a week. Emile, Connie, and I kept sitting at the same table, and the longer we sat together, the more the other kids avoided us. When the next week started, some of the kids I'd known before started talking to me a little, but they kept their distance from Connie and Emile. And I knew why they wanted to stay away. Connie smelled terrible, and nobody could understand Emile, but the three of us still sat together at lunch. As school got going with homework and everything, I had enough to do without worrying about the two of them.

"I've got to say, Emile picked up English quickly. He went from zero to understandable in about three months. Day after day, he'd learn new words. He kept going to classes and learning to read. He put words together in the strangest way, and some kids mocked him, but I never did. He spoke English far better than I'll ever speak Arabic.

"Connie stayed quiet for the most part. She sat with Emile and me at the table but didn't say anything. A guidance counselor came by once and tried to get her to talk, but no dice. One of the special education teachers tried to talk to her, and Mr. Mullins, the history teacher, sat at our table one day and tried to have lunch with us. Connie would act mean when one of the teachers tried to talk to her. She didn't bark, but she came close. She let everybody know they'd better stay away.

"The more English Emile learned, the more often he'd sit with other kids at their tables. After a few days away, though, he'd come back and sit at the table with Connie and me. He had a lot to say about the other kids and confided in me. Maybe because he knew I had Indian parents or because I had darker skin, but he complained to me about the 'American children.' He had an argumentative per-sonality. He fought everybody and everything. He played chess a lot because he said his father told him kings learned about war from playing chess. He couldn't wait to run track after school, but he didn't want to be on the track team. For him, a race on the track meant one winner, and everyone else lost. He didn't understand football, but he played soccer with reckless abandon. Whenever he got a chance to play soccer, he'd run around in circles screaming in Arabic when someone scored a great goal or missed a kick. Most kids gave him a lot of space, and the rest hurled epithets along with soccer balls.

"At lunch, he'd tell me about the weak students surrounding him. He tried to explain the power of commitment and dedication in strange, broken English. He had this fierce loyalty to a code of some sort, but he couldn't explain it. His vocabulary couldn't keep up. He made one thing clear though. It involved a lot of judgment. He said the boys 'lived for fat and lazy,' and the girls 'for immoral.' I realize how unusual this kind of talk might seem to you, Tom, but I'd heard my parents express similar sentiments over the years. Maybe in more polite and reasoned tones, but it amounted to the same thing. Emile didn't stop there though. He saw it as his duty to fight and conquer the evil he saw around him. He told me, 'One day, I triumph over enemies.' He told me about his plan to humiliate the boys at the school by making them sit on the dirt behind the football field. He had a plan for the 'immoral' girls too. He'd 'correct' them and 'wrap them in clothing,' although I never understood how he planned to make his 'correction.' This Emile kid had an intense view of life."

Frank took a moment to think about that and sipped his coffee. He continued, "The kids and the teachers would talk to Emile in class when they had to, but mainly they stayed away. Then one day Emile came to me and told me something about Connie. He said someone hit her. I asked him how he knew, and he said, 'Ask to raise the shirt of she.' I asked him, 'How do you know what she looks like with her shirt off?' Emile answered, 'She say one man, friend of father, hit.'

"The next time I saw Connie at the lunch table, I told her Emile said someone hit her. She stared at me with these laser beam eyes. Her face got red, and she screamed at me. She yelled, 'Leave me alone. You don't know anything about it!' She exploded into tears, and all the kids in the lunchroom looked at us when they heard the yelling. It looked like I made her cry, and I wished I hadn't said anything. The other kids had one more reason to dislike me, all over a fat girl who smelled terrible. I wanted to run out of the lunchroom, but I couldn't. I didn't want to get in trouble for being out there without a hall pass. I didn't know what to do. I sat there across the table from her, frozen to the spot.

"She stopped crying after a few minutes, and it all came out. She said, 'My mother died five years ago. My father's friends come to the house, and they get drunk. One of the men tried to do it to me last night. I hit him hard, and he hit me back. He left a red mark on my side.' I said, 'Holy smokes, Connie! Did your father see it? Did you tell anyone?'

"'My father doesn't care. He never does anything. I told Emile,' she said. 'Why did you tell him?' I asked. 'What's he going to do about it? You have to tell the school or the police or someone like that.' 'No!' she answered. 'And don't you tell anyone either. If my father or one of his friends gets in trouble, they'll kill me. They will. They'll beat me until I'm dead.' Then she said, 'I told Emile because I had to tell someone, and I didn't think he'd even be able to tell anyone else.'"

Frank looked away and said, "I've wondered about the whole situation over the years. At first I thought Emile might have been in on it. I even thought he'd done it. He walked around, ready to blow all the time, and what if he lost it one night? I also thought maybe he'd been over at her house and seen someone else hit her. That's not what happened though. I'm sure. He didn't even know where she lived, and he couldn't have known her father or anyone who knew her father. I think she told Emile because she knew he would sympathize with her. She hurt, and she knew he had a lot of anger. Maybe, in her mind, she thought Emile would hurt her father. I don't know, but Connie remained convinced her father or one of his friends would kill her if she said anything to the school.

"Then it happened again," Frank said. "Connie missed two days of school, and when she returned, Emile told me 'the father of Connie hit.' This time I asked her to pick up the side of her shirt. Someone had bruised a roll of fat on her right side and hit her hard enough to scrape the skin off. She told me two guys beat her, and they said they knew enough not to hit her face so it wouldn't show.

"I told Connie she had to report it. I got her to agree that she had a dangerous problem, but she said she wanted to think about it. Reporting it might stop the beating for a while, but if her father got in trouble with the law, it might get even worse for her. I agreed, but it didn't sit well in my heart. I asked her if she had any friends or places she could go to get away, and she said no.

126

"I wanted to tell someone, but I thought I'd make things worse somehow, and everyone would blame me as usual. Later that afternoon, Emile saw me in the hall before school ended. He waved me to the side and asked, 'Connie, one worker, for you at hotel?'"

Frank looked at me and said, "Tom, that one sentence in broken English set the course for the rest of my life."

I returned his gaze and raised an eyebrow to acknowledge the importance of what he'd said and to ask him for clarification at the same time. He took another sip of his coffee.

"Okay, let me back up a minute," he said. "As I told you, my parents came to America from India. My father's brother helped them put a down payment on a hotel in Jamestown. After they got the hotel going, they bought a donut shop franchise. That's how it works for Indian families sometimes. Someone saves enough money to buy into a business. They open up, spend twenty-four hours a day at it, and send word back home to tell the rest of the family how great things are. They say anyone who wants a chance at life in America can come and work at the business. My parents had my older brother a year after they got here, and I came along a year and a half after that. My parents accomplished something. They made it to America, ran two businesses, and had sons born here.

"So that night, I talked to my parents about Connie. I laid out the whole situation and asked them what to do. They did not say she should tell the school or call the police, which might have been the more appropriate reaction. That's what most American parents would say. But Emile had another idea, and my parents knew exactly what he had in mind. My parents also knew how to put it into play. They didn't hesitate. They said, 'She should come with us.'

"They offered Connie a place where she could stay and work at the hotel. They converted a storeroom into a bedroom. She had a bed, a desk, a chair, and a small refrigerator. She worked off the books for the room and a few dollars."

Frank paused for a moment and continued with hesitation. "Did my parents take advantage of Connie? Did my parents exploit a vulnerable girl for their good? Sure, but the deal got her out of danger. Okay, maybe she didn't understand all her choices. Did she have any other way to escape her father and the threat of danger? Maybe. She could have told the school, and they'd bring in county services. Except that doesn't always go the way it should, and sometimes it doesn't end well at all. The only thing I can say is this worked.

"Connie's father came to the hotel looking for her once. He sounded drunk, and my father yelled at him to leave. Her father argued that he had 'rights to his daughter,' which sounded as strange then as it does now. My mother stepped in and threatened to report him and his friends for the attempted rape of a minor. Connie's father slinked away, and I only saw him once after that.

"It's a gray area," Frank explained. "It's not how we think things should be done in America, but it's how they do things in India and other parts of the world. Connie worked at the hotel and the donut shop. She said she liked her converted storeroom, and the security she found with my family did her good. Before living at the hotel, she said she hadn't had a full night's sleep in years. Her father's drinking and loud noise kept her up late, and when the commotion ended and got quiet, she worried about some drunk sneaking into her bedroom. She never let her guard down.

"My mother recognized that Connie had missed some basic training without a mother. She took over remedial repair, and two needs intersected. I mean no criticism by this, but it's true. My mother needs to tell other people what to do. She gets her strength and purpose from directing. My brother and I were sick of it. We couldn't wait to graduate high school and move away from her nagging, but Connie saw it the other way. She needed direction and saw my mother as the first person who ever took a genuine interest in her. My mother started by showing Connie how to clean the rooms. They put together a work schedule around guests, school, and homework. Connie couldn't get close enough to her while my brother and I tried to escape my mother. She explained to Connie how to buy clothing at Goodwill, how to wait for bargains, and how to keep her room neat. She handled everything a young girl needs a mother to explain. Connie took hot showers in the hotel rooms before she cleaned them. My mother also suggested she clean her clothes by washing them with the sheets and towels.

"My parents taught her how to check people in at the hotel desk after school and on the weekends, which meant both my mother and father could work more hours at the donut shop. Also, around this time, two aunties arrived from India. They shared a guest room in our home. One auntie went to work at the donut shop, and the other worked at the hotel. My mother and father expected Connie to teach one of the aunties the daily routine at the hotel, but the auntie only spoke a little English, and Connie spoke no Hindi. Again, needs intersected with abilities. Connie started teaching the auntie basic vocabulary for the hotel, and the auntie returned the Hindi words for the same things back to Connie."

Frank's eyes lit up, and he laughed out loud. He said, "Connie picked up Hindi better than the auntie learned English." Frank gulped his coffee and continued, "After learning several words in Hindi, Connie tried them out on my mother. Language lessons became one more thing my mother could direct. I'd heard my mother and father speaking Hindi all my life, so I understood it. To this day, Connie and I can talk to each other in Hindi. It's important for business, and it comes in handy sometimes. Think about the two of us ganging up on a furniture salesman."

I didn't want to break Frank's stride, so I let this comment pass. I didn't understand what he meant about speaking Hindi with Connie for business, but I thought some clarification would come from context.

"After the auntie learned the hotel routine, my mother moved her to the donut shop. The auntie, who had been at the donut shop, went to the hotel. She moved Connie to the donut shop too, even though she continued to live in her converted storeroom at the hotel. My mother thought everyone should know all the jobs and took over training the other auntie at the hotel. I'd been working at the donut shop with my father for years by this time. He'd start at three in the morning, and I'd get there at five. I'd open at five thirty, take care of early customers, and put in a few hours before school. After school, I'd finish the day at the hotel. Connie and I did our homework at the front desk while I fixed things around the place, and Connie did the laundry in the basement. When Connie began at the donut shop, we'd meet every morning. We opened the shop and served customers until we left together to walk over and start the school day. If the other kids noticed us coming in together every morning, we didn't think anything of it. Now and then we'd freak them out on purpose. We'd share a joke or start talking in Hindi.

"Because Connie listened to what my mother told her, my mother accepted Connie. Nutrition became another thing they worked on together. Connie had a refrigerator and supposedly enough money to buy food, but she only bought potato chips and soda. When she moved to the donut shop, she'd eat three or four cream-filled crullers in the mornings while waiting on customers.

"My mother told me Connie ate junk because she didn't know better. After a week or so at the shop, my mother took her aside. She explained we never eat the donuts. They're full of cheap flour, imitation fruit, and fake sugar. My mother said, 'We sell the donuts, but we don't eat them.' While someone else might wonder about the ethics of selling something you wouldn't eat yourself, Connie only heard my mother use the word *we*. After that, my mother and the aunties took Connie into the kitchen and taught her about Indian cooking.

"Eventually, after a year or so, Connie could hold her own in the kitchen, but it didn't come easily. It's tough to pick up Indian eating as a teenager, but the foreign spices and textures only had to compete with the potato chips and frozen dinners of Connie's world. Working in the kitchen with the other women also allowed her to practice her Hindi. Things changed for good when Connie started losing weight. The first year Connie spent with the Indian women eating vegetables and learning to balance the proteins and vegetable fats, she lost forty pounds. The following year, she lost another twenty for a total of sixty pounds.

"Take a look," Frank said. He got up from his chair and walked to his desk. He picked up a framed picture and handed it to me. "You can't see her as a fat teenager, can you?"

My eyes went wide. In the picture, Frank stood in his blue suit next to a beautiful blond woman of medium build, about his height, dressed in a brightly colored green and blue Indian sari trimmed in gold. "Wait." I said, "This is Connie?"

"Yeah," Frank answered with a touch of nonchalance. "We do all kinds of Indian stuff here, and she dresses in traditional clothing now and then. We had this picture taken last year."

"Last year?" I asked, "You still see her?"

"Sure," Frank answered with a huge smile. "I married her." He laughed and took another swallow of his coffee.

"Okay," I said. "Now I have to hear how that happened."

"Well," Frank began, "as I explained, Connie needed a family, and my mother needed a student. I don't think either one of them consciously planned anything. They fell into it day after day, and their relationship evolved. They cooked together for my father, brother, and me. They looked for bargains at the thrift shop together. They cleaned the hotel, sold donuts, watched over the aunties together, and did it all in Hindi.

"You might think I'd come to see her as a sister, but I never did. She lived at the hotel. She didn't live in our home, and as close as she got to our family, my mother kept clear boundaries. Although she included Connie, she never included her as one of the family. Also, as she ate better and lost weight, I found myself attracted to her. Her skin cleared up. Her hair got stronger, and she let it grow long. My mother taught her how to dress and walk, and Connie's confidence grew. After we left high school and went to college, she looked even better. I'm telling you, Tom, I married the American dream girl."

I laughed at that. "You stayed in touch through college, then?" I asked Frank.

"Yeah," he answered. "We went to the same school."

It felt like he might be setting me up again. "Really?" I asked. "What college?"

"The Cornell School of Hotel and Hospitality Management," he answered proudly.

He laughed again, and I remember thinking that I'd met a man who relished life's drama, comedy, and possibilities.

"Well, how about that!" I said.

"Yeah," Frank agreed. "When I started senior year, I had to begin applying for college. My parents assumed I'd go to college. There's no other option in our culture. My brother had completed half of a premed program by then, and my parents wanted me to follow. They wanted me to do something in science and technology. That makes sense. I understand that, but I had a different idea.

"Whenever my parents talked about the other kids in the Indian families, it always had to do with success. The best of them, the doctors and engineers, had advanced degrees, but I couldn't see that for myself. One night Connie and I saw the movie *Dirty Dancing*, which gave me an idea. The film takes place at a resort hotel in the Catskills. I looked into it, and the way I understood it, Jewish people from New York City would drive up and go to these resorts in the mountains all summer long. Jewish people ran the resorts, and they knew what Jewish people liked. City people could go to the country, but they'd be comfortable there because they'd be around familiar people and accommodations. That got me thinking. I wondered where Indian doctors, engineers, and business owners went on their vacations. I found a few places, but I knew I could do better.

"I thought about it for a while and put the idea to Connie. I said, 'Let's go to hotel and restaurant management college. We'll learn about the business in school. Then we'll buy an old place and turn it into a resort for successful Indian families.' Connie didn't give it a second thought. She said, 'I'm in. And, sweetheart, don't even think about doing it without me.'"

Frank said, "That's where the idea started, and my parents couldn't be more against it. To them, the world only rewarded hard sciences. They said, 'Let someone else wash the dishes and change the bedsheets.' They'd done that, and they couldn't see why I'd want to do more of it. I stayed with the idea though. I kept arguing my case. I had super-high grades because the family didn't accept anything less. I nailed the SAT, and I had a shot at Cornell. I reminded them of what the Ivy League meant in America. And since Cornell is in Ithaca, a few towns over from Jamestown, I told them transportation would be cheaper than any other big-name school. They agreed but didn't truly get on board until after they'd seen our first million-dollar season."

Frank laughed. He said, "I didn't tell them how much of that went into loan payments, but they didn't have to know that."

I placed the picture of Frank and Connie back on his desk where we both could see it, and Frank continued, "But it didn't go that way for Connie. She had good grades, but not great. My mother made sure she did all her homework and taught her how to study, but Connie had trouble with school. After years of neglect from elementary school through junior high, she couldn't bring her grades up to high levels. She did okay on the SAT but wouldn't have even taken it if my parents hadn't insisted. Here's where my father came through in a way no one expected. He went into action. He made appointments with the guidance counselors at the high school and got the name of every teacher Connie had in all three years. He tapped his friends and buddies in the community and got in touch with every Cornell grad in the Jamestown area. One by one, he went around and told them Connie's story. Most of the teachers knew some of it already, but he made sure they knew all of it. He mentioned the abuse, but he mainly told them how well she worked at the hotel and donut shop. He made sure everyone knew she'd learned Hindi and Indian cooking. To top it off, he mentioned the sixty pounds she'd lost. That got everybody's attention. He took a portrait photo of her with his favorite camera and left an eight-by-ten print with each person he talked to. He'd taken an excellent picture of blond American Connie dressed in an Indian sari. My mother suggested red and green, the Jamestown High School colors, and Connie stood in front of our hotel. He asked each of them to put the photo on their desk, look at it carefully, and write a letter recommending Connie to Cornell. Every one of them did it. Forty-seven letters accompanied Connie's application, each raving about the small-town girl who had conquered disadvantages and wanted to study hospitality, international culture, and cuisine. In their own way, each one of them said the girl would become a successful woman and be a credit to the school.

"We requested our interviews scheduled for the same day to make the transportation easier. We borrowed my dad's Chevrolet, left early, and drove back that night. I remember it as one of those adventures you have when you're young—when a car ride across the state becomes a voyage to a new and far-off land. I did well in my interview, but I wish I could have seen hers. Mine came first, and two others followed before hers. The interviews took place in a conference room, and Connie and I sat together in the hallway outside. I had my interview, and while we waited for hers, I noticed several people who looked like college professors milling around. They wanted to sit in with the admissions committee for Connie's interview. I had to wait outside, but there wouldn't have been any room for me anyway. By the time they called her, people from the college had packed the place. They wanted to get a look at the blond wonder girl who lost sixty pounds and who all of Jamestown wanted to send their way. The entrance department even asked two Indian professors from the engineering college to talk with her to see if she knew the language. She did not wear a sari. She wore black platform heels, a red jacket over a white blouse, with a gray skirt—the Cornell colors. She answered their questions and told them how she made her way through high school working at the hotel and donut shop. Then she told them how she fell in with Indian culture and learned the language and cuisine. She said she wanted to continue her studies to further her understanding. I think Connie sealed the deal when she spoke with one of the professors in Hindi. She told me she listened to him politely as he told her how his mother prepared Pindi Chana. Speaking in Hindi, Connie thanked him and said she couldn't wait to get back in the kitchen to try his suggestions. The acceptance letter arrived a month later. Connie won a full ride."

"That's fabulous, Frank. You and the family must have been so proud of her."

Frank took another pull at his coffee. "A great day, no doubt," he said. "One of those days we live for."

He continued, "That fall, we took off for Cornell together, and, wow, I'm telling you, college is a different game. I'd studied in high school and got good grades, but I had to pour it on at Cornell. Connie struggled in some classes but did better than I did in others. Connie and I stayed in separate dorms and apartments all the way through. We had an odd relationship—not boyfriend and girlfriend, not brother and sister. Maybe business partners would be more like it. Not a week went by when we didn't run into one another two or three times. We traveled back and forth to Jamestown on the bus together for holidays but took different paths at school. There are many ways to approach the business. We each put together a view of what an incredible resort would be, which helped us over the years. Working outside of school helped too. One summer, Connie took a job in the Catskills so she could see how they really did it there, and I went back to town and worked at Chautauqua for a season. That's the Chautauqua Institution," Frank explained.

"I've heard of it," I acknowledged. "World-famous." Frank looked pleased that I'd recognized Chautauqua.

"They had an Indian social group at Cornell," he continued. "And I spent time with them. I went out with three Indian girls and didn't try to keep it a secret. Connie knew about them. One time I mentioned I had a date for a party on the weekend. I wanted to see how she'd react. She looked at me, I saw a smile in her eyes, and she said, 'I'll be waiting.' Sometimes I'd see her at campus parties. She'd be drinking a beer and talking to some of the other students, but that didn't bother me. I never thought much about it until one time in the fall of our senior year. I saw her on a date with a guy at an Italian restaurant. I recognized him as one of the stars of the Cornell football team. This time it scared me, and I proposed that winter break. I asked her to marry me and start the resort project right after graduation. She answered, 'Of course, let's get going.'

"We waited until after New Year to tell my parents because we knew it would be a difficult conversation. All my life, I'd heard more than ten thousand times they expected me to marry an Indian girl. They even had a few lined up for me. We met with them in our family living room a couple of weeks before returning to school and told them we wanted to get married. My parents met us with stone-cold silence. They didn't say a word. The four of us sat looking at each other, and my parents wouldn't respond one way or the other. I almost wanted them to say no so I could argue with them. After several minutes, Connie and I got up and left the living room. The silence went on for days, and that made it worse. After almost a week, they called us back into the living room. They had a bottle of Sula Dindori Reserve set aside with four glasses on a table covered with a small green cloth.

"My father did the talking and started with what we already knew. He said he and my mother had always wanted me to marry an Indian girl, and they'd been living an emotional tug-of-war for the last few days. He said they recognized how they had come to a new country and wanted to accept the ways of that new country, but they had to express their disappointment that I wouldn't be marrying an Indian girl. My father said he needed to say that because that's what he felt. He believed his son should marry an Indian girl and didn't want to bury those feelings. On the other hand, my parents also said they had come to know Connie. My father ended by saying he now believed we would make a successful team in America, and, after much thought and discussion, my parents decided to give us their blessing. With that, he poured the wine. He filled the glasses and said, 'No small sips tonight. It's a new year and a new life for our children.' Connie jumped up and ran to my mother. They held each other and cried tears of relief and joy. My father shook my hand.

"We went back to school with one more semester to get through. Connie wore her diamond and gold engagement ring, but we kept separate apartments. Maybe it doesn't matter, but I'll tell you, Tom, we hadn't ever slept together. We might have wanted to from time to time, but never at the same time. It hadn't happened, and now we thought it would be in keeping with tradition to hold off until after the wedding. It would be the first time for both Connie and me. I found a way to communicate that to my parents, which helped their acceptance.

"We didn't have much time for romance anyway. Our final semesters at Cornell took everything we had. We tied up loose ends, finished projects, and made it through. We had a splendid graduation day. My brother took a break from medical school, where he'd started two years before, and shared the ride from Jamestown to Ithaca with my parents. My father drove the same Chevy Connie and I drove over for the interviews. Holding their heads up and looking around, my parents told another couple nearby that they had two graduates, and my brother couldn't resist. He said, 'And after that, my brother and sister are getting married.' We exploded in laughter.

"We didn't lift a finger for the wedding. My mother, the aunties, and the Indian women in the community took over, and I mean they took over. It wouldn't have happened without them. With school finishing, we only had minutes to spare. Organizing a big event would have been impossible. They put on a fabulous wedding, as traditional as they could manage, and Connie looked radiant in her *lehenga*—that's the bridal gown. In Indian culture, the more colorful the *lehenga*, the better. In India, white is the color of death, so we don't use it for brides. Connie chose the old high school red and green but had it trimmed with gold this time. My parents invited Connie's father, who showed up in jeans and work boots. He looked and smelled like he had a few before he got there, and he spoke with Connie briefly. He cracked some joke about how much money the wedding must have cost and ducked out early. At least he didn't start a fight, and Connie didn't ask after him.

"The day before the wedding, we got the news that started us on our next adventure. My father and mother called us into the living room again and handed Connie an envelope. My parents told us later they assumed Connie would get married someday. They also knew her father wouldn't provide a dowry. Connie opened the envelope and took out a statement detailing how my parents had opened a savings account in her name. Deposit notices listed contributions every month going back to her high school days. The account had grown to $5,000. Connie looked at my parents. With tears welling in her eyes, she asked, 'You're giving me a dowry?' My father said, 'Yes, it's yours, given to you in gratitude for the work and joy you've given us. Take it with our blessing and build a wonderful life,' and then my father laughed. He said, 'We never thought it would go back to you, Frank.'"

Frank observed, "What counts is the time spent making ideas come alive. Many of the graduates we knew left for New York City or California, but this didn't make much sense to us. Why mix it up in the world of cutthroat competition? We also decided we didn't want to move far away. We wanted to stay close to home so we could get back to Jamestown to see my parents, but we didn't want to take over their hotel. We wanted something more extensive. That left the Finger Lakes. Why not? It had all the possibilities. We wanted a place to plant a sapling and grow it into a tree.

"We took two of the five thousand, bought a car, and drove it all around the middle of New York State, looking for a place to start. We kept our eyes and ears open. We learned about the lakes and every town around them. We checked for zoning restrictions and boating access. That's when we found this place. It had seen better days, but it had a great location on the lake. I remembered how important Lake Chautauqua had been to Jamestown. We applied to the hotel as a couple of Cornell grads with experience. They desperately needed us but couldn't afford to pay, so we took less. That didn't matter though. We had bigger fish to fry. Ironically, they didn't listen when we told them we both spoke Hindi. The manager who interviewed us asked why that would be important, and I answered that we could speak with Indian people in their own language.

"The manager said, 'We don't get many Indian people here. That won't be necessary.' Connie and I looked at each other, and we couldn't resist a smile. I think the manager noticed, but he didn't say anything. He needed us more than we needed him, or so he thought. We worked the holiday season, and then we came up with an idea to get us through the winter. In America, successful, well-off people ski in the winter. If you're successful, you might want to ski also, but what if you needed to learn how? We put together a weekend package for successful Indian people who want to learn how to ski.

"Sometimes people want to learn something as adults but fear stepping off familiar paths and looking foolish. Our natural tendency keeps us away from where we might fail. On the other hand, successful people have learned the way to be successful is to reach and learn new things. Our weekends gave successful Indian people an opportunity to learn skiing without embarrassment. The packages included gourmet Indian food and transportation to the slopes with ski lessons. We had brochures made with pictures of my parents, along with Connie and me, dressed in expensive ski clothing. We sent them around to every Hindu temple and Indian community center we could think of.

"We had a few responses the first year, but we hit the lottery when those people went back and told their friends they went skiing, ate butter chicken, or full vegetarian, and spoke with the people at the resort in Hindi. In our second year of the ski program, we had the biggest Presidents' Day weekend in Walworth Resort's history. It dawned on the people who owned the resort that we had a plan in mind. They initially collected the money and tried to tell us better ways to run our programs, but that wore thin. They liked our success but wanted to change our style and direction. They knew their days were numbered and decided to get out.

"The hotel owner talked with some people he knew about the best way to sell. We talked to a lawyer from the Indian community in Syracuse. We hired a woman from Cleveland who came over and did a 'going concern' appraisal. She spent three days looking through past bookings and balancing them against every cost, tax, and expense you could think of. Her reports went to the lawyer, and his firm came up with a figure. The owners went through the same process, and their lawyers came up with a figure. Surprisingly, our people valued the place at $7,000 more than their people.

"We split the difference and agreed to put 25 percent down and pay the rest in installments plus interest. Our lawyer put us together with a wonderful older woman he knew from temple. The woman told us stories of how her great-grandfather had escaped India. During World War I, men faced starvation, so they went along with conscription which turned out to be a ticket to slaughter in Europe, fighting for the British. She said, 'For him, it was death, war, or a new life in America.' She spoke with Connie in Hindi for two hours. The woman loaned us $50,000 and wrote on her stationary in perfect cursive, 'Ganesha be with you. Please repay at regular intervals when you are able.'

"That almost did it. We borrowed some more and made the 25 percent. The hotel's original owners bought a condo in Florida and used their Social Security to keep the gas tank full on their boat.

"Going into our first summer season under new management, we had another piece of good luck. A sailboat club decided to have their annual regatta on Seneca Lake that year, and the club asked if they could use our facilities as their headquarters."

I got up and went to the service for more coffee. Foraker Macreavy flashed into my mind, and I couldn't resist a smile. "Is there a lot of sailing on your lake?" I asked.

"Oh, sure," Frank answered. "And this particular booking came at precisely the right time. Connie and I hired extra staff for the weekend, and we worked around the clock. Seventy-five sailboats and hundreds of sailing people showed up in July that year. The other resorts and restaurants around the region got some of the business, too, and it looked like we brought good luck to the whole area. Talk about framing your first dollar. That's what that large picture is beside the window in the upstairs bar."

"I didn't see it," I told Frank. "I haven't been up there yet."

"Yeah," he said. "It's a picture someone took out on the water. It's a great shot of a group of sailboats. All the guys are leaning out of the boats trying to round the mark. It's a dramatic scene, especially since Connie and I were also going for a mark. I can't remember who, but someone gave us the picture to say thanks, and we had it blown up and framed. Every time I see it, I think back to those days, and I want to grab Connie and kiss her. That's the story, Tom. The resort kept us busy, and we've had a great life. We managed to have two sons with all of it, and now we're looking at what might come after us. That brings us up to now, more or less."

I asked, "You had sons, Frank?"

"Yes, two American boys. They're amazing guys, and we couldn't be more proud."

"Any interest in the family business?" I asked.

"No, they've got other ideas," he said. "But we're behind them a hundred percent, and we can't wait to see what they come up with."

Frank got up from his chair, and I took that as a signal he needed to get back to work. He stepped toward the door and said, "Let me show you around the place if you're interested and then this evening we'll treat you to dinner."

I thanked him for a tremendous morning and told him I'd be honored to take a tour. He took me to the main dining room. "We specialize in Indian food. Our chef came from India and has been with us for a few years. We have patrons who return and ask for him season after season."

We passed by tennis courts on our way to the boat launches. Poured concrete ramps allowed boat trailers to back into the water, and four well-maintained docks jutted out into the lake. A beautiful pavilion overlooked the docks, and Frank showed me around inside. One end of the pavilion sported a stunning twenty-foot-long mahogany bar finished with bright glossy marine varnish. It stood at one end of a moderately large open area that could be used for receptions. A giant TV hung on a wall to the side of the bar. The locker rooms came complete with showers, washers, and dryers. The service kitchen in the pavilion had everything you'd need for a full-size barbecue. I saw several golf carts outside the pavilion's back door. Frank explained they could take you to the golf course about a mile away or to where you parked your RV camper nearby. Frank and Connie had thought of everything. On the weekends in October, they sponsored "leaf tours" on buses that took people through parts of upstate New York. "Every bit as beautiful as Vermont," Frank guaranteed. They used the same buses for their ski weekend packages through the winter, which ferried guests to three different slopes in the area.

As the afternoon began, Frank left me on my own. He said, "Please, have lunch, but excuse me if I don't join you. I've got several things that need attention, but I'll see you for dinner. Meet me in the dining room at about nine o'clock this evening. You should be good and hungry by then, and most of the dinner service will be through so that we can eat in peace. Also, Connie might be able to break free about then."

Frank had bowled me over. I told him I'd continue the tour on my own and looked forward to seeing him at nine that evening. For another hour, I walked around. I watched people playing tennis and saw two boats set out onto the lake. It surprised me to see that many people on a weekday in September. About half the people I saw looked like they might be Indian.

I'd been looking over the boat launches and walked out on one of the docks when a young college-age man approached. He said, "Good afternoon, Mr. Strongtree. My father mentioned I might run into you out here." The young man offered his hand and smiled.

"Well, fabulous," I said as we shook hands. "I'm glad to meet you. You know I'm Tom Strongtree, and you are?"

"Oh, please excuse me, sir," he said. "Frank and Connie are my parents. I'm home from school for a few days, making a pest of myself. My name is Emile."

"The grand circle!" I said. "They named you after the boy they knew in high school."

"That's right," Emile confirmed. "Did you know my parents then?" he asked.

"I didn't, but I've heard the story," I answered. "What a remarkable couple." I said, "You have extraordinary parents, Emile."

Emile agreed and brought me back to the main building for a soup and sandwich lunch. After lunch, I wished Emile a good afternoon and returned to my room to stretch out for a nap. It's pure luxury to take a nap in the afternoon. I woke up two hours later and felt great. At eight o'clock that evening, I changed into dress clothes, threw on a tie, and made my way to the dining room.

It had to be Indian food. After all the talk about Indian culture, I couldn't pass up the chance to taste some of the best of it. Frank arrived with Emile, and they brought me to a table off to the side. We sat, and a young waiter came to the table, presenting us with American and Indian menus. He asked for a drink order. I had coffee, and Frank and Emile had cold bottles of Kingfisher. Frank told me Kingfisher beer reminded people of India, so they made a point of keeping it on hand.

I looked at the Indian menu and couldn't understand a word. Translations in side-boxes promised help, but I thought better of trying to sort my way through. I said, "Frank, I'm hungry. I'm sure anything you serve will be exquisite. Please order for both of us."

He had the chef make up a sample tray, and I had a bit of everything. We had chutney samosas pastries, dal, curry, and leg of goat. As old as I am, I tasted flavors at that meal I'd never tasted before. Frank coached me, and I gave myself over to the experience.

A full-figured blond woman entered the dining room through the kitchen doors about an hour into the meal. She beamed a beautiful smile in our direction, and I knew she must be the woman I'd heard about. Her steps toward us whooshed on the dining room carpet under her European kitchen clogs. I sprang to my feet.

Frank introduced us. "Tom, this is my wife, Connie."

She wore a red chef hat and matching kitchen coat with a gold collar over a dark-blue skirt. She gripped my hand with both of hers.

"I'm glad to meet you," she said. "Frank tells me you've heard the story, and you're still here."

"And I'm glad to meet you," I said. I gave it a moment and continued, "Mrs. Patel, I am so impressed with all you've done and accomplished. I'm thrilled to share this fabulous meal with Frank and Emile. I congratulate you on all you've done to make this a spectacular resort. Thank you for having me."

"The pleasure is ours," Connie said. "Frank had a great time sharing the old stories. I'm sorry I can't stay and have a drink with you, but there are emergencies to attend to. Please forgive me, and please come back again."

We shook hands, and I wished her well. She turned away and went back into the kitchen. As we settled in again, Emile gave me a sidelong glance and said, "Life and work in the kitchen never ends."

I returned a nod in his direction. I'm sure there are challenges for the sons of successful, dedicated restaurateurs. I looked over at my host and said, "Frank, she's an amazing woman. You are a fortunate man."

"Don't I know it!" he answered.

Our evening ended shortly after that, and I returned to my room for a beautiful night's sleep. I kept trying to reconcile the difference between the woman I'd met that evening and the scared, abused teenager Frank described. Remarkable.

I made it to breakfast around seven the following morning. I had a day's drive ahead and wanted to get up and out on the road. Frank came into the dining room, greeted me warmly, and thanked me again for making the trip. I thanked him for the hospitality, and he reiterated Connie's invitation to come back.

I remembered the upstairs bar and asked Frank, "Will you show me that picture of the sailboats you told me about yesterday?"

"Sure," he said. "I'll take you up there now."

We took the stairs. A door opened onto a medium-sized room with tall bar tables and stools near a large picture window. The window showcased an impressive view of the lake and the boat docks. He pointed to a framed poster-sized picture hanging next to the window, and I crossed the room to look closer. Frank explained, "We put it here so you can look at the picture and see the lake at the same time."

The photograph showed six different colored sailboats heading for a mark. The camera captured a bright blue sky, and, from the white caps on the surface of the water, there must have been a good wind blowing that day. A tangle of white sails marked with the Snipe insignia, and racing numbers filled the center of the picture. As Frank had mentioned, the sailors on board were leaning out over the sides of their boats. I could feel the wind and hear the boats slamming onto the water after they jumped the waves. I could imagine the competitors calling warnings.

One light-colored boat drew my attention. A young Black man in the crew position held the jib line with both fists and leaned heavily away from the sail. The helmsman held the tiller in his left hand and managed a smile as he gripped the line for the mainsail in his teeth. With his right hand, he waved at the camera. I called Frank over to the picture.

"This is Foraker Macreavy," I told him, pointing to the guy waving at us, "the policeman who picked you up off the living room floor at Andrea Lange's. He's also the guy who arranged for the regatta to be held at your place that year."

The two of us stood looking at the picture. For a moment, I wanted to let on that I knew the Black man in the crew position and that he had also done well in life. But something told me I'd best maintain his anonymity. Instead I commented, "Frank, you extended the compassion you received."

I've considered the parable of the Good Samaritan many times throughout my life. I've always wished the story had more to tell. The Samaritan is the hero. He gets the notoriety, but what about the other guys in the story? What about the innkeeper? The Samaritan drafted him into service, but he went along with it. What if he didn't want to? And did the man attacked by robbers survive? What if he needed extra attention? The innkeeper would have to pay for it, and then he'd have to figure out how to collect from the Samaritan. What if the Samaritan didn't return? Frank and the Patel family answered my questions. They showed me how it's done.

CHAPTER 8

Darla Rhinesmith: The Woman
Caught in the Act of Adultery

D arla Rhinesmith must have looked directly into the camera when they took her picture at the police station. Her dark eyes and thoughtful expression told me she had a story, but I'd put it off until now. I didn't want to admit that a fourteen-year-old girl scared me, but she did. Her eyes and countenance signaled intensity, and I knew I'd have to be at my best. I wanted to be ready.

Phil Troxel found an address for her at a medical clinic in Buffalo, New York. In his later research, Phil found that Macreavy donated money to a clinic in Buffalo after he died. I wondered if it might be the same place, and I made a note to check into it. I sent my letter care of the clinic.

She returned an email.

Darla Rhinesmith RN, MBA,
Administrator
Cheektowaga Health
Genesee St.
Buffalo, NY
To: Mr. Thomas Strongtree
Subject: Foraker Macreavy
Mr. Strongtree,

I've been smiling since I opened your letter!
Yes, it's me, and yes, I can tell you about Officer Macreavy.
I will be available Wednesday morning, the 16th.
I'm anxious to meet you. How about 8 AM?
Please call the clinic and leave a message to confirm.

In Gratitude,
Darla Rhinesmith, RN

So she runs the clinic. That surprised me, and her enthusiastic response surprised me even more. It sounded like she'd put the time and date on her calendar as an appointment. I called the clinic to say I'd be there, and then I went out and bought a new suit. I'd worn my best clothes for the interviews so far, but something in her email's informal but direct tone told me I had to step it up to better-than-best for this one.

I drove to Buffalo the day before our appointment, stayed at a motel, and arrived in front of Cheektowaga Health at 7:45 that morning. I noticed a large bus stop in front of the clinic, and I got an idea of the patients there. Add this to the long list of my quick judgments and assumptions that proved to be far less than accurate. I walked in and up to the reception window. When the receptionist looked in my direction, I said, "Tom Strongtree for an eight o'clock with Nurse Rhinesmith."

The receptionist surprised me with a huge smile. "Yes, sir," she said. "She's expecting you and told me she's looking forward to your meeting. Please take a seat."

I found a place in the waiting room on a blue vinyl-covered chair. While they may have served in the waiting room for years, none of the chairs showed cracks or rips. I thought, *Good for you, Nurse Rhinesmith, administrator. You've got your eye on the details.*

A television blasted into the waiting room, and I remember this as part of my first impression of Nurse Rhinesmith. A commercial came on with pounding drums, heavy bass, and a loud guitar. Music from the commercial filled the waiting room while a tall athletic dark-haired woman in a classic nurse's white uniform, complete with white cap and white shoes, threw open the door to the examination rooms. From her card, I expected Darla Rhinesmith to be fifty-four, but she could have passed for ten years younger. She focused on me, flashed a brilliant smile, and caught me off guard with bright red lipstick and eyelash extensions. As the drums beat and the guitars wailed on the TV, she raised her voice over them and called to me, "Good morning, Mr. Strongtree!"

I stood up and answered in a voice that matched hers, "Good morning, Nurse Rhinesmith."

She held the door open behind her with her left hip and offered her right hand to shake. "I'm so glad to meet you," she said. "Come this way. We'll go to my office, and please call me Darla."

"Thank you, Darla," I said. She brought me along a hallway to her office, opened the door, and ushered me in. A beautiful violet-and-black oriental carpet covered a polished cherry wood floor, and the light orchid walls of the office set off her white uniform. An ornamental iron desk with a glass top faced the wall, and the feet of an antique wooden office chair beside it had been updated with modern noiseless casters. Across from the desk, maple filing cabinets stood against the wall next to a walnut barrister's bookcase. Light came from two standing floor fixtures, an antique desk lamp, and a picture window that looked out onto a city park. On the wall next to the window, an enormous framed photograph of a bicycle racer crossing the finish line ahead of a pack of other riders with her arms held to the sky looked toward us. Nurse Rhinesmith's comfortable, well-appointed office felt like an oasis amid the city and the functionality of the clinic. Grateful for my new suit, it occurred to me that men with money would be comfortable in this room.

She motioned me to one of the four leather chairs with side tables and asked if I wanted coffee. She told me someone at the clinic made a run to a coffee shop down the street every morning at a little past eight. "It's a bunch of hippies," she said with a wry grin. "They claim to use exotic blends, and they do make great coffee. They also keep a quart of heavy cream because I ask for it. Would you like some?"

"Great coffee would be great," I answered. "I'll have a large cup, and make mine the same as yours."

She flashed her smile again, and I felt like she'd turned up the heat and the air-conditioning at the same time. Darla Rhinesmith leaned out her office door and called to someone down the hall to add another large coffee with cream. She turned back into the room and took a seat at her desk. She sat on her chair and swiveled away from the desk to talk with me. Although her white uniform skirt fell well below her knees, I noticed white stockings when she crossed her legs.

I ventured carefully. "Nurse Rhinesmith," I said, "you're wearing a traditional nurse's uniform. I haven't seen a nurse in uniform for a while."

"Yes," she answered. "I am a nurse. Nursing is important to me. It took a lot for me to become a nurse, and I'm proud to wear the uniform." She continued, "I've also found the uniform speaks volumes. It tells patients I care for them, I care about them, and I expect the best."

I couldn't tell if I'd touched a nerve from her reaction, and I hoped I hadn't offended her.

"It's not just the patients either," she continued. "The donors and supporters appreciate a nurse who looks the part." She paused for a moment. "You've heard the saying 'Clothes make the man'? Well, it's true."

Nurse Darla Rhinesmith got through the greeting, the smile, the makeup, the coffee order, and the explanation of her uniform in minutes flat. She changed the subject abruptly and kept up the pace.

"What's this about my police record?" she asked. "I've had a lot of dealings with my past over the years, but this sounds like something else."

I went into my backpack, took out the envelope, and handed it to her. I told her the story of the flea market and how I'd been around meeting the people. She held the envelope without opening it as I explained this, and when I finished, I pointed to it and said, "That's it, and it's the only copy I know of."

She slid the card and photo out of the envelope, and I let her take her time.

Without looking up, she said, "What a scared girl, and so much ahead of her."

I followed suit. "I'd like you to tell me about her," I said. "And I'd like to record your comments. I'm interested in whether or not early contact with the law made a difference in your life?" I added, "Of course, you don't have to tell me anything. I've delivered the card and photo. I can leave anytime." She didn't say anything more for a full minute, and I didn't speak either.

When she did look up at me, I saw the same serious expression I'd seen in her police photo. I did not try to make a case for myself. As a medical administrator, I sensed her understanding of people went far beyond my experience. If she wanted to talk, she would. She looked at me, and I waited.

Finally, she broke the silence. "Yeah," she said. "I'll tell you about it, and I don't mind if you record."

She waited a moment more, and with the hint of a smile, she said, "Officer Macreavy picked me up for forgery."

"Forgery?" I repeated as a question.

"Yes," she responded. "A fourteen-year-old forger," and she looked at the photo again.

"Maybe you remember when Nicorette first came on the market," she said. "The advertising said it made quitting cigarettes quick and easy. I concocted a plan to get my mother to quit smoking. I'd get some Nicorette gum and leave it around the apartment. In my mind, she'd take a stick, chew it, and suddenly she wouldn't want to smoke anymore."

She paused and said, "Let me explain, Mr. Strongtree. My two most significant characteristics have always been that I am tall and I am naive."

No question, this woman got right to the point. I wanted to slow things down a little, so I deflected. "Please," I interrupted. "Please call me Tom."

"Okay, Tom," she said, but she wasn't having any part of slowing down. "So I went to the drugstore to see if they had any Nicorette gum."

"Wait," I said. "Forgive me for interrupting so soon, but that seems like an elaborate scheme for a kid. Most kids badger their folks for a while, and sometimes it works. I've known a few guys who quit because their kids asked them to."

"That's right," she answered. "But when the badgering didn't work, I got serious. Cigarettes killed my father. His death certificate said he died of 'alcohol and nicotine poisoning.' I didn't want my mother to go the same way."

"Wow," I said. "He had it bad."

"Yes, he did," she observed. "And I wrote him off for years as a stupid old man. Who dies of 'alcohol and nicotine poisoning?' How embarrassing. But I've come to understand addiction is not that simple."

She paused and brought the conversation back. "I'll tell you about my arrest if you're interested," she said, and I thought I may have irritated her with my interruptions.

"Please," I answered. "That's why I'm here."

"Okay," she said. "My mother and I had an apartment on Main Street in Jamestown, close to downtown. I walked to the drugstore on Third Street, and they had the Nicorette gum, but at that time, you couldn't just buy the gum. It came as part of a program. The box said it contained directions and everything you needed to quit smoking, but it cost $30, and you had to be over eighteen to buy it. I thought being tall would make me look older, but as a fourteen-year-old living with my single mother. I didn't have $30. She cleaned houses and offices, and we got Social Security survivor benefits from my father's death, but I'm not sure she had that much either. I knew where she kept her checkbook, though, and I planned to buy the Nicorette with a check from her account. I'd sign my mother's name, take the gum home, and leave it around. Then she'd try some and quit smoking. By the time she figured out I'd bought the gum with her money, she'd have quit smoking. She'd be so happy to be free of the cigarettes that she'd thank me and forgive me."

In a tone I took to be self-deprecating, Darla said, "Things didn't exactly go the way I'd planned. Mr. Selligman, the druggist at the pharmacy, called the police. I suppose he might have just told me to 'go home, little girl,' but people had a way of watching out for one another in those days. Mr. Selligman called the station and asked for Officer Macreavy. That's when I first met the guy who showed me how to save lives. He started with mine."

I held my reaction. Her statement sounded melodramatic, but it somehow fit with Darla Rhinesmith's office, uniform, makeup, and intensity. "You say he showed you how to save lives," I repeated. "How's that? Did it have to do with the police?"

"Yes, and no," she answered. "Mr. Selligman scared me senseless. He told me to wait behind the counter because he'd called the police to arrest me. He had me in tears when Officer Macreavy walked into the store dressed in his uniform. The two men had a conversation about me as I looked on. Officer Macreavy said we could walk over to the police station together. He told me I didn't have to ride in the patrol car and wouldn't put handcuffs on me as long as I didn't try to get away.

"As we walked along, he told me I'd committed a serious offense. He said I'd have to go through the full intake procedure because the banks demanded prosecution of all attempts at forgery. He also told me to stay quiet while they took my picture and fingerprints. He said my time would come when I went to court. That's when I should tell my story, and the judge would probably dismiss my case. He explained I would be called a youthful offender. There wouldn't be any more problems if I didn't try to sign my mother's name on any more checks.

"That's about what happened. They called my mother, took my fingerprints and this picture, and gave me a court date about a week later. They said my mother had to appear with me, and she made it the worst week of my young life. She yelled at me every day about what the judge would say.

"It might have been a humorous moment for everybody in the courtroom. First, I got a woman judge, which somehow made it easier. She asked me about the check, and I told her about the Nicorette and how I wanted to buy it so my mother would quit smoking. I remember how the judge looked at me. She had kind eyes, and I didn't expect that. I thought she'd yell at me like my mother had, but she didn't say anything. She looked at my mother too, and the judge stared at her for a long while.

"This judge did what we wish all judges would do. She came up with a creative solution. She told my mother and me about a weekend health fair at the Jamestown Community College. She explained they did cholesterol screenings and blood pressure checks. They looked at your glucose levels and gave suggestions about diet and exercise. She said it started on Friday afternoon and went throughout the day on Saturday. She directed both of us to go to the entire thing, take all the tests, listen to all the talks, and answer all the health questions honestly."

Darla said, "I remember this next part verbatim because I've replayed it and thought about it thousands of times. The judge addressed me directly. She said, 'Darla, you did the wrong thing for the right reason. You can't sign someone else's name on a check. That's stealing. You can't do that even if you think it's for the best. That's the kind of thing that gets people in trouble.' She asked me, 'Do you understand that?' and I answered, 'Yes, ma'am.'

"The judge said, 'I think you probably do after all this. If you don't get into any more trouble, we'll seal the whole thing when you turn eighteen. In the meantime, I want you to go to the health fair and enjoy the day with your mother. These things can be fun in their own way.'"

I could see Nurse Rhinesmith's question coming. "So, Tom, tell me, how is it you got this card and picture if they sealed everything?"

"Believe me," I answered. "I don't know, and that's part of what started this whole thing in the first place. The only thing I can tell you is some people think Officer Macreavy had something to do with it."

"Well, that could be." She shook her head and said, "'Kin' guy is still surprising me."

Darla seemed to accept my explanation for the moment and picked up her story. "Well, anyway," she continued, "at this point, my mother spoke up to the judge. She tried to sound like a lawyer on TV. 'Your Honor,' she said, 'why should I be punished when she committed the crime? I haven't done anything wrong.' The judge focused a withering look at my mother from the bench. It must have been devastating. The judge said, 'From where the law stands, your daughter is guilty of a first-degree misdemeanor. She tried to pass a stolen check to buy a stimulant drug, and she's only fourteen years old. I'm wondering what you've done right.'

"She let that ring out in the courtroom while everyone looked at my mother. Then she said, 'There must have been something though. You've got a daughter who cares about you. She wants you to live. Thank God for her! Take her to the health fair, pay attention, and try to learn something.' She banged the gavel and said, 'Case dismissed.'"

Darla had broken into a full smile, and I laughed out loud. It must have been a fabulous moment for her. We heard a knock at the office door. The young receptionist I'd seen before delivered two coffees in paper cups with lids. She smiled and said, "Two extra-large with heavy cream!"

Nurse Rhinesmith smiled back and said, "Thank you, Jen, just what we needed."

We opened our coffees and sat for a minute, enjoying the aroma. After a sip, I placed mine on a coaster on the side table next to my chair.

Darla Rhinesmith swiveled sideways and placed her coffee on her desk. She continued, "We went to the health fair and did it all. I learned to take a blood pressure reading with the cuff and stethoscope. It fascinated me to hear my heartbeat. The technology of medicine impressed me more than anything I'd experienced before. The nurses impressed me too with their uniforms, and I couldn't believe how much everyone knew about the body. And who should be there but good old Officer Macreavy. He gave a talk about exercise and eating to fuel muscles.

"After his talk, he came over and said, 'Hi, Darla.' He remembered my name, and he also said hello to my mother. I told him I enjoyed his talk about exercise, and he explained to my mother and me that he learned most of it from riding bicycles with a local club. He said bicycles are a lot of fun, a great way to exercise, and he asked me if I'd like to go on a ride with the club. He told us the club got together every Wednesday night for people who wanted to get in a ride after work, but young people could always join in.

"My mother asked him if she had to buy me a bicycle, but Macreavy said he had one I could borrow. He told us he knew a woman who came to town now and then, and during her visit, she usually wanted to ride around the lake with Macreavy and the club. She kept her bicycle at his place because she didn't want to drag it with her on the airline. He said she wouldn't mind if I borrowed it, and it would give him an excuse to pump the tires, polish it, and keep it going for her.

"My mother didn't answer. She looked past Macreavy, and I saw the side of her mouth tighten. I thought about the difference between my mother and a woman who would travel on an airline. When she did speak again, she said, 'It must be fifty miles around the lake.' Officer Macreavy laughed and said I wouldn't go that far at first. I'd start with the slower riders who didn't go as far and work up to it. I'd ride with them, and they'd teach me how to do it.

"My mother told Macreavy that I already knew how to ride a bike, and I started thinking she might agree to let me go. Macreavy told her, 'We learn balance and trust as kids, but we learn to focus as we get older.'"

Darla's coffee had cooled by now, and she took a sip. She looked at me, raised an eyebrow, and said, "For the first time, I felt like my height helped me. Around then, I must have been five eight or so, and Macreavy thought the woman's bicycle would fit. He told my mother if I wanted to come riding with them, he'd bring the bike and the woman's helmet. All I had to do was meet everybody at the starting place.

"Speaking to my mother, he said, 'Let her give it a try. The folks at the club will help her get going, and it'll be fun.'

"My mother agreed, and Macreavy said I should show up at the grocery store parking lot by the Third Street Bridge that following Wednesday night at six.

"When I got there, Officer Macreavy introduced me to the other riders and set me up on the borrowed bike. He said I had to wear the helmet too, and he handed it to me. I noticed two long black hairs caught in the chin strap buckle, and I knew they must have come from the woman who owned the bike. It felt strange to put someone else's helmet on my head, but I didn't say anything. I pulled the hairs away and clipped the buckle.

"I did my first club ride that night. I rode with the old guys, and now I know how much of a kick they got from having a young girl ride with them. I didn't mind though. They were nice to me, and I learned a lot. I went back the next week and the week after that. I started improving too, and after a few weeks, I kept up with a group that went a little faster. This group had some women in it. As we rode along, they talked about their husbands, their kids, their bosses, and the people they worked with. I enjoyed listening to them.

"Macreavy brought the bicycle every week, but at the end of a ride one night, he said the woman who owned it would be in town the following week. He said she'd want her bike for the ride. One of the women I'd been riding with said she had a bike I could borrow. It surprised me that someone had two bicycles, and she also said I could use her 'last year's helmet.' I'd get to ride another week, and that made me happy.

"The woman brought her other bike the next week and adjusted it for me. She said, 'It might not be as nice as that Cinelli you've been riding, but it should be okay.' Until then, I hadn't paid attention to what made one bicycle different from another.

"The woman loaning her bike had almost finished adjusting the seat height for me when Macreavy pulled into the lot. He had his bicycle and the bicycle I had been using in the back of his truck. He also had the woman with him. I remember she may have been the first beautiful woman I'd seen outside of TV. In the years since, I came to understand she'd been given the gift of beauty. She jumped out of the truck and said, 'Hey, everybody!'

"The whole group leaned their bikes against whatever they could find and crowded around her. Everybody got excited. One chubby guy named Paul said, 'Now that you're here, Nel, it's going to be a great ride!' The group agreed, and as they returned to their bikes, the woman came over to me.

"I'm telling you, Tom, this woman, at that moment, made a lifelong impression on me. I learned over the years that although she might be beautiful, her confidence came from her world-class mind.

"She said, 'Hello, Darla. I'm Nel Bell. Mac tells me you've been keeping my wheels spinning this season.' I smiled at her play on words, but it amazed me that she knew my name. Macreavy must have told her, but still, she remembered it. She said it always thrilled her when she met a young woman who wanted to ride and how a good bicycle made it so much easier. She said her bike always made her want to ride better. She laughed again and told me that because I'd been riding it, she didn't have to argue with Mac to keep it tuned up."

Darla paused for a moment, and I saw the faintest shift in her smile. She said, "I never heard anyone other than Nel Bell call him 'Mac.'"

Darla continued, "I also remember she had incredible hair. That night she had it tied back into a thick black and gray braid that fell down her back. The hairs I found in the helmet the first night were undoubtedly hers. I also remember her eyes. They were large and bright, but the word deep always came to mind whenever I saw her. Her eyes made me wonder if she could be happy and sad at the same time.

"The group rode away from the parking lot, and I kept up with Macreavy, Nel Bell, and the faster riders for about a mile or so. When we came to the open stretches out of town, though, they hammered the pedals, and I couldn't believe anyone could ride that fast. They flew off, and I had to ease up and ride with the slower groups. When we all returned to the parking lot, Macreavy and Nel Bell had finished the ride and stood talking and laughing with some of the other riders. While Macreavy hoisted their bikes into the truck, Nel Bell spoke to me again. She made it to a few more rides that summer and always remembered my name. She went out of her way to talk with me, and one time, she brought me some new sunglasses and riding gloves. She told me the glasses would protect my eyes against the wind, and the gloves would protect my hands if I fell. I appreciated that. She cared about me, and I looked up to her. I wanted to be her.

"The lady who loaned me her bike said I could keep it for as long as needed. She knew I couldn't afford one and saw how much I enjoyed riding. She said she'd rather see me riding her old bike than have it collecting dust in her garage. Hardly any old bike though. She'd loaned me an Italian Bianchi Superleggera in this unique bicycle color called Celeste. I rode it home and kept it in my bedroom."

Darla paused. She drank some of her coffee and continued, "So, yeah, I rode bicycles on the club rides with the older people. I heard about jobs and politics and things happening in the world. I didn't understand everything, but I listened. That Christmas, my mother gave me a Bianchi riding jersey and a new helmet in the Celeste color to match the bike. She went to the bicycle store and ordered it specially. It may have been the best present she'd ever given me, but she couldn't just give me a nice thing. My mother hurt me then, and I don't know if I ever got over it. The jersey and helmet looked good on me, and I said I couldn't wait to show Officer Macreavy and everybody at the riding club. She said, 'Don't get your hopes up about him, honey. Men like that don't care about girls like us. He'll look you over in your fancy bicycle shirt, but a man like that will never throw in for good with someone like you.'"

Darla looked at her coffee cup. She twisted it in her fingers. She said, "You don't know how something like that can sound to a fifteen-year-old girl. She might have been trying to give me a clue about the world, but it hurt."

"I can only imagine," I said.

"No, you can't," she snapped. "I've been fighting that moment ever since."

"I'm sorry," I said. "I stand corrected. I can't imagine."

Darla refocused. "Oh, I'm sorry." She said, "I didn't mean to act like that. You didn't have anything to do with it, and maybe someone has said something like that to you. It shows how much it affected me though. Here it is decades later, and I'm still learning to let it go. She sipped her coffee and sat back in her chair.

"Anyway, that spring," she continued, "I did bicycle rides with the club, and I also started riding on my own. I improved enough to ride on weekends when the club went around Lake Chautauqua. I thought of it as 'training,' and I saw myself racing up the mountains in the Grande Boucle Féminine Internationale. That's the Tour De France for women. Years later, Nel Bell and I stood outside a cafe at the foot of Col du Tourmalet in the French Pyrenees. We both cried as the women raced past, and we thought about how much we missed Macreavy.

"Bicycle riding attracts an odd mix of people," Darla observed. "Factory workers ride next to heart surgeons. Business cutthroats try to keep up with male nurses, and women aerospace engineers like Nel Bell block the wind for divorce lawyers. Men and women put on tight shorts and revealing jerseys, and no one thinks twice about discussing the pros and cons of how a bike saddle fits your bottom. I rode bicycles around Jamestown and Chautauqua County all through high school, and it made for an unusual introduction to the world.

"One club ride before my senior year, some of the riders asked me about my plans for after graduation. I told them I figured I'd get a job and ride my bike. They told me I'd better figure again. Using cycling analogies, they said if I did that, I'd always be off the back, out in the wind with no draft, and I'd never bridge the gap. I thought about my mother. That described her and our life together—never enough money, never enough time, and no way up. They told me about certifications and entry-level jobs and talked about their different colleges. I asked the group what they thought I should do, and they said I should get a license or qualification of some kind.

"Two of the riders worked at the Jamestown General Hospital, and they recommended nursing. They told me about vocational schools where I could get a license in two or three years. They said I already knew something about nutrition and exercise and could use that as a start. One guy, a nurse who worked at Jamestown General, said if he had it to do all over again, he'd go to California and do the nursing program there. He told us how everybody in California is into health and fitness. They spend their days riding to and from exercise classes on expensive super-light bicycles. He said it never rains in California, and you can get together anytime with movie stars who do club rides over the Pacific Coast Range. Everyone had a good laugh, but I didn't get the joke. I didn't pick up the sarcasm at the time and asked the guy, 'Would you? Would you really go to California?' The group stopped talking, and we pedaled along for an awkward moment. I think I stumbled onto his secret desire but didn't know enough to let him keep it hidden. I remember he answered, 'I just might.' Then I asked him how I could go to nursing school in California.

"As we rode on our bicycles that day, the group made a plan for me. They said I should go to the office at the high school and tell the guidance counselors that I wanted to attend a nursing school in California. They said I should ask the counselors to help me find a school that gave out-of-state students financial aid, and I did that. In the meantime, my friends in the bicycle club put me in for an Optimist scholarship, an American Legion Scholarship, and a scholarship from the Chautauqua Lake Yacht Club. At the time, I didn't know why these people would care if I went to school or not, and the idea of me having anything to do with yachts seemed crazy. I didn't understand the essential nature of community and connections back then. The Optimists said they'd give me $500, the American Legion gave me $300, and the Yacht Club said they'd stake me $1,000. Amazing!

"The guidance office had me take the SAT that fall. Later they found an opening for out-of-state students at a junior college near LA. Students went to school and worked part-time at a retirement home as nurse's aides. The program granted certifications for different levels of nursing. If I kept going to the school for a full three years, I'd be eligible to take the exam for the California board. If I passed, I'd be a registered nurse. I couldn't wait.

"My chance to get out into the world had come. Before I left, I tried to return the Bianchi to the woman who loaned it to me, but she said she wanted me to have it as a graduation gift. She said she'd never be able to sell it, knowing how much it meant to me. She said she'd keep it in her garage after all, and I could come for it anytime. I didn't understand this kind of generosity back then. I couldn't see why she'd give me a thousand-dollar bicycle, but I found out later she'd given me even more than that. She helped me preserve a piece of my youth and innocence."

Darla paused for a moment and took a sip of her coffee. When she spoke again, she said, "I still have it. It's in my living room right now. I got even taller after high school, so it's too small for me to ride, but I keep it hung on the wall like a piece of art."

"So did you go to the school in California?" I asked.

"Oh yeah, I sure did," she said. Darla collected her thoughts and continued, "That September after graduation, I took a bus across the country. California is a long way from Jamestown. I made it to the school, and they housed all the students, primarily girls, in subsidized dorms. I didn't realize it then, but finding an apartment would have been a nightmare, and the reduced-price dorms were a good deal. As nurses' aides, we helped older folks who couldn't help themselves, and I learned a lot. I liked the patients, but after classes started, I quickly discovered how expensive the school would be. My scholarship money got me there and got me going, but I ran out of money by February. As part of the program, the school paid us to work with residents and patients at their nursing homes around a class schedule. That left me with $20 a week cash after I paid for room and board. The school showed me how to borrow money from the State of California to cover tuition for the second semester. The school said once I earned my nursing license, I'd make good money and be able to pay back my student loan. They had testimonials from nurses who said they'd been through the program, and the brochure had pictures of nurses in scrubs working in fancy operating rooms." Darla held up her coffee cup and flashed a sardonic smile. In a sing-song voice, she said, "Let's cheer again for naive Darla. I signed up."

She laughed and continued, "As time passed, going to class and working at the nursing home began to grind. I needed more hours in the day. I learned about time management the hard way, but I never shorted the patients. They say most people get sick during their first year of nursing. You catch every cough and cold until you develop immunity. That's what happened to me just as my first year ended. Wow, did I get sick! The flu put me in bed for two weeks and way behind at school. I'd also missed shift after shift at the nursing home, so I didn't get paid. I had no money. On top of that, the school told me if I didn't finish and get a license, I'd still have to repay the loan.

"They set up a schedule where I'd double up on clinical hours until I caught up. I worked that semester like never before, and I got it done. By Thanksgiving, I'd caught up to my class. I felt relieved and then at Christmas, my mother died."

"Oh no," I said. "Darla, I'm exhausted just hearing this. How did she die? Did you expect it at all?

"Not that surprising." She shrugged. "Months before, during the summer, she sounded depressed over the phone, but I couldn't do anything about it. I didn't want to leave school and go home just because she felt bad and then I got sick. I hardly had enough money to eat, let alone enough to take a trip home to listen to her complain."

"So, since you left," I asked, "you hadn't been back to Jamestown?"

"No," she answered. "I hadn't left on the best of terms. My mother didn't want me to go. She didn't understand any of it. Even though she bought me the jersey and the helmet, she didn't like cycling. She said the riding group had talked me into being a nurse, and I shouldn't go. She thought being a nurse meant bagging a doctor, and she said no doctor would want a stupid overgrown girl who rode a bicycle anyway. Thinking back on it now, it would have been easier to do a program closer to home, and maybe we'd have smoothed things over if she'd lived, but I had to get away right then. I had the scholarships, I'd told everybody about California, and I wouldn't let myself back out."

"I get it," I told her. "You did what you had to, but it's still a shame she died when you were so far away and involved in school."

"Yeah," she agreed. "But I decided I should at least get back for the funeral. Thankfully, she had a brother who took care of the details at the funeral home in Jamestown. He had just enough to cover it, but I had no money. I talked to the other girls in the dorm, and one said she'd loan me $300. That gave me enough to get a flight home and back to California in time to start the next semester. I didn't want to fall behind again. That's how I got to the funeral. Her brother had her cremated, and hardly anybody came. Not much to it. Still, no one could say I skipped my mother's funeral.

"I made it back right after the New Year, and I told the girl I borrowed the money from that I'd pay her back as soon as possible. She said not to worry and told me she had a secret. She piqued my curiosity by saying she had $300 to lend, and I didn't. That got my attention, but she didn't let up. She said I might be interested in her secret. She made me ask her about it several times, and finally, she told me she danced at a topless bar the next town over."

I interrupted, "Ha! Darla! Did you know anything about this?"

"No," she answered. "The girl told me that once or twice a week, she took the bus an hour across town to the Villa Capri Lounge and took her top off. She'd dance on stage and told me she came home with $500 one night. She admitted that most nights she picked up closer to $200, but she thought that would be enough to get to graduation. Then she asked if I wanted to take a shift with her. I said no at first, but the more I thought about it, the more it seemed to answer my money problems.

"When I asked her about it a few days later, she told me the guys at the club make a lot of noise and stuff ones and fives in her underwear. The club owners kept the cover charge and the money they made on drinks, but the girls kept the tips. She said the men give you more money if you do more suggestive dances. She laughed and said she didn't even have to buy striptease costumes because guys always want to see nurses take off their hospital scrubs. On the nights she danced, she took off the same clothes at the strip bar she'd worn that day on the med-surg floor. She even danced in her hospital shoes. She assured me I could make a few hundred dollars every week, easy money, no sex, and we'd take the bus together."

Darla looked at me, and I saw her eyes laughing. "Yes, Tom," she said, "that's what I did to get through the rest of that year. I even had a natural flair for it. Everyone wanted to see the tall girl take off her clothes, and with my cycling body, I made plenty in tips.

I'd prance around and dance to the music with nothing on but my underwear, a stethoscope, and the same white shoes I wore on the wards. They never knew that dancing also allowed me to memorize anatomy homework. I'd chant the Latin names of all my bones, muscles, and body parts as I flashed them to the boys. I'd yell them out, and the music overpowered everything. I breezed through my written tests and aced the clinical examinations that spring. I got a licensed practical nurse certificate in May and took my first real job in a hospital."

"Bravo! Darla!" I cheered and said, "If I ever see a stripper again, I'll be watching her lips."

"Yeah," Darla agreed. She put a twang in her voice and said, "I'm sure them boys weren't lookin' at my lips."

I said, "Darla, I see from your email that you are an RN. Did you stay at the school then, or did that come later?"

"No, I got that right away," she said. "I did well at the hospital with the LPN. I could read charts and do some treatments, but I couldn't administer complicated medications without registration. It felt good when the patients, the other nurses, and the doctors called me Nurse Rhinesmith, so I signed up at the school for the RN. The program took another year, and I started that July.

"For the first time in my life, I had some money, and it seemed like a lot, but I needed a car to get from my job at the hospital to the new clinical assignments. Also, RN students couldn't live in the dorms. I had to live off campus, which meant getting an apartment. My stripper partner stayed on for the RN program too, and we got a place together. That helped, but I also had to start paying back my student loan. The state wanted repayment for the LPN classes, while I took another loan to pay the tuition for the RN.

"With pay from our new nursing jobs, my friend and I thought we'd be able to make it without the strip club. She found a spot working at a family practice, and after my mother died of cancer, I went into oncology. My friend worked in the suburbs, and I worked in a city hospital. This might surprise you, but we could make more money as strippers than we made as nurses. That brought on lively discussions and complaints around our apartment, but we tried to stay with our original plans. The weeks turned into months, and I spent my first Christmas as a licensed practical nurse on a cancer ward.

"As the new year began, I realized I couldn't make it. I 'bonked' in the middle of January. That's a word from cycling. It means you're so depleted you can't turn the pedals another stroke. My car needed brakes and tires, and I couldn't afford the grocery store even though I didn't buy anything. I fought my way from paycheck to paycheck. I told my roommate I didn't think I could go on, and she admitted she'd been taking shifts at the topless club again. She said the lack of money had stressed her too, and she promised herself she'd only dance long enough to get through school. I went back to the club with her, and things got better. The work at the hospital and school didn't get any easier, but at least I didn't have to worry about money.

"One night in April, my roommate came home with a proposition. She said a customer at the club asked her to do a porno film. He told her that shooting porn in California is considered 'artistic expression,' so there's no danger of being arrested for prostitution. He offered $1,000 a day for two days 'on set.' That's the euphemism he used. The guy promised she wouldn't have to do anything she didn't agree to, and everything would be in writing. She asked me what I thought about it, and I told her I didn't know what to think. Then she told me the guy offered her $1,200 a day for each of us if she brought me along."

Darla paused to take a sip of her coffee. I took some of mine also, and I tried to mute any expression that showed judgment. I never expected our conversation would lead in this direction.

Darla looked directly at me, "Tom," she said over her coffee cup, "maybe it's not a good excuse, but stress and anxiety had overwhelmed us. Years later, I realized this turned out to be the biggest lesson I learned in nursing school. We might have been able to make it without our extracurriculars, but we didn't budget well, and we'd become addicted to the money. Even though I thought of myself as strong and smart, something set me up to experience how addiction takes hold. We had board exams hanging over our heads, I'd maxed out my credit card paying for the car repair, we hadn't kept up on the rent, we ate nothing but fast food, we owed a bunch of money for loan payments, and, along with class work and clinicals for school, we worked all day and danced topless at night. That's what my version of 'strung out' looked like, and I couldn't stop. We only had two months more of school, so we had to keep going. We had money coming in, but we thought we needed more."

"Darla," I asked, "did you ever think of asking Macreavy for a loan?"

"Funny you would bring him up," she said. "But at that point, I hadn't spoken with him for over two years, and I didn't know anything about his money. So, no, I didn't think of asking him."

Darla sat quietly. She recrossed her legs, and I didn't say anything. When she spoke again, she said, "I'd had sex before, but not much. I'd call myself inexperienced, but it didn't matter. My roommate and I went to the shoot together to do what they called a 'scene.' We had to take STD tests, and while we waited for the results, we signed 'model-release' forms. The man my roommate had spoken with explained that the forms gave him permission to produce and sell the movie on VHS tapes with our consent. He made sure we understood we would receive no royalties. He gave us each twelve one-hundred-dollar bills and said we'd get the second payment when we came back the next day. We agreed to the common sex positions with no violence but insisted on condoms, and he didn't have any problem with that."

It occurred to me that Darla might have conveyed this event with more emotion. She seemed matter-of-fact about it, and that intrigued me. What I learned later in our meeting explained how and why she'd developed indifference towards it. She'd told this story before.

"The crew directed everything," she said. "They told us how to tie our hair back, what lipstick to use, and exactly when and how to take our clothes off. Guys followed us with movie lights and microphones. Two guys ran the cameras, and a woman touched up our makeup when it got smudged. We had sex with men who didn't say a word and participated with the enthusiasm of robots. One of the guys in the crew told us we should act like we enjoyed it. He had to say that because everything seemed so mechanical, like none of it counted for anything. My roommate and I finished the day and tried to act like everyone else, like nothing unusual had happened. We went out for pizza and broke one of the hundred-dollar bills at the restaurant. The next day, the man gave us each another twelve one-hundred-dollar bills. We played our parts again, and the man never called us back one way or the other.

"The last few months at school went by quickly after that," she said. "My roommate and I had an extra $2,400 each, and that got us through. We aced the finals, and both of us passed the boards. The day we got the notification, we went out for pizza again and broke the last hundred-dollar bill. We thought we were putting a lid on the whole episode.

"At the end of June, the school had a 'capping ceremony.' In the old days, the hospital schools gave nurses caps to hold their hair up. Each hospital had a distinctive cap, by the way. You could tell where a nurse went to school by her cap. Anyway, I didn't want to go to the ceremony. I didn't have any family, and, as complicated as the school had been, I had no time to make friends, but my roommate talked me into it. She invited me to share the day with her mom and dad, and a few days later, she said two of the girls from the strip club wanted to come to see us get our caps. So that did it. I had to go, and it turned out to be a fantastic day."

"Darla," I said, "you do know how to tell a story."

"Yeah," she said. "It's a story, all right. About twenty of us graduated and got our caps that day. We wore nurses' white uniforms instead of graduation gowns, and I felt proud sitting with my classmates. About five minutes into the program, I looked around at the people who came to see us. I couldn't believe it. My hands started to shake. Officer Macreavy looked back at me from an aisle seat with the biggest smile I'd ever seen. I wanted to jump up and run to him. He came to see me receive my cap.

"He told me later that he thought about me as he got his bicycle out after the winter and wanted to get in touch. He found out my mother had died when he tried to call the old number, so he asked the high school if they knew how to contact me. They gave him the number of the nursing school in California. When he called, the school told him I would be 'capped' that spring, and he took a few days off to fly out and surprise me at the ceremony."

Darla took another pause. Her coffee couldn't be more than warm, and she took a mouthful. When she could speak again, she said, "Now, Tom, at this point, I had no idea about Macreavy beyond being a nice-guy cop who rode bicycles. The Yacht Club scholarship confused me, and I never considered it further. I'm sure you've heard about his will, but as I told you, I had no idea about the money."

She noticed a lipstick mark on her coffee cup and turned it around. She said, "The ceremony ended, and I dashed for him. I must have been a sight—a big, tall girl in full nurse's whites crying and laughing and hugging this guy. He held me away by my shoulders with his strong hands and looked into my eyes. He said, 'Congratulations, Nurse Darla Rhinesmith.'

"He told me he'd arranged a party and had me gather my friends. I corralled my roommate, her parents, and the two girls from the club. Macreavy made a phone call and led us to a waiting limousine. We piled in, and no one could believe it. It's a testament to his understanding and skill that Macreavy kept the conversation past judgment and criticism. I wondered how everybody would get along. Our group consisted of a Midwestern mom and dad, two nurses in whites, two strippers, and Macreavy in a two-thousand-dollar custom-tailored summer-weight silk and wool suit. I'm sure he knew what the girls were all about, and my roommate's parents weren't blind either, but Macreavy brought us together that evening. He pointed to big events and bright days in the future. He made us feel thrilled to be there with each other. We wound through the streets of Los Angeles until we stopped on a side street, and a doorman came out to meet us. The outside of the building looked like a regular old warehouse, but that disguised a private club inside. What an incredible place. It had dark wood tables and floors, red leather chairs, and silver light fixtures. A man in a tuxedo played the piano, and the maître d' brought us to a table set for seven. One of the girls from the club whispered to me that she'd been there before on a date, and people spent months trying to get a table.

"Macreavy took care of everything and had the limo bring us back to our places. My roommate and I were last, and Macreavy walked us to the front door of our apartment. He kissed me on my forehead, said, 'Let's keep in touch,' and left just like that, almost like he hadn't been there."

Darla paused for a moment and looked out the window. She said, "I'll tell you, something took my father away but gave me Macreavy in his place."

"Did you see him again?" I asked.

Darla answered by continuing her story. "Along with my California registration," she said, "I qualified as a specialist in oncology nursing. I got a job at a hospital near Palo Alto, which paid well. The hospital used the word 'outstanding' in my evaluations, my patients smiled when they saw me, and I heard some doctors ask for me to look after particular patients. I paid off my loans and bought a new car. I also bought a new bicycle and started riding with some locals."

Darla paused again. She drained the last of her coffee. "It happened in my second year at the hospital," she said. "I showed up for work one day and found a note on my time card. It said to report to the administrator's office before my shift. I thought it might have something to do with a patient, so I changed into my scrubs and shot right up to the office. The administrator told me to take a seat in front of his desk and shocked me to the core when he said he had to terminate me.

"It knocked the wind out of me. At first I thought he must have mixed me up with someone else. He told me I had to turn in my personnel badge immediately. I would be denied access to the floor where I'd been working and would not be allowed to speak with anyone. He told me a female security guard would take me to my locker in the changing room. I could empty the locker, but she would examine my things before leaving with them. She would then escort me to the door. They do this when someone gets in trouble with drugs and steals narcotics from the hospital, but I didn't have anything to do with that. 'What's going on?' I asked. 'What did I do?'

"The administrator said, 'We are dismissing you on morals charges.' He read from a prepared statement, 'You are dismissed immediately concurrent with a breach of the morals clause in your contract. The legal department has instructed the hospital staff and me to have no further comment. A formal statement will be delivered to you personally or sent to you by certified mail.'"

I saw Nurse Rhinesmith's eyebrows tighten. She said, "The administrator sat behind his desk, stone silent. He wouldn't talk to me. He wouldn't let me say anything or ask questions. Years later, when I saw him again, I remembered the whole thing verbatim, so it's probably best he didn't say anything else. I dragged my feet to his office door. A guard stood waiting for me in the hallway and kept her face blank as she walked me to the elevators in silence. People came in and out of the elevator. I became aware of how some people looked at me, and others looked away. Some of them tried scanning reports, but I could tell they were only acting preoccupied. When we got to my locker in the basement, I put my street clothes in my backpack. The woman security guard didn't search it. In a quiet voice, the guard told me she'd heard a rumor. She said one of the x-ray techs recognized me in a porn tape he rented. He brought it to the hospital and played it on a VCR in the room where they read heart scans. The guard said she hadn't seen it, but apparently, several others had, and they recognized me as well."

Darla Rhinesmith spoke to me while she looked out her office window. She said, "My skin boiled and froze under the hospital scrubs. My face turned red, and I had to walk past a hundred people on my way out of the building. I didn't know who had seen me having sex and who hadn't. I hung my backpack over my shoulder and walked out to my car on autopilot. I don't know how I drove home without getting into an accident. I turned the key to my apartment door as quietly as possible. I wanted to avoid seeing my neighbors and locked the door behind me. I dropped my bag on the floor, fell on my bed, and broke into tears. I cried and cried. I asked myself over and over, 'How did this happen?' They fired me for morals, which meant I'd never work in a hospital again. I'd left my hometown in a huff and ignored my mother in the last months of her life. I put it all on the line to do something I thought might make me a better person, and I'd lost. I'd thrown my life and career away in two days for a lousy $2,400 dollars.

"The hours passed. Night came, and I didn't even turn on the lights. I hadn't changed out of my scrubs, and they'd soaked through with sweat and tears.

"I got up at about two that morning, I felt more alone than I ever had, and I'd run out of tears. An idea came to me while I sat at the kitchen table.

"I thought about when I tried to buy the Nicorette, and I remembered Officer Macreavy's kindness and understanding as he walked me to the police station. I wanted to talk to him again. After the party, he'd left me his home number, but I didn't want to wake him up in the middle of the night. I assumed the Jamestown Police Department would be open, so I tried to reach him there. Someone answered on the second ring. I introduced myself and said I wanted to leave a message for Officer Macreavy to call me when he could."

Darla broke into the same smile I'd seen when she first greeted me. She said, "Whoever picked up the phone said, 'Hold on a minute. You're in luck. He just walked in the door.'"

Darla said, "I'm telling you, luck didn't begin to describe it. Old Officer Macreavy picked up the phone. I said hello, and he recognized my voice in one word.

"'Darla!' he said. 'How are you? I'm so glad to hear from you! What's going on?'

"I didn't think I had any more tears left, but they started again when I heard his voice. I couldn't stop crying, but Macreavy hung on. He stayed on the line and listened. When I let up enough for him to get in a word, he said, 'I'm here, Darla. Take all night if you want to.'

"He calmed me down, and I pulled it together enough to tell him about all of it. I told him about the school, the money, the porn tape, and getting fired from the hospital. I almost collapsed off my chair after going through it again."

Darla's eyes teared up at the memory. "I had no one else, and I threw everything out in front of him. He didn't answer me though. I didn't know if he'd heard me or not. He didn't say anything, and when I had nothing more, we let the silence linger between us.

"After what must have been close to a minute, he spoke up in his 'instructor's' voice. He started by saying it's a situation that's ruined people, but he also said people had come back from much worse. He said he had an idea kicking around, and the time had come to make it work. He gave me three days to live out my depression and self-pity. He told me to cry and eat ice cream, take baths, listen to Neil Young, stay up late, wake up late, watch TV, and kick myself for being the stupidest girl ever. He said I'd better be over it when he called at the end of those three days. He told me he had a way out of my problem, and he'd let me in on it then.

"He asked if I remembered the bicycle I borrowed back when he first took me riding and said he wanted to talk to the woman who owned it. I reminded him I'd met Nel Bell several times, and he said he needed her help with a few more contacts. He also said he needed my assurance I'd do whatever he told me to do. I had nowhere else to turn, so I agreed. He laughed and said, 'Now life's going to get interesting. Are you up for it?'

"I said, 'I guess,' and he changed his tone. He had a penchant for drama and said, 'Not good enough. This is your call-up. This is the big show.' He said he'd be my coach, but he needed 'total commitment.'"

Darla smiled briefly. She said, "I think he realized he might be getting overexcited and backed off. He told me to get some sleep and that he'd be in touch, but right before he hung up, he said, 'Oh, and by the way, you'll never have to worry about money again.' I remember he said it so casually I didn't think I'd heard him correctly."

Darla opened her eyes wide. She said, "I didn't know what I felt when I hung up the phone. I didn't know if I'd been comforted or kicked. I hurt, and I'd been awake for hours. I'd been fired from a job I fought for. I'd been humiliated and embarrassed in front of an entire hospital in the worst possible way, and the only guy I knew to call started talking about baseball. I couldn't go another minute, and I passed out on my bed. I slept for twelve hours and woke up the following afternoon with a bruised psyche.

"I didn't have to go to work and didn't want to stay in, so I got out on my bicycle and rode twenty miles. After getting cleaned up, I ate a sandwich and started feeling better. I went to a coffee shop down the street and sat looking out the window. As I thought about what to do, I worried about becoming my mother again, living by myself in cold apartments and driving a worn-out car. I kept asking myself what Macreavy had in mind and how I could agree to anything before knowing what he wanted me to do. I told myself I'd qualified as a registered nurse. I thought there must be someplace that needed a nurse, but then I reminded myself I had a dismissal on my record and the worst kind. People are more forgiving of drugs. I liked the part about not having to worry about money, but what would I have to do for it? I'd learned that lesson, at least. I couldn't go back to dancing again. I'd die if anyone from the hospital came in, and I knew they would. I kept trying to convince myself that Macreavy wouldn't be into anything illegal, but what did I know about him for real? Where did that money come from for the party anyway? Maybe he had some scheme going and wanted me to get into it. 'That's good old Miss Naive Darla again,' I said to myself. 'Drinking his champagne and eating at his fancy restaurant. What a fool!'

"When I got through wondering about what he wanted, I asked myself what I wanted. That boiled down to one question. When he called, I'd ask if his plan had anything to do with the medical world. If it did, I'd say yes no matter what. If he said no, I'd pass and look for someplace that had trouble finding nurses. I kept telling myself I'd fine someplace or someone who wanted me.

"He called when he said he would, and before he started, I asked him if his idea had anything to do with nursing or medical. He asked me what I'd do if it didn't. I told him I'd say no and find someplace that needed a nurse bad enough to hire me. That's when he melted my heart. He said, 'Yes, Darla, it has to do with medical, and because you'd give up gold to follow nursing, I know it'll work.'"

Darla Rhinesmith got up from her chair and paced back and forth across her office. Her height and the white uniform energized the room as she related the rest. She said, "I remember he asked me, 'Are you ready to do this?' and I told him I trusted him.

"He wanted me to take notes." She walked over to her desk and picked up a picture frame from her desk. "Here they are," she said and handed it to me. She'd framed a sheet of paper torn out of a notebook. I could read some of it, but she'd scrawled the rest, and I couldn't make it out. I saw lists written in pencil. Words had been circled, crossed out, or underlined. Numbers might have been dates, phone numbers, or street addresses, but it didn't matter what any of it said. The page documented the intensity of the moment.

Darla took the frame back and placed it on her desk again. "He told me it would be best to leave California. He said I should pick a medium-sized city with a good airport. Next, he wanted me to enroll in any university in that city. I would study nursing and health administration, but I had to take at least one accounting class every term. He said, if I could, I should keep my nursing registration active until I could transfer it to wherever I landed. He warned me to bite my tongue and go along with whatever remedial action they recommended regarding the dismissal. He said, 'Some arguments are a waste of time.'"

Darla stopped her pacing. She said, "This sounded exciting, but I asked him where I'd get the money for all this moving and college. Macreavy told me to 'shift onto the big ring,' which is what bicycle riders say when it's time to go fast and hard. I didn't realize at the time that my new life had already begun. Macreavy told me not to worry about the money. He said, 'Send me the bill.' He gave me his home address at the lake and told me to use it for my home address too. He said he'd send me money every month so I could concentrate on the project. When I asked him, 'What project?' he answered me by asking me if I'd ever heard about the camel and the eye of the needle. I said, 'Sure, that's the story about how rich people can't go to heaven.'

"Macreavy laughed and said I'd missed the second part, the part that talks about possibilities.'" Pacing again, Darla said, "Macreavy couldn't get enough of these dramatic moments. He set them up so he could deliver big theatrical lines. He said, 'Darla, prepare to ride the camel.'"

Darla laughed out loud. Her eyes lit up with enthusiasm. She said, "Macreavy told me he'd been in contact with several celebrities, doctors, health experts, and what he called 'good-hearted souls.' He said I'd get to know them all, and I have. They each pledged a million dollars to start a clinic specializing in recovery. He told me I would lead that clinic. He said, over the next few years, these people would put money into an account we'd use when I graduated from university. We'd have ten million to start. He said that wouldn't be enough, but he figured it would get the project rolling. After that, fees from patients, additional donations, and in-kind benefits would build and maintain the operation. There's something else I didn't understand at that time. He could have floated the whole thing himself, but he saw the strength of having a small group of smart people involved. I cannot tell you how valuable that group has been. He explained that each of the donors he'd spoken with had some experience where they needed a clinic like the one he wanted me to open. He said it would involve all the usual stuff—drugs, mental rehabilitation, and terminal illness. Still, the private funding would allow the clinic to skirt the strict application of laws that sometimes got in the way of effective treatment. He told me none of the people he'd contacted wanted repayment in dollars. They all had more money than they'd ever need and were paying tithes on their good fortune. They wanted access to successful treatment. If they had someone who needed help, they didn't want to hear about 'waiting lists.' Macreavy told me, 'You're going to build that place, Darla. And you're going to run it your way on your terms. It will be your life, and you'll give it the twist to put it over.'"

I could see Darla's smile growing from ear to ear. She said, "I could feel the drama building and gave him the setup. I asked, 'What's the twist?'

"Macreavy shouted the banner headline over the phone, 'Ex-porn queen runs rehab clinic!' He didn't say anything for a moment and then asked me. 'Are you ready, Darla?'

"I shouted back, 'Yes!'

Darla Rhinesmith looked at me. She said, "That's where this clinic came from, Tom."

I couldn't resist the smile. I had a million questions, but she kept talking. She said, "I looked around the country and picked Buffalo because of its proximity to Jamestown, and I didn't want to be too far away from Macreavy. I went to the University of Buffalo here.

They had a public health policy program, along with nursing and accounting. Only a year's worth of nursing credits transferred from California, so I started as a sophomore. I knew a lot, but I had a lot to learn. One of Macreavy's donors helped me smooth over the dismissal until I registered in New York State. After my bachelor's, Macreavy talked me into staying on for the MBA. He made his point when he said the Bible has more to say about money than sex, and understanding business is essential. He kept telling me to meet people and build a network. I remember him warning me about 'the competition trap.' He'd say, 'You don't compete to win. You compete to cooperate.' That might have sounded like empty nonsense from anybody else, but you'd be amazed at who called him to talk things over.

"I found out more about the money over the years too. He paid for my schooling but said he hadn't given me anything for free. He told me he'd exchanged money for my services. He said he'd paid to develop my talents because I brought passion to his project. He always made me feel good when he told me I could do things he couldn't. His mover-and-shaker friends made it happen because they'd all been through situations where a specialty clinic could have helped. They called me when a friend or family member called them."

As I looked around, I had an observation and tried to bring it up tactfully. I asked, "Say, Darla, I don't mean to be critical, but I have to ask, is this a multimillion-dollar clinic?"

"Oh no!" she said. "This is a small part of it. You're looking at the public side of what we've got going. We also have two residential facilities and another one of these clinics on the other side of town."

Darla explained, "When I joined up with Macreavy, I grabbed a lifeline. Once I realized I wouldn't drown, I thought more about it. I wondered about people like my mother and my father, and me, for that matter. When I talked to Macreavy about something we could do for regular people, he said he'd been waiting for me to ask. That's when we put the rest of the plan into action. The high dollar fees we charge the ultrarich put them first in line, but those fees make the clinic possible for everyone else."

Darla said, "I'm not going to argue about what's fair. Waste someone else's time with that. I can tell you that the patrons are okay with what we charge because we're responsive and have a good track record. Most of them keep us on their contributions list much longer than expected, and the people receiving subsidized care get the best available. We've scaled slowly and carefully. That's the only way I know how to do it."

Nurse Rhinesmith eased off her passion and explained, "The paradox is people become wealthy through generosity, but you have to care enough about your life to accept the grace that comes from generosity. That's the first step. If someone thinks that's unfair and wants to bring me down to make themselves feel righteous, I tell them to get out of the way. If they don't, I make calls. Believe me. The people Macreavy organized to start and keep this place going taught me how to fight for human dignity. Grace brings its own brand of fairness.

"We do a lot with end-of-life cases and plenty of addiction work. I cringe a little when I hear about addiction to pornography, but I've never tried to hide my past. Macreavy had me own it from the start. No lies around here. But if you call me a porn queen, you might as well call a bar band guitar player a rock star. Still, I get a lot of mileage out of it. No one feels judgment coming from an ex-porn queen. A priest can tell you about forgiveness, and that's fine if it means something to you. An ex-porn queen can show you a way past shame and guilt. Recovery comes from finding something bigger than your misery. I remember that judge in Jamestown who sent me to the health fair. She opened the door to a larger world, but I'm not sure about her idea of 'wrong for the right reason.' Would I have found nursing without trying to sign my mother's name? Maybe. Would I have found Macreavy or the cycling people? Who knows? And what if they hadn't fired me from the hospital? There are people alive today because of our clinic. People have regained their lives. The Spirit lives in consequences the same as it does everywhere else. Besides that, if you want to see what I looked like having sex as a young woman, carefully directed and well lit, have at it. If anyone wants to see what I looked like with no clothes on at twenty-two years old, I don't mind. I've got other worries. Once, we admitted the daughter of a politician you'd recognize after she had an illegal abortion during his reelection campaign. She didn't want a video of her leaving a clinic showing up on the six-o'clock news, so she went to an off-label scrape shop. They botched it, and after she almost bled to death, she caught MRSA. Now that's a sex problem.

"I heard from my old roommate several years ago. She said the tape never came up for her, and she's been working as a hospice nurse for years. They'll be more than sorry if anyone tries to fire her from that."

Darla paused. I remembered she said something about meeting the hospital administrator sometime later, and I asked her about it.

"Yeah, poor guy," she said. "He called me for a family member."

"You're kidding. Did he call you to get someone into the clinic? I asked.

"I can't tell you," Darla responded. "But I can say that call couldn't have been easy for him, and he didn't sound good. I heard frustration and anxiety in his voice, so I put him on my call list. I checked in with him on the phone every Friday for a few weeks. Anyone and everyone will talk to an ex-porn queen, and I told him he wasn't allowed to clam up this time. Once I got him going, he couldn't stop, and we'd talk for an hour or so. He mentioned he rode bicycles on one of those calls, so I invited him to ride with me. He flew here to Buffalo and rented a bike. I drove us to Chautauqua, and by the time we finished a ride around the lake, I'd hired him to run one of the residences."

"You hired him!" I said, "The man who fired you?"

"It's involved," she answered. "He fired me because he had to, and I knew that. The job and the position called for it. He explained and apologized, but he also told me he'd come to the end of the line at the hospital. He had questions about life. You'd understand this, Tom. There's something that happens to a man around fifty years old. My friend, the administrator, needed a purpose. He wanted one more shot at life, and I needed an experienced administrator with the desire to help people find healing. The joke is he and his wife left California to move to Buffalo. Did you know they call this city 'winter's home office?' Well, they do. His wife told me the two of them were on their way to a divorce, and now they're having the time of their lives.

"So that's my story," Darla said. "That's why I got arrested, and that's what I know about Macreavy. I couldn't believe he died in a bicycle accident, of all things. I get to Jamestown once or twice a summer to ride around the lake, and I pray for him every time I pass that spot on the road where he got hit. It's odd. In cycling, it's called a 'false flat' because it looks like the road is flat, but it's actually a slight uphill that goes on for longer than you think. A woman in a van said the sun got in her eyes, and she didn't see him. His life on earth ended one glorious evening, and I can't wait to see him again. We'll laugh about him riding off into the sunset."

I asked her, "What about your personal life, Darla? Did you get married? Any kids?"

"No," she answered. "I poured myself into this clinic, and it's been a great life. I came close a few times, but we couldn't make it happen after all. Funny how God works. With sex so much a part of my life, I never got married, and although I gave my life to nursing, I've never had a baby at my breast."

Nurse Rhinesmith sat back in her chair and looked into her empty coffee cup. She took a breath through her teeth and shook her head slightly. She said, "'Kin' guy."

I thanked her for her story and congratulated her on the work she'd done starting and running the clinic. Getting up from my chair, I remembered to ask her about the bicycle photograph on her wall.

She said, "That's Mary Riddle winning the mountain stage at the Women's Western States Classic in Colorado a few years ago. Nel Bell took that picture. We sponsored one of the clinic patients and went out to cheer her on."

"Did she do well?" I asked.

"She sure did," Darla answered. She got the bronze medal. That's her crossing the line behind Mary Riddle. Her name is Linda Turek from Atlanta, Georgia. She told all the cycling magazines about it then, so she wouldn't mind me telling you. Five years before that picture, she'd overdosed, and a pimp kicked her half to death trying to wake her up. A couple of paramedics revived her with naloxone and hauled her into Grady Memorial. She miscarried, and the kick punctured her left lung. Look at that picture. Have you ever seen anyone so happy to win third place?"

Bible scholars tell us it's unlikely the woman caught in the act of adultery ever existed. They say a scribe added the story to John's gospel later on. But nobody doubts the truth brought to the confrontation if it had occurred. The situation de-escalated, and we assume the woman left her life of sin. And yet I've always wondered what happened afterward. How did she get along later with the men who wanted to stone her? Darla Rhinesmith got into trouble, which put her in a position where she could help people find the grace to lift them out of it. Blessings to you, Darla.

CHAPTER 9

The Lawyer Letter: Shouted from the Housetops

It came as I had almost completed my project. I'd written to the last guy on my list, and this close to the end, it concerned me that he hadn't responded. One day in the early afternoon, about a month after I'd sent him the letter, I heard a loud pounding at the front door as I sat at my desk reviewing notes. Our dog growled instead of his usual bark, which hurried me downstairs. A postman in full uniform stood on our front porch holding an oversized envelope. He even wore a post office hat and thrust a registered letter at me. The letter required a signature, and the postman pointed a pen at me. I noticed my hand shaking as I signed for it and took the envelope. The postman whirled heel to toe and bounded down our front steps back to his delivery truck.

The letter came from the law firm of Leatherford and Berry in Syracuse, New York. I read it over several times and had to lay it down as I kept smudging it with my fingers. My wife hadn't been home then, and it terrified me to think of how she'd take the news.

I'd like to reprint the letter here, but getting too involved in the jargon is useless. The long and the short of it is I'd touched a nerve. The lawyer's letter said my contact endangered his client's professional standing in the community, the affection of his spouse, and the respect of his children. Holy mackerel! I couldn't help wondering what this guy did. The lawyer said, "Disclosure of youthful indiscretions would significantly and negatively impact current lifestyle." The letter notified me to "anticipate legal action." The way I read it, they were bringing out the big guns.

I didn't know what this could mean for my wife and me because the figure quoted would be about fourteen times our total worth, including our house, cars, and savings. It sounded like they'd even come after our dog. That night at supper, I couldn't eat. I told my wife I felt sick and left the table, but that's all I said. I went to bed early, but I couldn't sleep. When my wife came to bed later, she brought me a glass of water and checked for a fever. I didn't know what I'd tell her, but I'm sure she knew I had something on my mind.

I thought about my project as I lay in the darkness that night and for the entire week following. I tried to distract myself with jobs around the house. I'd get involved in something, and for a while I'd forget about the lawyer's letter, but then I'd think about it, and my heart would sink again. It had been an enjoyable project. I'd met great people and heard fabulous stories, but I'd been playing with fire. I kept asking myself if any of it had been worth losing everything in court. I thought about calling the lawyer who waved me off the project initially, but I couldn't bear hearing him say "I told you so." I checked the mailbox every day, worried about more letters from the lawyer. The more I thought about it, the more it ate away at me, and the more I realized I had to tell my wife.

Bless her. She couldn't have been more understanding. She said she knew something had been bothering me and thanked me for telling her about it. She reminded me that lawyers usually make things worse than they are. She said she'd always believed in my project, and if worse came to worst, we'd get our own lawyer. She knows me well and told me not to get too upset before we had all the facts. I felt relieved but exhausted from worry. I must have dozed off sitting on the sofa, and my wife let me sleep. She said she knew I needed it.

Our dog woke me up the following morning, and I let him out. Watching the sunrise, I thought about the people I'd met from the police cards. I didn't know anything about being in trouble with the law, and it occurred to me I'd happened onto my own way of sharing their experience. I asked myself what they'd tell me. I let our dog in, went upstairs to my desk, and wrote back to the lawyer.

Dear Mr. Leatherford,

Please extend my most heartfelt apology for causing any anxiety or disruption to your client. As I wrote to your client in my original letter, I came by the records innocently and assure him I plan no further contact.

I am sending you your client's police fingerprint card with the photo. Please pass them along. I've made no copies. Since the card says only "released to parents," the nature of the offense, judgment, and sentence are still secret. Furthermore, from conversations with other subjects of my inquiries, I believe you will find there are no official mentions of this incident whatsoever. If you went into the police files for this period, you would find your client's records are better than sealed. They are missing. The entire event remains a mystery.

Respectfully,
Thomas Strongtree

P.S. On a personal note, I suggest you have your client recall whatever Officer Macreavy tried to show him. It could be more relevant now than ever, whatever it may have been.

I sent the letter with the envelope containing the fingerprint card and photo to the lawyer's office, registered mail, and checked the box that said "signature required." I received a handwritten note a week later.

Dear Thomas Strongtree,

Sir, I owe you an apology and am deeply indebted to you.

When I got your letter, I overreacted. Call me a hothead, but I assumed the worst and got in touch with my lawyer. He told me to calm down. He said he'd send you a letter and see what happens. When you sent the fingerprint card and the picture, it reminded me of my younger days, and when you told the lawyer to remind me about Macreavy, I had a talk with myself. The lawyer had no idea what you meant, but I did. That night I went home and told my wife.

I thought I'd kept it a secret from my wife and her family for many years, and I assumed my children didn't know about it either. As it turns out, my wife knew all along. Her brother told her and her parents long before we were married. They thought of it as a crazy prank and nothing to hold against me. When I told my kids about it, they thought it sounded like the coolest thing their dad had ever done.

Thank you for bringing it out in the open. Oh, the things we worry about!

Yes, I'd be glad to have you at our home for dinner if you're ever in the area. I'll tell you all about it if you're still interested, and I'll also tell you whatever I can about Macreavy.

Regards,
Eddie Moretti

CHAPTER 10

Edward Moretti: Water to Wine, the Wedding at Cana

He'd written the note on office stationery. Although I no longer had his police card and information, I remembered Phil Troxel had written "dentist" next to his name. This fit. The stationery had "Brilliant smile, Edward Moretti, DDS" printed at the top of the page in red capital letters, along with a phone number and an address in Fayetteville, New York. I found Fayetteville on the map. It looked like a suburb of Syracuse, New York, which gave me an idea.

The meetings I'd had with the "caught thirty" brought my imagination to Jamestown and the areas around Chautauqua Lake, but I'd never been there. To end my project, I thought it might be good to make the trip to Jamestown. If Dr. Moretti agreed to meet me, I'd take a detour through Jamestown on the way. I called his office and left a message. The doctor himself called me back.

He started with a laugh and spoke in a loud, clear voice. He said, "Hey, are you Thomas Strongtree? Eddie Moretti here." His laughter and rhyming name made me smile. "My wife and I were talking about you this morning. Are you coming to see us?"

"Sure," I said, and I had an invitation just like that. July had almost finished, and we discussed meeting sometime in August. I mentioned I wanted to drive through Jamestown to look at the place, and he came up with a better idea. He said he and his wife planned on returning to Jamestown for their annual summer visit in two weeks. He said they drove over once in a while to visit relatives, and they'd be glad to take me for a look around. He said they usually stayed at the Hotel Lenhart in a town called Bemus Point on Lake Chautauqua, and he suggested I take a room there also. He said the hotel had a long porch that looked out on the lake. They put over-sized rocking chairs on the porch, and, all summer long, people sit and enjoy the breeze from the lake. He said some people watch the sailboat races from the porch, but mostly they come to watch the sunset. He confided that he and his wife looked forward to sitting on that porch with tall gin and tonics all winter. He said, "It's like floating on a cool cloud."

Dr. Moretti said he'd take care of it right then. He must have logged on to reservations for the hotel while talking to me on his phone. He sounded distracted for a moment, and then he said, "Okay, we're on. I confirmed reservations for two rooms, Thursday night, two weeks from now. Let's meet that afternoon. Is that all right with you? What do you say? We'll sit on the porch. You can tell me again about buying that fingerprint card, and I'll answer anything you want to know about it."

He caught me off guard by reserving rooms before checking with me, but it sounded great, so I agreed. "That's more than I'd hoped for, Dr. Moretti. I'm looking forward to it."

"It's settled, then," he said. "I'll get the rooms. How about you pick up dinner?"

Again, he made the plan, but I had no objection. I said I'd get the better part of the bargain, and Dr. Moretti laughed. He said, "Well, that's how I like to do things. My wife will be there too. We'll talk on Thursday, drink gin on the porch, and watch the sunset. On Friday, we'll take you on a tour of Jamestown. Half a day ought to cover it, and you'll be on your way in the afternoon. We'll stay on for the weekend and catch up with family."

So we had a plan. Efficient, and I had no argument, so I thanked him for getting back to me and told him how much I looked forward to meeting him. Before he hung up, he dropped a bit of information that intrigued me. He said, "Oh, and by the way, the hotel is on the lake, not far from Macreavy's old place. I've got some good stories about that old boy."

"Great!" I responded.

"See ya then," he said, and the call ended.

As I looked back on them, the people I'd come to know through my project were an unusual mix. Something set them apart, but I couldn't put my finger on it. The trip to Chautauqua Lake would put me near their hometown. Maybe I'd get a better feel for it there, but at any rate, the trip would be the high point of my summer.

The Thursday of my meeting with Dr. Eddie Moretti arrived hot and clear. I hoped the weather would hold for that evening as well. After Dr. Moretti's buildup, I wouldn't want to miss the sunset from the porch of the hotel. I pulled off the Southern Tier Expressway into Bemus Point on Lake Chautauqua at around two o'clock that afternoon. I had no trouble finding the Hotel Lenhart. In the best sense, it looks exactly like what you think of when someone says "old hotel."

I parked my car, followed a path lined with carefully trimmed hedges, and walked up six or eight wooden steps to the front porch. I saw the oversized rocking chairs looking out onto the lake and assumed I'd arrived at the right place. A booming voice from inside the front door confirmed it.

"Good afternoon, Thomas." An old-fashioned screen door with a wooden frame opened out, and a large Italian man stood holding his hand to me. He laughed in the same loud voice and repeated the greeting, "Good afternoon, Thomas. I'm Eddie Moretti."

"Good afternoon to you, Dr. Moretti," I answered. "Please call me Tom."

"I will, Tom," he said. "And I go by Eddie."

Eddie Moretti wore lightweight black slacks and a short-sleeved white shirt. The big man had a big handshake, and while he held on firmly, he said, "Tom, why don't you check in and take your bag to your room." He released my hand and continued his directive. "You unpack. Get comfortable, and we'll meet you out on the porch. I'll make sure we have three chairs off to the side. You'll see us, and we'll wait for you before ordering."

"Great!" I said, once more agreeing to the plan and giving him the lead.

The Hotel Lenhart couldn't have been more perfect for a reminiscence of the past. The beds, plumbing, and electrical system had been updated, along with the furniture, but the overall feeling had me stepping back in time. I could imagine a summer years ago when people wore afternoon attire for cocktails while watching sailboat races.

I changed into a fresh polo shirt, light cotton pants, and soft fabric shoes. I wanted to look like I belonged on the porch. When I made it back outside, Eddie Moretti and his wife had situated themselves in a prime location on the side of the porch farthest from the comings and goings of the front door. They'd saved a rocking chair for me.

Moretti jumped up and introduced his wife. "This is Mary Ann," he said. Some others I'd met through my project mentioned significant populations of Italians and Swedes in Jamestown. I could see right away the Italian Eddie Moretti had married the Swedish Mary Ann with blond hair, a beautiful smile, and bright blue eyes. She stood and shook my hand also.

"We're happy to meet you," she said. "Eddie tells me this will be an old-home weekend, and I'm always glad to get back here. This is our first time this summer."

I didn't know how much Dr. Moretti had shared with his wife about the nature of the meeting. I assumed he'd said something, but I proceeded with caution. "Well," I said, "I hope I don't dredge any bad memories."

Moretti laughed. "Ha!" he said. "Let's get some drinks and toast to the craziest days of our lives."

I stopped him at this point. I said, "Listen, Eddie, I have to tell you. I don't drink. I used to, but those days are past. Please, I don't mind if you do. I wish you would, but it's best if I don't."

He gave a nod of acknowledgment, and I continued, "What I'd truly enjoy right now, more than a single malt, is a special dark, preferably with cream and no sugar."

"Then that is what you shall have!" Eddie Moretti declared. If he had a gold-encrusted ebony staff, he'd have planted it firmly on the wooden slats of the porch floor. As king of the porch, he motioned for a waitress to take our orders. He continued the announcement, "Mary Ann and I will have two tall gin and tonics to celebrate this fine afternoon and bring my newfound friend here the largest cup you have of your very best freshly brewed dark coffee with a generous side pitcher of cream."

The waitress smiled and stood by to make sure he'd finished. "Will that be all, sir?" she asked.

"No," our magistrate answered. "Please tell me your name."

"My name is Janet," the young woman answered.

"Well, Janet," Eddie continued, "it's a beautiful afternoon, and it looks like there will be a spectacular sunset this evening." With only a hint of discretion, he handed the waitress a hundred-dollar bill and continued, "We'll be here this afternoon for drinks," he said. "We have dinner reservations for six o'clock, and afterward, we'd like these same chairs, off to the side here, to sit and enjoy that sunset."

"Very good, sir," Janet responded. She smiled, but if the porch of the Hotel Lenhart had been in another country, I think she might have curtseyed.

When the waitress left, I held out my iPhone and asked him for permission to record our conversation. Moretti glanced at me momentarily, pointed to the phone, and gestured that he didn't mind. "So I suppose you want to know all about my breach of the law," he said.

By way of an answer, I held my palms up and raised my eyebrows.

"Sure, I'll tell you about it," he said. "B&E."

"B&E?" I repeated as a question.

"Yup," he responded. "Breaking and entering."

Mary Ann looked at me and asked, "How did you find out about this again?"

I repeated the flea market story, how I hired an investigator to find current addresses, and how I'd been in touch with those who would talk to me.

"Who were they?" she asked.

"I'd rather not say," I told her. "I promised anonymity, and I'd like to keep everything quiet."

"Fair enough," Eddie agreed. "But for me it doesn't matter. It happened long ago, and it turns out people knew about it anyway. And you want to know about Macreavy too," he said.

"Everyone in the group had something to do with Officer Macreavy," I said, "And you said you had stories about him."

"Sure glad for his girlfriend," Mary Ann interjected.

Eddie Moretti chuckled, and at that moment, the waitress arrived. She told us the bartender took extra care to ensure the drinks would be delivered as cold as possible, and she said the kitchen staff had brewed a fresh pot for my coffee. She left momentarily and returned with a bucket of ice, a bowl of limes, and a glass pitcher of cream.

"Thank you, Janet," Moretti acknowledged. "You're doing a fine job!"

When the waitress left, I repeated the word as a question, "Girlfriend?"

I assumed they might be talking about Nel Bell, but I didn't want to get too far ahead.

"Okay," Eddie said. "I'd better start from the beginning. The police arrested me for breaking and entering. They hauled me in at the ripe old age of sixteen. I had my scheme going for almost a year before that, so I must have started it at fifteen. My father had a plumbing business in Jamestown and got repair calls from all over town. His plan had me taking over the business after him, so I'd been riding along in the plumbing truck for as long as I could hold a pipe wrench. By thirteen or fourteen, I could do basic repairs without him. A call came from a liquor store on Second Street downtown. My dad dropped me off to look it over while he finished another job. I went down to the basement and found a leaking supply valve. Easy job. It needed a new washer, and I had one in my tool kit. I shut the water off from the outside and got to work.

"Buildings on Second Street back then had been built on the riverbank. The fronts opened onto the street level, but you could walk out the basements. What a row of fire traps! The city tore them down years ago. Anyway, as I replaced the washer, I noticed some of the boards making up the wall in the basement had rotted away. I could see daylight coming through from the outside. I got this idea I could leave a rotted board loose enough to push it aside and sneak in after the store had closed. I could take anything I wanted. I left a few nails holding the board, so it looked like nothing had changed, but it would move just enough for me to squeeze past it."

Eddie Moretti laughed and took another swallow of his gin and tonic. He touched his belly with his fingertips and said, "No chance I'd get through there now."

"Well, it worked like a charm," he continued, "until the store owner got tired of losing good whiskey. I'd been careful about it too. I never bragged, and I never took too much. I only took a bottle at a time, and only now and then. A weekend would come, and I'd magically show up with a bottle. My friends and I would have a great time running around a football game or checking out the girls at a dance. But I didn't understand what I'd let myself in for. The worst part is I put my father's business at risk. After I got caught, my mother told me I couldn't tell anyone about it. I had to keep it a secret forever. I'd been skating on thin ice and didn't know it. She said if word ever got out that a plumber came back to a repair job and stole from a customer, that plumber would lose his business and never be able to work again. She scared me halfway to hell, and I'll tell you, Tom, it's a relief to have the whole thing behind me.

"I didn't understand back then how they controlled liquor inventory. There are strict laws, and the state makes sure everybody keeps accurate records. A store owner can lose his license if the bottle counts are off."

Eddie Moretti took a sip of his drink. "Everyone has surveillance cameras now," he said. "They have nanny cams, and people aim cameras at their front doors and backyards, but they'd just started coming out in those days. The liquor store owner bought one from a 'spycraft' mail order catalog. One Friday morning, he walked in and checked the videotape. He had a clear picture of me walking around inside the store with a bottle of Austin Nichols Wild Turkey Bourbon. He called the police, and that's when I met Officer Macreavy for the first time. He came to my house and picked me up. When he explained everything to my father, my poor old man collapsed onto a chair in the kitchen. He put his elbows on the table and his hands on his forehead. He couldn't even stand up."

"The police processed me with the fingerprints and the mug shot and released me back to my parents. The city called two days later with a date for my hearing in juvenile court, but in the meantime, Macreavy stepped in. He got together with my father, and they went to talk with the liquor store guy. My father begged the guy not to press charges, but Macreavy informed him the guy didn't have that option. An arrest had been made, a date had been set for a hearing, and the State Alcohol Control Board could ask for the verdict if they wanted to. They might not, but everybody had to keep the record clean just in case. Macreavy explained the laws went back to the days of prohibition. Everybody had to follow through, even though I'd be a youthful offender. The only good part would be they'd seal my record after I turned eighteen."

At this, Mary Ann jumped in. "Yeah," she said with one word that expressed resentment, irritation, and annoyance all at once. "Ed's record is supposed to be sealed!"

"I had the fingerprint card and the photo," I answered. "But that doesn't tell anybody anything. It's got Eddie's name, personal information, and the arrest date, but it doesn't allege a crime or give any idea of the disposition. All it says is 'released to parents, juvenile court date pending,' and I sent it to the lawyer to give Eddie anyway. But I'm with you, Mary Ann. The mystery is how and why the card and photo left the police station in the first palace and how they wound up displayed out on a table at a flea market. That's where this whole thing got started."

I looked at Moretti and continued. "But it's better than sealed," I told him. "I've heard the records are entirely missing for you people with these cards I found. Nothing exists. It's like none of it ever happened."

I let that register even though he'd probably heard it before from his lawyer, and after a moment, I said, "My guess is you've never had any trouble with background checks. I'd bet you sailed through when you applied for your dental licenses."

"That's right," he answered. "No trouble, and I worried about that. When they said they had to take my fingerprints, I didn't want to say 'you've got them already.' I just went along, they took the prints, and nobody said anything."

"So what happened with the liquor store owner?" I asked.

"Well, Macreavy came up with an idea," Eddie explained. "He suggested my father talk to some of the carpenters he knew and pay them to rebuild the back of the liquor store. That way, the store owner would get the repair done for free, which would be worth more than what he lost in liquor. We'd show up in court and explain everything to the judge. Macreavy had us play up the idea that I had good men watching out for my best interests, which would be better than sending me to the youth facility in Buffalo. It cost my father about $2,000, but he saved his business from embarrassment, and I think I've paid him back about a hundred times over by now."

Eddie Moretti put another ice cube in his gin and tonic. The waitress noticed and called over, "I'll bring fresh drinks, sir."

Eddie winked at her. He said, "Thanks, Janet."

He continued, "So we all went to court for my hearing. My father made me get a short haircut, and my mother said I had to wear my good suit even though I'd grown out of it. The liquor store owner told the judge that he had me on tape, and that's why he called the police. He explained that my father would assume the damages and have the back of the store rebuilt. The judge asked my father if he agreed to that, and my father produced a signed contract and receipt from a carpenter. The agreement said the repair would start soon, and the receipt said my father had already put down a thousand dollars with another thousand to go.

Eddie looked away from me and out onto the lake. He said, "The judge looked at everybody for a long time. When he spoke, he said he wanted me to consider myself fortunate that I had parents and a community that cared about me. He told me I should honor that community. He said most kids who appeared in court didn't have families who cared about them the way my parents cared about me. He wanted me to know that, and he asked if I understood. Office Macreavy had explained how to address the judge, but I meant it. I said, 'Yes, Your Honor.'

"The judge must have been satisfied, but he didn't want to let me off the hook. He told me to serve twenty hours of community service and left it up to Officer Macreavy to find something useful for me to do for three Saturdays."

Eddie finished his drink and looked at the ice cube left in the glass before continuing. "Macreavy had this feeling about the Chadakoin River," he said. "That's the outlet for Lake Chautauqua. No white water rafting or anything exciting on the Chadakoin." Even though I'd heard about Macreavy's river cleanup on Saturdays several times before, I let Eddie continue as if I hadn't. "It's just a rambling old industrial river. A long time ago, Jamestown used water to power the mills and the furniture factories. I know his family went back to those times, and that's where his money started, so maybe he felt he owed the river something. Whatever the reason, he talked the city into these cleanup brigades every spring and summer. Now and then he'd take a bunch of volunteers and some of the community service people and spend a Saturday picking up beer cans, trash bags, and whatever else the fisherman left behind. He told me picking up an old tire would be worth five hours off my community service time. He had a thing about the river, but he lived out on the lake. He had a place right on the water near Greenhurst." Eddie motioned to his left and pointed down the lake. He said, "You could almost see it from here except for the tall trees. His family liked to keep the place secluded, and I don't blame them, but anyone could see it from the water.

"You might not think so, but we had some fun cleaning up the river. The young guys and gals would get wet and muddy, and we'd laugh at each other when we fell in the water. The older people even volunteered for it because they could pat themselves on the back for helping the environment. Macreavy had this colossal rowboat he'd pull along. We'd fill it up with junk and float it down the river to a dumpster at the end of the day. People signed up for as many trips as Macreavy would lead. On one of my Saturdays, Macreavy talked to me about plumbing. He told me his house had been in his family for over a hundred years, and he thought it might be time for some maintenance. Someone installed indoor plumbing years ago, but he figured it probably needed additions and upgrades. I told him it probably did, and in my mind, I thought if I sold a plumbing job, it would be a way for my father to make back some of the money he lost because of me. Macreavy asked me what he had to do to have someone look at his place."

Moretti gave us a view of his younger self. He said, "I told Macreavy to call us at the office. I said, 'We'll come out to your home and do an estimate. We'll talk it over with you, and together we'll decide what you'd like us to do, exactly how much it will cost, and precisely when the work will be finished.'"

Eddie Moretti said, "I gave him the full sales pitch, and the 'kin' guy made me feel like a million bucks. I told him, 'It's just that easy. We're the best in town. You'll be delighted with every aspect of our work. I guarantee it!' Macreavy let me think I'd sold the job, and for years I believed I had."

Eddie had used the expression "'kin' guy," but it slid past, so naturally, I didn't want to call attention.

The waitress arrived with a tray of fresh drinks and another cup of coffee. After she passed the drinks, Eddie put his empty glass on the tray. Mary Ann had only finished half her drink, but she placed it beside his. I exchanged the waitress's coffee for my empty cup, and we all thanked her. After she left, Eddie looked at his new drink, leaned back in his chair, and said, "Come to think of it, maybe I did sell that job. If any sixteen-year-old kid I know came up with a line like that, I'd buy."

Mary Ann and I laughed, and I asked, "So did Macreavy have you renovate his plumbing?"

"Yes, he did," Moretti answered with unrestrained enthusiasm. "And more than that! My father and I drove the truck out to his place, and what a crazy old house. It had different-size rooms everywhere, two stories high with a flagstone basement. He needed a new water heater and all the plumbing for the kitchen. He also wanted to convert one of the upstairs bedrooms into a second bathroom. That meant new fixtures too, and he wanted the best.

"My father worked on that estimate for two days and figured it with a sharp pencil. He called Macreavy and set up an appointment to go over the details. We went out again, and as we pulled up to the house, Macreavy called out for us to come on in. He had a pot of coffee going and poured out three big mugs. We sat at a heavy oak table in his kitchen, and my father laid out all his drawings and calculations. He told Macreavy he'd cut it as close as possible, and the job would cost $3,000.

"Macreavy didn't flinch. He asked my father, 'Do I pay you now?'

"My father answered that most people pay half to help buy materials and then they pay the second half when the job is done."

Moretti looked at me and said, "I don't think I'll ever forget what happened next. Macreavy told my father, 'I trust you and your son completely. How about I pay for everything now?' He got up, walked over to a sideboard, and pulled out a drawer. He handed my father a check he'd already written for $5,000. On the way home that night, my father didn't say anything. I saw him tear up, and that's the closest I ever came to seeing him cry."

Eddie looked out onto the lake again. He said, "It turned out Macreavy knew more about money and people than any of us understood back then. I believe he did the calculations and knew precisely what my father would ask for. Then he added the two thousand to cover the liquor store. The funny part is that Macreavy got way more than he bargained for by the end of it. For anybody else, my father would have charged twice as much for all the extra work he did."

With a massive smile, Eddie Moretti held up his glass. He announced, "And now it's time for dinner. Afterward, you'll hear about the shower and the Carlsons."

Mary Ann laughed. She looked at me and said, "That's my favorite part of the story."

My watch said six o'clock, and I realized the man had paced the story to match the afternoon. I had to hand it to him. If Eddie Moretti wanted to be the smartest, most entertaining man on the porch, he'd achieved that goal.

We made our way to the hotel dining room, where another waitress had a table near the front window waiting for us. The waitress suggested the Lenhart Sampler, and we had a wonderful meal.

Intermission from Eddie Moretti's story lasted an hour and a half at the table. Over dinner, he told me about Jamestown. Factories there made furniture for the gilded age and ball bearings for warplanes from the beginning of flight through Vietnam. The Crescent Tool Company forged their iconic wrenches in town, and a company called AVM manufactured automatic voting machines, which counted votes from 1900 through the seventies.

Mary Ann told me about the Swedish craftsman in her family and the beautiful homes they built on Lakeview Avenue in town. She smiled when she told me you could see the lake from their upstairs sitting rooms. I heard how the original settlers used red bricks to make streets because bricks stood up best to the long winters. I heard again about the unique maple trees native to Western New York.

With dessert, Eddie finished the meal by proudly claiming Jamestown as the original home of the American Incense Company. He told me he'd met the owner once. Eddie asked him, 'How's business?' and the owner shot back, 'It stinks!'

I asked for the check and added a two-hundred-dollar tip. From the excellent care that went into her service, I guessed the waitress had been primed that Dr. Moretti tipped well. So far, my day had been worth every penny.

The three of us picked up our after-dinner cups of café au lait and headed back to the porch. We sat in the same places as before and took in the full glory of the last light of the day. The sunset had begun, and once again, Eddie Moretti had timed things perfectly.

The hotel kept the lights low outside to limit mosquitoes and give the evening its due. As the sunset faded, we found ourselves in the glow of candlelight. Eddie Moretti resumed. "So we started the plumbing job at Macreavy's house," he began. "We did a good job. My father wanted to do most of the work himself, but he wanted me there too. He also put two of his best guys on the job to help him. About a week into the project, the carpenter my father hired to fix the liquor store showed up. He told us Macreavy had called him about adding a shower to the job.

"We saw Macreavy talking with the carpenter on the back porch overlooking the lake. The carpenter had a measuring tape out while Macreavy drew pictures and scratched notes on a yellow legal pad. When my father asked him about it, Macreavy said he had an idea, but that's all he said. A couple of days later, the carpenter showed up again. This time he had plans with him. They met in the kitchen, and the carpenter left half an hour later. On his way out, he called upstairs, 'See ya in a few days, fellas.'

"After the carpenter left, Macreavy asked my father and me, along with the two additional plumbers, down to the kitchen. He laid the carpenter's drawing on the table and said, 'I want you guys to plumb in an outdoor shower.'

"The drawing showed an open-air shower using a new water-proof material as a deck. He said he wanted to rinse off after sailing or riding his bicycle without going into the house. He told us he wanted to stand naked and shower in the bright sun and open air. Holy mackerel! The four of us looked at each other. Then we looked at the plans. Sure enough, the drawing called for a deck, but it had no walls, and he wanted us to make it into a shower.

"After taking in the design, Macreavy showed us where to set up six risers to hold the showerheads. The water would fall through the deck, and he wanted us to plumb a drain into the septic system.

"My father looked at the drawings and gave it another try to be sure. He asked, 'What about the walls? Can we attach the shower-heads to the walls?'

"Macreavy said, 'No, there are no walls.'"

Eddie Moretti explained, "The risers had to hold the heads and deliver the water. And then he said he wanted the biggest shower-heads we could find. He said he'd seen some ten or twelve inches across and wanted his shower to 'feel like rain in the sunshine.'"

Eddie Moretti had me imagining Macreavy, standing naked, out in the open sun, with six massive showerheads raining water on him. It might have been uncomfortable talking about this in front of Mary Ann, but I'm sure she'd heard the story, probably more than once. Moretti paused, his eyes wide open in the candlelight, and low-ered his voice while the image lingered. "My father said, 'We can do it, Macreavy. We just have to figure out how.' When the rest of us went back to work, Macreavy pulled my father to the side. He opened the same drawer he'd opened before and took out another check. Macreavy had added to the job, so he added another payment.

He gave my father a check for $2,000, much more than my father would have asked for."

Eddie paused for a sip of his coffee. When he resumed, he sang out, "You should have seen that shower, Tom! Caesar Augustus himself would be jealous. I worked on it with the guys, and I even added an improvement. I put in a valve to drain the pipes at the beginning of the winter. Then I added a fitting on each showerhead so Macreavy could pour antifreeze into the lines to save them from exploding when Chautauqua County went into the deep freeze.

"All the time the guys and I worked on it, we kept thinking about what it would be like to take a shower out there, naked, open to the world. We decided it would be great. The next house over couldn't be less than a quarter mile away through the woods, and maybe someone could see if they happened to be passing by on a boat, but so what? They'd probably wish they had their own shower like that.

Moretti paused and raised his cup. He looked from Mary Ann to me and said, "Now let me tell you about the Carlsons."

Mary Ann laughed. She said, "This is where I come in."

Another waitress must have seen Moretti lift his cup. She came by with a fresh pot of coffee and a serving tray of cream and sugar. We topped off our cups, settled in, and the evening felt grand.

"In Jamestown," Eddie Moretti began, "we went to different schools depending on where we lived, but starting in tenth grade, we all went to the only high school in town, Jamestown High. I went to the Catholic school for elementary and junior high, so I didn't know many other kids, even in my neighborhood. That fall, after we finished the plumbing job for Macreavy, I started at the high school. My mom drove me to school now and then, and one morning in October, as she drove along Lakeview Avenue, I happened to look out the car windshield. At that exact moment, I saw the most beautiful girl I'd ever seen in my entire young life. The wind had picked up a pile of leaves, and she struggled to keep her hair from blowing away with them. I couldn't pull my eyes away from her. She saw me, but she didn't look away either. She looked back at me with the most amazing smile I'd ever seen. And she had braces! That might seem like an odd thing to be attracted to, but that's what got me, Tom. Yes, she had braces, but she wanted to smile, and she let it fly. She didn't care. What a great attitude. Fabulous!"

Mary Ann couldn't resist showing the smile as she looked on.

"What an angel!" Eddie declared. "I guessed she must be on her way to school too, and I kept an eye out for her all day. I wanted to see her again, but I couldn't find her out of the 1,800 kids at the school. One day, though, maybe a month later, I saw her again. Amazing! I stopped in my tracks, but she didn't notice me this time. I saw her from time to time after that, and one of those times, I asked a guy I knew, 'Who's that girl?'

"He said, 'Mary Ann Carlson. She's going out with Doug Williams.' That crushed my heart, but it made sense. Why wouldn't a beautiful girl like that have a boyfriend? All through high school, I'd see Mary Ann Carlson now and then. I always considered her the most beautiful girl I'd ever seen, but I also figured she'd never be interested in the Italian plumber kid, so I looked elsewhere. I had a few girlfriends, and I even went to the prom. Mary Ann went to the prom too."

Eddie looked at Mary Ann. He said, "I had to force myself to look away from you. If my date saw me looking at you, it would make her feel bad."

Mary Ann laughed. She said, "Oh, she saw you, all right. And I heard about it too, but it didn't matter. She had her eye on Wayne Lindquist."

Eddie laughed and let it roll off. He continued, "We all graduated," he said. "And I wrote Mary Ann Carlson off as my high school crush. Everybody says they had a crush in high school. *That's life*, I thought. I took up plumbing with my dad full-time and began to study for my license.

"Then one day, I came down with a toothache," he said. "I called the dentist, and he got me in right away, but who's the hygienist?" he asked, full of irony and drama. "None other than Mary Ann Carlson! I think she recognized me from high school, but you recognize people you went to high school with in Jamestown for the rest of your life. It's not that big a deal. She took x-rays and cleaned my teeth. All the while, I'm thinking my high school crush has her hands digging around in my mouth. Yes, I had a cavity, and she watched me wince from the novocaine needle. In the end, she also got to watch me walk out of the office with half my face drooping over." Eddie winked in my direction. He said, "Now that makes a guy feel like he made a good impression.

"After the dentist," he said, "I worked the rest of the day. My tooth felt better, and I decided to reward myself that night and head out for a drink. I had to work the next day, so no dancing or loud stuff. I just wanted to get out of my apartment for an hour, take it easy, and head back before it got too late. I walked over to this quiet place, a little more sociable bar than I usually went to, and I saw Mary Ann Carlson there. I smiled and gave a wave. She had two other girls with her, and it looked like a girls' night out in the middle of the week. I hadn't seen Mary Ann Carlson since high school, so what were the chances she'd work on my teeth at the dentist's office during the day and I'd run into her again that same night? I sat at the bar, ordered a scotch and water, and proceeded to take in the atmosphere.

"I had my mind on a job coming up when I heard her voice behind me. She asked, 'A little more anesthesia for the day?' When I turned around, I saw that smile again, but this time without the braces. Before I knew it, she had me looking into her eyes. I told myself, *Ed, say something. You don't have to be funny, but you've got to say something.* I said, 'Hi, Mary Ann. I think you did a great job today.' 'Well, thank you,' she said. 'Cooperative patients like you make it easy.'"

Ed allowed that the scotch gave him more confidence than usual, and he said, "I had the perfect subject to keep her talking. I asked her how often she saw a patient during the day and the same guy at a bar that night.

"She wound me up," he said. "She told me it may have happened before, and it could happen again, but she felt lucky because it happened with me this time."

Eddie Moretti gripped the arms of his chair. He said, "I thought to myself, *Hold on! Am I hearing this right?*" He mocked his own surprise at the moment. He asked, "Could this be Mary Ann Carlson flirting with me?

"Well," he said, "I decided to go for it. I said, 'Mary Ann, I've wanted to ask you since high school. May I call you and take you to dinner on Saturday night?'"

Eddie Moretti said, "Tom, to this day, I can still remember how she stunned and amazed me when she reached into her pocket, took out a pen, and wrote her number on a bar napkin. No sweeter numbers have ever been assembled in that exact order in the entire history of humankind."

"Oh, for crying out loud!" Mary Ann scoffed, and the two of us burst out laughing while Ed sat feigning a hurt reaction to the reproval.

"Well," Eddie continued when Mary Ann and I had settled down, "that's how it started, and I've been a happy man ever since."

She said, "Eddie, tell him about the wedding. That has something to do with Macreavy."

"Yes, it does," he agreed. "But first I have to tell him about the Carlsons."

Mary Ann laughed. She smiled again and said, "Ha!"

"The Carlsons are great people," Moretti began. "My dad told me once that if you want to see what a woman will be like when she gets older, look at her mother. Well, if that's true, then I'll have no problem. My mother-in-law is one of the kindest, happiest, and most caring women I've ever met. She's content with life. She's a woman who wakes up in the morning, looks out the kitchen window, and says, 'Good morning, world. I'm grateful to see you, and I hope everybody is feeling well today.' Over at the house one evening before Mary Ann and I got married, her mother mentioned breast-feeding her babies. She called it 'wonderfully pleasurable' and said it without a hint of embarrassment. That kind of thing has endeared me to the whole family for as long as I've known them. I think Mary Ann got her joy in life from her mother.

"I knew Mary Ann's older brother from the trades. Her father had a cabinet shop, and her brother worked for their father the way I worked for my dad. I'd see her brother on kitchen remodel jobs now and then, and somewhere along the line, he heard about the liquor store. It must have been hilarious around the dinner table the night he told the rest of the family about Mary Ann's new boyfriend."

Eddie and I both looked at Mary Ann as she sat quietly. Then she smiled again, and even in the candlelight, she dazzled us.

Eddie laughed and continued, "If you have a picture of an old-world Swedish craftsman in your mind, you're looking at Mary Ann's father. Once at his shop, he pointed to an antique desk he'd repaired. He told me one of the legs had been smashed and broken, and he had to replace most of it. When I asked him which leg, he said, 'You tell me.'

"Tom, I looked over every part of that desk for five minutes, but I could not pick out the new leg. He'd matched the wood, the grain, the stain color, and the finish gloss. He even put a few charcoal marks on it to make it look like it matched the age of the other three. A fantastic craftsman.

"Well, as I said, the Carlsons are great folks," Ed continued, "and I'm proud to be their son-in-law, but we had one problem. They're Lutherans, and they don't know about big parties. Even though I'm a Catholic, that didn't bother them, and they gave us their blessing, but it surprised them how many of my relatives wanted to come to the wedding. Mary Ann got nervous and had a talk with me. She explained a big wedding would be a stretch for her parents. That disappointed me at first, and I brooded about it. Weddings are a big deal in my family, and I wanted a blowout. Mary Ann let me think it over, and then she said, 'Eddie Moretti, we're going to go to bed every night and wake up together to start every morning for the rest of our lives. That's what we're going to do. It's the marriage, not the wedding, that counts.'

"Okay, so that settled that," he said. "We agreed on a guest list of one hundred. That's big enough to be noticeable, but nothing like the enormous Italian weddings I'd been to. Sometimes in Jamestown, families invite every other person in the phone book.

So anyway, everything went well, even if it turned out to be the hottest day in August that year. My family didn't embarrass anyone, and her family put up with all our Catholic kneeling and sitting and standing.

"Father Crimmins said the Mass, and for a minute, I thought he'd been talking to Mary Ann when he wrote his homily. He said, 'Marriage is a great adventure. Two people leave the comfort of their families at home and set off together to find meaning and new experiences. They're looking for value in their existence, and the marriage of these two people makes life better for everyone they know. If they do it right, the adventurers find their purpose and return to help the rest of us understand something about God and ourselves. We remember people who have found value and purpose. Their lessons live on in our hearts.'

"Father Crimmins said, 'Ed and Mary Ann, let your lives and your life together be a blessing to everyone around you. We don't need any more buildings with marble columns. Let your good and honest lives be your blessed memorial.'"

It impressed me that Eddie Moretti remembered what the priest said at the wedding. Something about it sounded familiar, and I looked it up later. The priest had been referring to Proverbs 10:7.

"To be polite," Eddie continued, "we invited Macreavy. I didn't think he'd come, but he responded right away. He wrote on his response card that he wouldn't miss it and marked '2' in the box asking how many would attend. Holy smoke! Someone told me once that his wife had died, but I didn't know anything about that. I assumed he had a social life, but I hadn't thought about who he might go out with. He showed up with a woman on his arm I'd never seen before. Trim and athletic, she looked about his age, and we all took a second look. She wore a light-blue cotton dress and carried a navy shoulder bag with matching heels. She had large brown eyes that looked wet, not like she'd been crying, just bright and shiny, but she stopped the show with her hair. She had this thick black and silver hair tied up in a fancy twist. I commented to one of the plumbers, an older guy who worked at Macreavy's place on the lake. I said, 'Leave it to Macreavy to show up with a hot one,' and he told me I didn't know the half of it."

"She did cause a stir," Mary Ann remarked.

Eddie nodded at her and continued, "That plumber and some of my dad's friends at the wedding knew Macreavy from high school, and they seemed to know her too. She had everybody smiling and laughing in no time. I asked another one of my dad's friends about her, and he told me, 'That's Nel Bell, Macreavy's high school girl-friend.' He said he didn't know the whole story but heard they broke up when they went to different colleges.

"We had the wedding at Saints Peter and Paul Church on Cherry Street," Eddie explained, "and we held the reception down-stairs in the church basement. After the Mass, Mary Ann and I stood on the steps and received guests. That's when Macreavy introduced us to Nel Bell. She took my hand in both of hers. She told me she went to school with some of the guys I work with, and it made her happy to see how we'd all found a way to stay in town together. Then she complimented me for doing a great job on the shower at Macreavy's place. I didn't expect anything like that. I didn't know how to respond, so I said, 'Thank you,' but she hadn't finished. She said, 'Sometimes I ride the bicycle or go sailing with Mac just to get hot and dirty enough to wash it all away in that shower. It's fantastic!'

"I'll tell you," Eddie admitted, "for a split second, I thought about the two of them in that shower together, but I didn't dwell on it. As a married man, I had to learn to be polite. I said, 'That's great! Officer Macreavy has been an important part of my life, and I'm happy you two came to celebrate with us. Please have a marvelous time.'"

Eddie alerted me. He said, "Now this is funny, Tom. Macreavy's date said, 'Oh, we will. I'm planning on lots of dancing, and since Mac's got the wheel tonight, no doubt I'll have a few too many.'

"She let go of my hands, and Macreavy escorted her in. At the same time, Mary Ann's father opened the door on the other side of the church basement and carried in a case of beer. As more guests filed past, I kept looking over at the buffet area. I thought he'd bring in more beer and a few bags of ice, but no. The Carlsons had only planned on one case of warm beer."

Eddie laughed. "It never crossed my mind to check what the Carlsons had planned for a reception. I figured they had everything covered. I told Mary Ann we had to have more than one case of warm beer, and she reminded me her dad and mom didn't drink. Mary Ann said her father had never bought a case of beer in his life.

And on top of that, they had a problem with bringing beer into a church anyway."

Eddie said, "I couldn't do anything about it. I talked to some of my buddies and asked them to make a beer run. They agreed to go, but they all had full plates of food from the buffet and said they wanted to eat first. When I saw my dad, he said I looked worried and made a joke about being married. I told him I didn't think Mary Ann's folks brought enough to drink, and he told me to let it go. He said it would all work out, and I should get back to the guests and thank them for coming. I saw Macreavy by himself and asked where his date had gone. He said he'd been looking for her himself and asked me if I'd seen her. When I said no, he changed the subject."

Although he continued telling me the story, Eddie looked at Mary Ann. He said, "Macreavy congratulated me again for getting married. He told me I'd come to understand what a wonderful woman Mary Ann is. And he said, 'Do whatever she tells you.'"

I held up my coffee cup in salute. I said, "Sounds like good advice, Eddie."

"Absolutely!" Eddie agreed. "I've always trusted her, and I always do what she says."

"Oh, please," Mary Ann scoffed.

Eddie continued, "We had a DJ, and he played soft music for dinner. When most people had finished, the DJ asked for attention, and we started the speeches. When it came to my turn, everybody sat at their tables, waiting for me to speak. I got about two lines into my speech when the church basement door burst open. The liquor store owner, the same guy from all those years ago, stood there holding a case of wine and two bags of ice. He walked in and looked around for a place to put it. Everyone sat at their tables, wondering what to do, and the door slammed open again. This time, Nel Bell, Macreavy's date, walked in with another case and stood next to the liquor store guy. I couldn't believe it. My dad and Mary Ann's father jumped up and then the women who set up the buffet table ran over. They took the cases into the kitchen and iced the bottles and the beer while we finished the speeches. The DJ played the traditional dances and then it was time to crank up the music and start the party."

Ed Moretti leaned back in his chair. "By then," he said, "they'd opened several bottles and poured glasses for the guests. I shot over to Macreavy's date and the liquor store owner as soon as possible. My face must have asked the question because I couldn't find the words. The owner told me how Nel Bell came into his store with a huge smile, all dressed up and asking for 'emergency service.' He said she'd walked over from the church in high heels by herself because she knew Macreavy tried to stay out of liquor stores. We all knew that Macreavy didn't drink, and only then did it dawn on me how awkward it must have been for him to arrange the meeting with the store owner and my father. Anyway, she told him I'd gotten married, but the bride's family only brought one case of beer. She picked out twenty-three bottles of assorted wines, some white, some red, and some champagne. The old guy commented, 'She knows her wine too.'"

I asked Eddie, "Twenty-three? Why twenty-three?"

"I thought the same thing," Eddie agreed. "But they'd brought more than we had. So what could I say?"

He went on, "The store owner explained when Nel Bell first came into the store, she asked for two cases of wine. He told her he would drive her back to the church and help carry the wine in case boxes. There would be slots in the boxes for twenty-four bottles. He told her to pick out twenty-three bottles so he could save one slot for himself. The liquor store owner went into the church basement kitchen and came out with a bottle of Austin Nichols Wild Turkey. The old guy handed it to me and said, 'This one's on me, Eddie Moretti, Congratulations!'"

"Eddie!" I shouted. "That's amazing!"

Mary Ann had her smile full on. She said, "I'll never forget that."

"It overwhelmed me," Eddie said. "I'd married the woman I most desired and been forgiven by a man I'd wronged. I told him I'd be forever grateful and get the money over to him ASAP. I also asked him not to mention the break-in to Mary Ann. The old guy told me Nel Bell had paid for everything already. He said he usually didn't take out-of-state checks, but he recognized her from when she went to high school. He laughed when he told me how he remembered her walking with Macreavy past the shop. They tried to hold hands while they each carried stacks of books. He said because he remembered she carried so many books, he figured she'd probably be good for the check. Her name printed on it made him sure of it. The check said 'Nelson Bell, PhD.'"

Mary Ann said, "What a fabulous wedding, the memory of a lifetime. Everyone had so much fun, and they danced till midnight."

Eddie added, "Macreavy and his date danced up a storm. They danced with a lot of the guests too. I smiled when I saw some of my dad's plumber buddies dancing with Nel Bell. I know what they had in mind too. They imagined her outside on that hot August afternoon under the sun, wet hair hanging down her back, standing naked in that outdoor shower they made."

Mary Ann gasped. "Ed, that's enough!" she said.

Eddie said, "Oh, for crying out loud. It's part of life, Mary Ann, and people like Macreavy and Nel Bell knew how to enjoy it!"

Mary Ann sat for a moment and then she laughed out loud. "I suppose you're right, Eddie," she said. "It does sound like fun. Maybe they found their own little corner of heaven."

I enjoyed hearing the two of them banter, but it started to feel like we were all getting tired. As it got close to ten o'clock, Eddie stood up, stretched his arms over his head, and took a few paces where he stood. He said, "I think I'll call it a night, Tom. You two can stay up if you want, but I've had enough for today."

"I'm with ya, honey," Mary Ann agreed. "Let's turn in. We'll give Tom a good tour around the old town tomorrow."

"Sounds great," I said, and the evening ended.

The following day I found a copy of the *Jamestown Post Journal* on one of the tables while I ate breakfast. I read stories of daily life and people in the town. I wish I knew some of them. Halfway through my omelet and the paper, Eddie and Mary Ann walked into the dining room. I stood to greet them, and Eddie spoke before I did. He said, "Good morning to you, sir. Are you ready for a journey into the past?"

He'd started already. The day of stories and nostalgia had begun. Eddie and Mary Ann thoroughly enjoyed the breakfast buffet and said they started every day with "the best in breakfast." This time Eddie wore blue jeans with an open-collar dress shirt. Mary Ann had on a red blouse and white wraparound skirt. Her blue running shoes gave the outfit a patriotic vibe, and her bright blond hair and perfect smile lit up the room.

Eddie suggested we take their minivan. Eddie drove, of course, and Mary Ann took her position in front. The seat in the second row let me see everything on both sides. As we pulled out of the lot, Ed explained it would take a few minutes to get to Jamestown. Almost immediately, he motioned to the right. He pointed to a small private driveway and said, "That's where Macreavy lived. I wonder how much the people who live there now know about him. So many years have passed." I looked, but I couldn't see the house through the trees.

While Eddie drove, I asked him, "How did you get from plumbing to dentistry?"

"Her idea," he laughed and gestured toward Mary Ann.

"And you're glad I talked you into it," she added.

"That I am, darling," he agreed. "That I am."

As he drove, Eddie Moretti explained, "We got married and moved into a nice little apartment. I kept working with my father, and Mary Ann stayed at the dentist's office. One day, about six months after we got married, Mary Ann said she wanted to have a serious talk with me. She said she'd always be proud to stand by my side. As a cabinet maker's daughter, she'd only ever hoped to be a tradesman's wife. She described her father and brother as master woodworkers and had no doubt I'd qualify for a master plumber's license in time. She said her father and brother could make their saws and clamps sing and dance, but people only paid for their work after paying for everything else first. When she got her braces, she saw dentists and orthodontists do the same work as her dad and brother. They rebuilt and repaired, but they spent a fraction of the time her father and brother did, and people spent much more on dental work. She took classes to become a dental hygienist and made more than her brother at her first job. When she had this talk with me, she made as much as her father ever did, and she also helped people relieve their pain and maintain their health."

As a retired woodworker, I understood the point.

Eddie took a breath and continued, "She said to me, 'Ed, I've been around craftsmen all my life. I know what it takes, and you're as good as any. You do fine work. You have intelligence, creativity, and hand skill. You could do anything the dentists I work for can do.'"

Eddie glanced back at me while he drove. He said, "I told her I didn't think I could do the schooling. A dentist had to go to college and then to dental school. She said we could break it up. We'd keep working our jobs, and I'd go to the community college. From there, I'd transfer to a four-year school. I could do plumbing jobs along the way, and she could get a job anywhere with a dentist. I could go as fast or as slow as I wanted, one class at a time to make good grades. I'd quit plumbing and go to dental school when we got far enough ahead. She'd keep working, and I'd go to school till I finished. It took years, but I finally graduated from the University of Buffalo Dental School. I worked at a clinic in Buffalo for five years and then the practice opened up in Fayetteville. I wish I could work in Jamestown, but I did well at the practice. Mayann and the kids built a life there, and I didn't want to uproot the family."

"Yeah, tell me about your kids," I asked.

"Two boys, Doug and Sam," he answered. "They're staying with friends this weekend, giving us a break. Tremendous fellows. I couldn't be prouder."

We started seeing some of Jamestown come into view, and I looked out the driver's side window. We passed Arby's, and I saw the Big N department store a little further on. I thought about Chauncey Cook and Patrick Williams. Ed took a turn onto Washington Street. He said Washington Street crossed through Jamestown, and I saw auto dealers and garages where Chauncey Cook's father and uncle might have worked.

Larger homes and older buildings came into view, and we might have been getting close to downtown. I asked Eddie to take me past the bus station. I saw his head move slightly, but he didn't ask me why. He said that would also give us a chance to pass by Saints Peter and Paul Church. We took a few turns, and he pointed out the passenger side. I saw a stone-block church with old-fashioned stained-glass windows. I also noticed the library across the street.

Darla Rhinesmith came to mind, and I asked him about a drug-store near the center of town. Mary Ann answered, "There used to be one across from where the Lucy Museum is now."

"What's the Lucy Museum?" I asked.

"It's a whole museum for Lucille Ball," Eddie answered. "She came from Jamestown."

"You don't say," I answered. "I didn't know that."

"That's right," Eddie confirmed. "Genius, the original wild girl Janis Joplin without the heroin. Do you need something from the drugstore?"

"No," I answered. "I thought I'd heard about it once."

"You heard about a drugstore in the middle of Jamestown, New York?" Mary Ann asked.

I answered her with a smile. "Yes, I did, oddly enough. Is it near the police station?"

"Kind of," Eddie said. "A few blocks. The center of town and the police station are both down the hill from where we are now."

Mary Ann asked, "How do you know about these places?"

"People told me different things about Jamestown when they told me about Macreavy," I answered.

"The liquor store I told you about stood over there," Eddie said. He pointed to a row of new townhomes. I glanced up at a street run-ning perpendicular to our direction and opposite the townhomes. I saw an old neon sign hanging off level that said "Jenny's Lunch."

"Okay," he continued as we drove along. "Here's the City Hall building and the police station where Macreavy worked." We took a turn to avoid a one-way street and then another turn. He said, "The high school is over there. This is Prendergast Avenue, where the bus station used to be. I'm not sure where it is now."

Mary Ann said, "Let's go up Lakeview Avenue."

"Yes, my darling," Eddie agreed. "Your wish is my opportunity to please you."

Mary Ann replied with a loud "Ha!" and added, "You see what I have to put up with? A man who wants to please me every time I have a wish. It's infuriating."

I laughed. The two of them were kidding each other like high schoolers as they cruised the streets where they grew up. Eddie told me Lakeview Avenue took us to the North Side. We wound through streets turning right and left until I'd lost direction. I thought about the Pridemore family welcoming Lee as a boy, and Rubin Gubbio casing houses after supper.

Eddie Moretti said, "That's my old house right there." He drove a little more, took a few turns, and said, "And that's where Mary Ann grew up."

They told me about days when the town froze over, and the kids took to the streets on ice skates. They seemed like friendly homes, and some of them remained well-kept. Some spots looked like they might have come from picture postcards, and I thought about the people who had lived all their years in these houses.

I asked Ed, "Do your folks still live here?"

"Sure," he answered. "We've got relatives all over town. They're mostly older now. Mary Ann and I will make the rounds tomorrow."

Eddie turned the van and said, "Now we'll go across town to the South Side."

He drove down Lakeview Avenue in the opposite direction and went through the "downtown." He pointed out the bar where he got Mary Ann's phone number, and we took another turn to go over a bridge. When I looked down, I saw water. "Is that the Chadakoin?" I asked.

"That's it," Eddie said and added with a note of sarcasm. "The mighty Chadakoin."

He took us up and down steep hills while driving for another half hour. He told me about the places we passed, and I took in the houses, the old maple trees, and the cracked sidewalks. We passed over McKinley Street, and I remembered Joyce Earl telling me about her second-floor apartment, but I couldn't guess which house. After a while, he announced, "That's about it. We'll head back to the hotel by way of the West Side. That will give you a better look at the river." He took another turn and started down a low flat street. "The factories used to be down here by the water," he said. As we came into view of the river, I saw a building behind a sign that said "Jamestown Board of Public Utilities," and again, I thought about Joyce.

Eddie said he'd brought me past every place to see in Jamestown, and I thought to ask about the Patel family's hotel. Eddie told me he did some plumbing work there once, but a city urban renewal project took the hotel down long ago. He remembered the Indian family who owned it. He told me they had two boys who left right after high school. He said he heard the mother and father went to live with one of the sons who became a doctor. He remembered the family also owned a donut shop across from Bigalow's department store downtown, but urban renewal took that too.

Eddie kept driving. I hoped he'd remember someplace else he wanted to show me, but he didn't, and Mary Ann didn't either. We got back to the Hotel Lenhart in time for a late lunch. It surprised me to see so many people there on a weekday. Eddie explained the curtain came down right after Labor Day for Chautauqua County, and every tourist dollar counted this late in the season. We had sandwiches, and I thanked them repeatedly for telling me their story and showing me around.

Mary Ann said Eddie never mentioned the whole liquor store thing, and she never thought to ask him about it. She didn't know he'd been keeping it a secret. She said she wouldn't have believed anything about the fingerprint card and picture until he brought it home one night. She asked me, "Did you learn anything, Tom? Did you get what you came for?"

I told her I had. I'd learned something about miracles. Some miracles are dazzling, like a shower in the sun on a hot afternoon turning into cold wine in the evening. Other miracles are less obvious, like two kids exchanging glances and a smile at the same moment on their way to school. Wonders and graces come to everybody. Some miracles last an evening, and some go on for a lifetime. Some come to boys as they fix things with their dads, and some come to young girls who have to wear braces.

As I left Chautauqua County on the drive home, I could see the lake from the top of a hill. I thought about Macreavy and Chauncey on the water in the old maple sailboat. I wondered if Macreavy covered that same road on his bicycle. He probably had more than once. I've sometimes thought of life as a pencil line or a scratch on the earth, almost meaningless. But I've learned lines and scratches can make pictures or write words. The miracle is how they fit together. It's a puzzle in a kaleidoscope and then it's over—time for the next kid to take a turn.

CHAPTER 11

Nelson Bell: The Woman with the Alabaster Jar/Mary Magdalene

W hile driving home from meeting with Eddie and Mary Ann Moretti, it occurred to me I needed one more interview. I had to meet Nel Bell. Before my wife and I went to the flea market that Saturday morning years ago, I'd never heard of Jamestown or any of the "caught thirty." Since then, Macreavy and the rest of them had occupied vast amounts of my thinking. I kept wondering what Nel Bell could tell me about Macreavy. She sounded fascinating, but what did he mean to her? By this time, I believed the cards and photos had to have come from Foraker Macreavy, but she might be able to tell me how and why he got involved. Then again, maybe she'd say I'd fabricated a grand coincidence, and I'd have to live with that.

I called Phil Troxel and asked him to find out about a woman named Nelson Bell who had something to do with Macreavy and Jamestown. I told him the only thing I knew about her is that I'd heard she graduated from Jamestown High School the same year he did. Phil said he'd have something for me in two days, and we agreed to meet at the usual place.

He pulled into the coffee shop parking lot on his motorcycle and made his way in, where I greeted him with a large cup and a smile. He pulled out a notebook and wasted no time. He said Nelson

Bell had been easy to find and described her as "queen of the mountain" in elements and materials research.

Phil sipped the hot coffee while flipping through his notebook. Without looking up, he asked me why I wanted to know about her. I explained how several of the people I'd spoken with referred to her, and it looked like she went back a long way with Macreavy. I told him she probably didn't have anything to do with the police cards, but maybe she could answer questions about Macreavy.

Phil stopped me, "Yeah," he said. "Did you ever find out more about that guy?"

I realized I hadn't spoken to Phil for a long time and explained how Macreavy and the rest of them had become a considerable part of my life. I told Phil, "He turned out to be a lone-wolf cop who went around coaching kids in trouble. At first, I had to prove to myself that he had something to do with the arrest cards. Then I wanted to know why. For some reason, he took an interest in these kids. I got as curious about Macreavy as I'd been about the kids. He must have been a real character. Everyone respected him, and it appears he had connections. Most of the people I talked to told me about the money, but only a few of them knew about it until after he died. Until then, he worked as a cop, but I can't imagine he needed the paycheck. They say he lived in his family's summer home on Lake Chautauqua near Jamestown. As I got further along in my interviews, some of the people I talked to mentioned a woman he knew named Nelson Bell. She may have been a girlfriend, but they broke up after high school, yet they seemed to have had some relationship later. It's quirky, but Jamestown is a small town, and things get quirky in small towns. That's why I want to get in touch with her. I thought if I told her about the fingerprint cards, she might fill me in on what I don't know about Macreavy."

Phil Troxel took another sip of his coffee while he waited for me to finish. "Well," he began, "she's alive. Dr. Nelson Sophia Bell is eighty-one years old and still working. She's probably semi-retired but keeps an office at her company. It's her company by the way, called Associates and Light. They do aerospace research. She started it years ago with a fistful of venture capital, and she must be what my dad would call a smart cookie. After college, she took a job as a junior engineer at NASA during the Apollo years. Afterward, she joined a group that developed the heat shield tiles for the Space Shuttles in the '70s and '80s. The company is about communications, they produce ideas and connections, and it's worth millions." Phil took a breath. "I can't tell you much about her business, but it looks like she coordinates projects. Her company puts other companies together with each other.

"She graduated from high school in 1960, the same year as Macreavy, first in the class. She has a doctorate from Texas A&M, and she's been in Seattle for the last forty years. She married a guy named Theodore Hickman. He did sales and marketing for Corning Glass."

I laughed. "A salesman named Theodore Hickman?" I asked.

"Yeah. Did you know him?"

"Theodore Hickman is the salesman in *The Iceman Cometh*," I explained.

"Is that so?" Phil acknowledged. "Do you want me to look into him?"

I laughed at his quick comeback and thanked him for what he'd found.

Phil left a folder of details for Dr. Nelson Bell but alerted me to a possible problem. He said, "You might want to talk to high-dollar people like this, but you can't just call on the phone." He said I might have to find someone who could pave the way. So far, none of the people I'd met in my project needed a special introduction, which brought fresh doubt. Even if she had something to add to Macreavy's story, why would she tell me about it?

I gave myself a task. I had to write my best letter. I stopped at a stationery shop located in an old brick building downtown. I'd passed the place countless times and always wanted to stop in. It had a heavy wooden door with a bell attached, and an older woman smiled and greeted me from the counter. The wooden floor squeezed and squeaked as I walked closer. I remembered that Chauncey Cook told me Nel Bell got her name from her parents' wealthy families. I explained to the woman at the counter that I wanted to write a letter to an older lady who'd grown up with the finer things. The woman sold me a packaged set called The Elegant Vintage Letter. It cost

$49.95, contained beautiful sheets of ivory-colored linen paper with matching envelopes, and came complete with a fountain pen. The box the set came in said the ink color had been "selected to compliment the paper." The combination promised to "project authenticity with a feeling of warmth." That inspired me. I practiced with the fountain pen, and after my cursive improved, I wrote this letter.

Thomas Strongtree
Spring Valley, Ohio
Dr. Nelson Bell, PhD
Chief of Science
Associates and Light
Seattle, Washington
Dear Dr. Bell,

I am a retired carpenter living in Ohio. Several years ago, I bought a pack of police arrest records at a flea market. The collection consisted of thirty Manila envelopes containing fingerprint cards and photos of young people who lived in the Jamestown, New York, area. The arrests took place from the mid-1970s through the '90s, and I contacted all of those who are still living. They are adults now in the prime of their lives. I felt drawn to these individuals, and they changed my life.

I wanted to understand if interaction with the law at a young age made a difference in their lives. The adventure came out of nowhere, and what an adventure it has been! The individuals I spoke with shared freely and enthusiastically about their lives. What links them all is their relationship with a police officer named Foraker Macreavy. He must have been an extraordinary and fascinating man.

Some people I spoke with also mentioned that Officer Macreavy had a female acquaintance.

They referred to her as a woman named Nel Bell. Some say they met her. After consulting graduation records from Jamestown High School, I believe you may be Nel Bell.

This project and understanding the man Foraker Macreavy have become a significant focus in my life. If you can add anything to what I have learned about him, I would be grateful to hear it. I am willing to travel to Seattle to meet with you. The place and time would be at your convenience.

I send my respect.

With gratitude,
Thomas Strongtree

The letter and the addressed envelope looked good. I got the lines straight and the centering perfect. I made sure to mark "personal" on the envelope, and three weeks later, I found the letter returned to my mailbox.

Phil Troxel had warned me about this, so I'd come up with an idea in the meantime. I don't know why I didn't think of this in the first place, but I called Darla Rhinesmith at her clinic. I could imagine her smile and red lipstick as I heard her voice. "Mr. Strongtree," she said, "wonderful to hear from you. How may I help?"

I explained that after meeting with the people in my project, I wanted to meet Dr. Bell, but my letter had been returned. Darla said she didn't think Nel Bell would mind talking to me, especially if it had something to do with Macreavy, and added that a handwritten letter would be appreciated. She said, "Letters used to be a huge part of her life, but there aren't many of you around who know how to write them anymore." She gave me a different address and explained that anything labeled "personal" at Dr. Bell's office would probably be considered advertising or menacing. Darla said she'd arrange a meeting if the letter didn't get through. Then she added, "But you'd better hurry."

"Is there a problem?" I asked.

"Do it soon," Darla answered.

"Is she sick?" I asked.

Darla Rhinesmith answered, "Tom, I'm a nurse. There are things I can tell you and things I can't. I'm saying you'd better send your letter sooner than later."

"I understand," I said and read the new address back to her.

I could imagine her lipstick and smile as she confirmed, "You got it. Is there anything else?"

"No," I answered. "Thanks a million, Nurse Darla."

I sent the letter using the new address, and I got a letter back this time. Dr. Bell had also used a fountain pen on linen stationery. She'd printed my address in a sublime engineer's script on the envelope, indicating a sure and precise hand.

I sat down at the kitchen table and opened the letter with a blade so I wouldn't damage it. I unfolded the paper and noticed a fragrance. The figure of a bell had been embossed on the top of the page with the name Nelson printed over it in a decorative font. A slight discoloration near her signature told me she'd placed a drop of perfume near it. The letter read,

Dear Mr. Thomas Strongtree,

I remember Foraker Macreavy as a light in my life.

I will be available to speak with you at my offices in Seattle next month on the morning of the 15th. We'll meet at 8 o'clock for coffee.

Please call my secretary, Raphael, to confirm. I've enclosed a card with details.

You've delighted me with your letter and reminded me of days filled with wonder.

You also sent me to an almost forgotten drawer in my desk searching for suitable stationery to reply to your own.

Looking forward,
Nel Bell

It worked! The card dropped onto the table when I unfolded the page. I called immediately, spoke with Raphael, and booked a flight online.

For most of my life, I have been afraid to fly. Working in shops and factories, I've seen hundreds of mistakes over the years. When I think of airplanes being built and serviced, I think of a young guy putting the wrong shim in place or cross-threading a nut and bolt. I see another guy rushing through a checklist and giving an inspection a cursory glance. I am aware of these mistakes because I've made them, and I've been anxious and hypervigilant my entire life because of them. But this project changed my thinking. I've learned there is more to life than my understanding. I've learned about trust, and I've come to understand that life goes on. Maybe I'll be here for it, and maybe I won't. Airplanes fly most of the time, and sometimes they don't. Fear of death has kept me from living, but I'm no longer afraid of that.

Phil Troxel mentioned Dr. Nelson Bell is a big deal, and a search on the computer told me how big. Associates and Light works with anyone who has anything to do with heat—guarding against it, transferring it, or generating it. Everyone knows that all technologies have problems with heat. It's a world of specialty ceramics, metals, and fabrics, but I kept asking myself how an eighty-one-year-old woman is still involved with building airplanes, spaceships, and nuclear reactors."

When I got to my hotel room in Seattle, I carefully hung up my suit and went out for coffee. As I sat, taking in the atmosphere, I went over the questions I wanted to ask. I'd been interviewing people who knew Macreavy for close to five years. Macreavy and Nel Bell had become familiar, but I didn't want to assume too much. I turned my coffee cup around and around.

I paged through the folder Phil Troxel had given me. The complete bio claimed Dr. Bell's worth at more than $20 million. I wish I could relate some of the other stories I heard about Foraker Macreavy and her. The caring nature of their generosity would astound you, but I've pledged confidentiality.

I made it to the appointment in plenty of time. Dr. Nelson Bell occupied a suite of offices and conference rooms on the third floor of a contemporary-style office building. A man with a shock of blond hair and extra white teeth stepped forward as I walked through the front doors. He introduced himself as Raphael, the secretary she had me call. His gold earring and bright red and yellow shirt made me smile and feel at ease. He said he would escort me to "a more comfortable meeting room." I nodded and followed him to an elevator that took us up.

From the elevator, Raphael led me along a carpeted hallway past open office doors. I saw workers sitting at desks, focusing on computer screens. We came to a room that had an aluminum door with a large windowpane more than an inch thick. I suspected it might be some space-age plastic. Raphael ushered me into the room, furnished in mid-century modern. It couldn't be anything other than a conference room, but it didn't feel like it. A natural maple dining set took the place of an imposing conference table. Chairs of the same elegant wood had been fitted with leather upholstery and placed around the table. Raphael said I should sit anywhere while motioning to a silver service set waiting on a side table. He offered coffee, and as he poured the coffee into an oversized china cup and saucer, he whispered to me in a conspiratorial tone. He said, "Dr. Bell is so looking forward to meeting you. Thank you for coming to see her. I can't wait to tell her you're here." He flashed a smile and left. I asked myself why he would thank me for coming to see her.

Raphael had offered a chair, but I continued to stand. I looked out a large picture window onto a field of grass shining in the morning sun. I noticed my hands sweating as I sipped the coffee and held the cup on the saucer. I didn't want to drop it, so I put the cup and saucer onto a side buffet cabinet made out of the same wood matching the table and chairs in the center of the room. I noticed a metal plaque held by four brass tacks on the side and toward the back of the buffet. It said,

Maddox Table Company
Jamestown, New York

I assumed Nel Bell had something to do with the table as she had grown up in Jamestown as a girl, and the plaque took me back to Eddie Moretti's tour of the town. As I looked out the window, I asked myself what gave Jamestown such a magic appeal. As I thought about it, I realized the feeling probably came to the people I'd met because Jamestown had been the place for their growing years when we first reach beyond ourselves and learn about the obstacles in our way. I thought about my own hometown.

I'd been musing about youth and looking out the window for maybe ten minutes when the aluminum door swept open and startled me. She walked in, and I remembered Darla Rhinesmith's comment about the gift of beauty. I'd never guess her to be eighty-one. Tall with a slight figure and perfect posture, she looked directly at me. Her liquid brown eyes drew me to her and held my attention. She walked across the room, took my hand in both of hers, and said, "Good morning, Mr. Strongtree. I'm Nel Bell."

I stood looking at the woman I'd heard so much about. As she held my hand, I couldn't speak for a moment. When I found my voice, I returned the greeting. "Good morning to you, Dr. Bell. It's a pleasure to meet you."

She let that stand. She did not say "call me Nel," and the formal address gave her a degree of distance that allowed me some comfort. The woman commanded respect with her presence. She'd locked my attention with her eyes, but when she released my hand to gesture for me to take a chair at the table, I saw her hair. She wore it swept back in triumph. Some people I interviewed described her hair as black with gray, and some called it gray with black, but everyone noticed it, and everyone commented on it. I saw her hair as entirely silver, contrasted with her dark-blue silk blouse and light-gray mid-length woolen skirt. Her polished black shoes only suggested a raised heel. A delicate chain held a polished bronze coin-sized pendant of a sailboat with a mast but no sail. She wore no other jewelry save for the slip of a wedding band on her right hand made from the same metal.

"Please," she said with a smile. "Would you like coffee? You're in Seattle now. That's all we drink."

"Thank you," I answered. "Raphael poured me a cup earlier, and it is delicious.

"By the way," I said as I pulled out the chair she'd indicated, "would you mind if I recorded our meeting?" I put my phone on the table and took a seat.

"Oh, that's fine," she agreed. "Everybody wants to document everything anymore. I'm used to it."

"So tell me," she began, "what's all this about Mac?"

I tried to remember who first told me she called him "Mac" while everyone else referred to him as "Macreavy" or "Officer Macreavy."

"Well," I began, "as I mentioned in my letter, I bought a pack of police arrest cards and photos at a flea market, and I got the idea that I wanted to meet each of the kids in the photos as adults. I made it a project. Something called me to do it."

"Called you to what?" Dr. Bell asked. "The project?"

"Yes," I answered. "But more than that, it felt like the people themselves calling me."

"That doesn't surprise me," Dr. Bell interjected.

"Why is that?" I asked.

"Go on," she said, "I think I know what's coming next."

I reminded myself that the same people who commented on her hair also told me about her intelligence.

"So I got in touch with an investigator who finds people," I said. "And he came up with addresses and phone numbers. Some of them died in the meantime, but I contacted the rest."

"That would be Philip Troxel?" she asked.

She stopped me with that. "Yes," I said. "Phil Troxel. How do you know about him?"

"From the government," she explained. "It doesn't happen to me much anymore, but there are people who care about such things. When someone searches for me seriously, the office gets an alert, and sometimes they think it's important enough to ask me about it. I thought something might be going on with you and Mr. Troxel. First, I heard about a man from Ohio looking into my past and then I received your letter with a return address in Ohio. I put the two together. Also, several of the people you spoke with called me after you met with them, which gave us a wonderful chance to catch up. It disappointed me to be left out of your party until now. Then again,

I've never been arrested, so I thought that might leave me off the invite list."

I smiled and held my hands out, palms up. "Well, that's what happened," I admitted. "I hope you're not offended. I meant no harm, and I'm sure Phil won't cause you any problems."

"Thomas," she said, "I'm flattered. I'm glad you went to the effort. Please continue."

"Okay," I said. "Everyone talked to me. They wanted to. They told me their stories even though some didn't want me to repeat them. The oddest thing came out though. Every one of them had something to do with Officer Macreavy. Some had a lot of contact, others not as much. But he changed their lives in one way or another. I added finding out about Foraker Macreavy to my project. I asked the people I spoke with to also tell me about him, along with their stories. When I told them Officer Macreavy might be responsible for holding out their arrest cards, none seemed surprised."

A thought flashed in my mind, and I asked her, "Do you remember the expression, ''kin' guy'!?"

Her eyes lit up, and she laughed out loud. She jumped up out of her chair and ran to me. She put her arms around my head and drew me to herself. This startled me to the point of paralysis. I had deferred to her formality, and the embrace confused me. I sensed strength and frailty in her arms at the same time and caught a whiff of her perfume as she held me. I believe she'd absorbed something from me in exchange for something of herself in the swirl of her enthusiasm. When she broke away, she said, "No one could know Mac without knowing about the ''kin' guy.' What a glorious project!" she said. "What a fabulous idea! Please go on." She walked back to her chair and sat down again at full attention with her hands clasped on her knees.

She'd overwhelmed me with her response. I didn't expect it, but I kept talking. "As I met with the people who had been arrested, I learned more about Officer Macreavy. But their experiences with him only went so far. They told me about the lasting impressions he made on their lives, but they couldn't tell me much about him. Some of them knew where he lived. Some said he rode bicycles and read books, and a few told me about his sailboat. If you think about it, though, that doesn't say much. The guy is a policeman. He lives by the lake, rides a bicycle, reads books, and has a sailboat. It's like describing a man as medium height and medium weight. But then, after he died, he left millions of dollars around town. Now that's unusual.

"All the arrests, except one, happened in and around Jamestown. That's all I know for sure. Everything else is speculation. I'm sure there's another side to the stories I heard, and I want to learn more about Foraker Macreavy from you. The guy fascinates me."

Dr. Bell said, "Give me a minute."

She got up from her chair and carried her coffee to the window. She looked out onto the field the way I had. I took a moment to sip my coffee and tasted vanilla and cinnamon. She stood while I sat in a chair at the maple table. Silence hung in the room. I remember thinking, *This must be what it feels like to share a room with royalty.*

I don't know how long she stood at the window. It would have been rude to look at my watch. Time didn't matter anyway. She'd mystified me. I picked up her fragrance in the silence between us. It reminded me of water and the sky.

Dr. Bell turned into the room, walked to a different chair at the table, and sat down. Her face tightened, and her eyes filled with tears. I noticed a box of tissues on the side table I'd seen before and rose to bring it to her. She gestured a thank-you, took a tissue, and held it in her hand, but she didn't dab the tears.

Another moment passed. She got up and walked back to the chair where she'd been. She acknowledged the tissue, gestured her thanks again, and this time held it to her eyes.

"Please excuse me," she said. "There are so many memories. I lost myself."

"Dr. Bell," I answered, "I had no intention of making you sad or reminding you of anything unpleasant. If I did, please accept my most heartfelt apologies."

"You didn't," she said, reassuring me with a smile. "I've been blessed beyond measure, and sometimes when I see all of it at once,

I can't take it in." She sipped her coffee and sat for another minute without speaking.

She looked at me, put her cup on the saucer, and spoke. "I'll start from the beginning," she said, "and assume you haven't heard any of this before. I'll tell you what I told him a dozen times to his face. Foraker Macreavy could have been a reincarnation of the rich young man in the Bible. Are you familiar with that story, Mr. Strongtree?"

I didn't know if she meant this as a metaphor or if she wanted me to understand she believed in reincarnation, so I answered her question as a way of acknowledging what she'd said as an observation. "Yes, ma'am, I know it," I replied. "But please call me Thomas."

"Well, Thomas," she said, pausing again as if she were looking for a place to begin, "Mac came from old blood and old money. He could recite the names of relatives going back to before the Civil War. After a long line of grandfathers, his father became the Jamestown 'financier.' His father had a seat at the Chicago Mercantile Exchange, and he partnered with a fellow who had a seat on Wall Street. Some in the Macreavy family joined the Exchange when it started as the Chicago Butter and Egg Board. My Uncle Dennis told me once that Mac's father and grandfather kept Jamestown alive through the Depression.

"I knew Mac as a kid in Jamestown. Our families always had a dance, a lawn fete, or a social get-together going on. The same families socialized over and over. Mac played sports with the boys, the sons, and I planned parties and dances with the girls, the daughters. My father, Brian Bell, met my mother late in life and died two days before my third birthday. My mother's brother, Dennis Nelson, stepped in and cared for my mother and me. I could say a hundred things about my fabulous gay uncle living in the middle of the last century, but I'll give you the top three. He cared deeply about humanity, he could keep people's failings a secret, and he had an undying appreciation of fine automobiles. Fortunately, he came along before electronic fuel injection. He probably would have taken fuel injectors as a personal affront to his ability to balance a carburetor, but he cared for me as a daughter and taught me everything he knew about old-time mechanics. That's where I got my start in engineering.

"Mac and I recognized one another from the social gatherings, but nothing sparked between us until the first day of our senior year in high school. We'd been assigned to a class called Health and Biology, and no one would come near me. I'd become the school pariah, and he came to sit with me. Bless his heart, he sat at the desk next to mine and laughed his fool head off."

"Laughed at the school pariah?" I asked. "I don't understand."

"Okay," she said. "I guess I have to back up. Chautauqua Lake is cool in the summer." She smiled and added, "That's cool as in comfortable temperature. Before the days of air-conditioning, people went to the lake to get away from the hot summers. Of course, Jamestown people went to the lake, but they came from as far away as Cleveland and Pittsburgh. All through the winter months in town, we girls would dream about wearing our bathing suits out to the lake on hot summer afternoons. But that dream rarely came true on a lake known for cool temperatures. Referring to summers and bathing suits once, Mac said, 'Hot days make scant showings on Lake Chautauqua.' He dropped that one right after calling the Memorial Day sailboat race the 'Mammary Day Regatta.'" Nel Bell smiled as she recounted the puns, and I smiled along with her.

"So anyway," she continued, "a hot summer day finally arrived in the middle of July, and I brought out my new yellow two-piece. I borrowed my uncle's car, and my girlfriends and I took off for Midway Amusement Park on the lake. Midway had a roller coaster and rides, but it also had a beach. My friends and I couldn't wait to get to the park to wear our bathing suits, lie in the sun, and watch the boys watching us. Mac used to call them 'baiting suits.' What a time! I had black hair in those days, and it went well with the yellow suit."

Dr. Bell raised an eyebrow. "Yes, I'm sure you guessed it. I had a boy in mind. I'd had my eye on Greg for a year at school, and wouldn't you know it, Greg just happened to be at the park that day. He got a look at my yellow suit with me in it, and he hung around all afternoon. We had pizza and pop for supper, which never happened in the winter, and went back to the lake to get in one more swim before the sun went down. Greg and I slipped away into the shadows when the lights came on. The calliope music started at the park, and we wanted to escape the noise and be alone. He wanted to get me out of my suit, and since I knew I couldn't get pregnant, I decided that would be my night."

Past stories and recollections about Macreavy and Nel Bell from the people I'd spoken with primed me for frank discussions of sensitive topics, but this stopped me, not unlike her sudden embrace earlier. I would have let it go any other time, but I'd come a long way, and she brought it up, so I raised my hand an inch.

She paused, and I asked, "Dr. Bell, I don't mean to be indelicate, but how did you know that?"

"Oh, I suppose that's part of the story too," she said. "Forgive me. It's so long ago, and this is the first time I've told anyone about it for years." She continued, "My parents had me late in life, and as I told you, my father died. My mother blamed the hospital for his death and didn't trust doctors after that. You could call her the original anti-vaxxer. My uncle Dennis snuck me in for a smallpox inoculation, and thank God the school gave me a polio shot with the other kids. I didn't care how furious that made my mother. I might not be alive today if they hadn't. Later on, my husband found out I'd never had a tetanus shot, and he made sure I got one before he married me, which sounds hilarious. I asked him what kind of rusty nail he had in mind. So I got past the big diseases, but I caught almost everything else as a little girl. I had chickenpox, measles, and, worst of all, I got the mumps. The mumps virus left me infertile. I'm not sure how they figured it out, but at age fourteen, my mother and our family doctor informed me I would never be able to have children. The doctor gave me a long clinical lecture explaining ovaries, irregular and absent periods, infertile eggs, and damaged fallopian tubes. I think that's more than a fourteen-year-old should have to endure, but at the time, I didn't understand enough to cry about it. The tears came later. It's my stone."

"I'm sorry, Doctor," I interrupted. "Your stone?"

"Yes," she answered. "My sharpening stone. Everyone's got one. The stone is difficult, but it makes the edge. A knife isn't a knife without an edge. A knife doesn't do what a knife does without being honed into form."

"I see," I answered.

"Something else came from my childhood diseases," she continued. "I couldn't get out of bed for months. When I could get up, I couldn't leave the house. I started school two years late. My mother and uncle taught me to read, but I began the first grade at eight, two years older than the other kids. The health problems kept me weak and small for my age, so I didn't stand out, but the fact is, I remained two years older than the other kids all the way through. I don't think it mattered much, and I didn't complain. I don't think anyone else did either, but I guess that's another thing I'll never know.

"So Greg and I had awkward teenage interactions a few times over the summer, and I liked having a boyfriend. I felt great about it until I walked into school that first day. It happened in front of my friends and a group of kids in the hall by my homeroom. This boy, Skip Robinson, called out to some of his friends loud enough for me to hear, 'Greg says he rang the bell out at Midway this summer.'"

Nel Bell paused and flashed a devilish grin. She said, "Apparently, word about Greg and me got around. Everyone knew what Skip meant, and they froze in place, looking at me. It may have been a clever thing to say, and I would've laughed if Greg said it only to me, but he hadn't. He'd told the other guys about us, and it came back to me. That finished him, and I couldn't let Skip get away with it either. They'd embarrassed me, and I wanted blood. I leveled my gaze and lowered my voice. I said, 'Listen. Gregory did not ring the bell. He's got a tiny hammer, he doesn't know where to hit, and he'll never be able to swing it hard enough. And as for you, Skippy, please understand that I will be twenty years old this year. Sexuality is a part of my life. If that's a new concept for you, check in with your mother and have her explain it, but you'd better not bother her while she's washing out your Popeye the Sailor Man pajamas.'

Nel Bell paused. She said, "The hall went quiet, and everyone looked at Skip Robinson. I'd blasted the kid, and I made it hurt."

"Dr. Bell," I said, "sounds like he got what he deserved."

"Well, maybe," she agreed. "But it didn't last long. By midyear, everybody had forgotten most of it. Then there's the old double standard. If they remembered anything, it would be something about my intimacies with Greg."

She brought the story back to Macreavy. "So by the time I got to the second class of the day," she said, "everyone in the school had heard about it. Half the kids wrote me off as disreputable, and the other half thought I might cut into them the way I had with Skippy. All except Mac. He laughed and came over to sit by me. He said he heard another kid call Greg 'Tiny Hammer,' and kids started singing 'Popeye the Sailor Man' wherever Skip went. Mac got the story when he overheard the math teacher telling the social studies teacher about it. He saw both women laughing in the hallway and wished he'd heard it himself.

"Even though we'd known each other as kids, that's when it clicked for us. The Health and Biology class had a unit on procreation, so Mac told everybody we met on the first day of sex education. He asked me out the following weekend, and I kissed him on our first date. All that year, we lived the kind of romance a girl dreams of. I remember autumn leaves, Thanksgiving, Christmas parties, and New Year's Eve. He'd borrow his mother's Mercedes to take me out on dates, and we'd huddle together in the car against the never-ending snows in Jamestown. What wonderful memories. I hope you've had hours like that yourself, Thomas."

"I have," I said. "I only wish I'd recognized how wonderful they were back then."

"Isn't that the truth?" she answered.

She smiled again and continued, "At least once every winter, the entire town iced over. They'd close the school, and we'd all skate right out on the streets. Mac and I skated for hours. I thought I saw the rest of our lives together that day, and I felt sad when the sun came out and melted the ice in the afternoon." Nel Bell paused for a moment and looked at the floor. She took another sip of her coffee as she relived the moment. I recalled Eddie Moretti telling me about those days of ice skating on the streets as well.

She looked up and resumed, "The holidays came and went. The New Year arrived, we had one semester before graduation, and we started looking toward college. He said he wanted to help people and thought sociology would give him a good start. He applied to Western Reserve in Cleveland. They had a sociology program, and Cleveland is only three hours away from Jamestown. He got in, which surprised all of us. Mac only had a C average, and that's usually not good enough for a place like that. It might have been because his father could pay full tuition, but that's where he went for whatever reason. They had an engineering school there also, but I didn't want to go to the same school. I didn't want anyone around to remind me of my family or who I should be. I wanted to try on new hats, so I went to RPI.

"Excuse me, Doctor," I asked, "RPI?"

She laughed and said, "I'm sorry. With all this talk about Jamestown, I have to remind myself you're not from New York State. RPI is Rensselaer Polytechnic Institute in Troy, New York.

"Oh, sure. "Excuse me, Doctor. I've heard of Rensselaer. That's a great school, and I think I also heard something about you being high school valedictorian."

"Yes," she said and repeated the word "valedictorian," but she didn't elaborate.

When she didn't say anything more, I spoke again, "And do I remember something about Texas A&M?"

"I see you've done your homework," she observed and answered, "Yes, Texas A&M for my doctorate." She paused for a moment and added, "Aeronautical engineering and material science."

Then, as if talking about herself might take her away from Macreavy, she said, "Cleveland almost killed Mac. He hated school, and he drank a lot. He had so many problems with the sociology faculty that he washed out of the program and finished in English. He knew a lot about old stories and wrote just well enough to pass. That's the only way he got a diploma."

I remembered Patrick Williams and how Macreavy opened the teacher's lifelong passion for reading.

Dr. Bell continued, "We had happy summers during college, but things gradually worsened each year when Mac returned to school. Eventually, we unraveled altogether. I went to see him in the city one time. I stayed with him at his apartment, and he just sat around drinking. I couldn't wait to get out of there. I'm not sure what happened, but college made him bitter and resentful. In his senior year, he totaled his beautiful red and black 1950 Mercury Monterey Cobra. He spent almost a week in a coma. Someone in his family had given it to him, and they were glad he hadn't died, but they were so angry with him over his behavior that they just about cut him off for good. He flipped the car near the old Rockefeller mansion and saw some significance in that. He tried to joke about it, but I never saw the humor. He said he'd 'wrestled with the snake.' I'm sure liquor had something to do with it. He claims he hadn't been drinking, and maybe that's true, but he spent so much time drunk back then that I don't know how he could ever be completely sober.

"He tried to explain it to me once, and it made some sense in the context of the rest of his life. Years later, at his place on the lake, Mac woke up in the middle of the night. He wandered down to the water in the dark. I thought he might jump off the dock and swim out into the lake. I didn't think he should do that so late at night. I got him to sit with me on the porch and look at the lights across the lake. As we sat together, he told me he died after the accident and came back. He said it changed him forever, and he'd never be able to forget it. He said he went to a world beyond imagination. Someone welcomed him home, but Mac said he didn't want to stay. He said he missed the experience he'd signed up for in the world and hadn't learned what he wanted to know. Whoever he spoke with told Mac if that's what he wanted, he should 'go back and get to work.' Mac said he thought he might have made a huge mistake when he regained consciousness in the hospital. He said he believed he'd find his way but felt lost."

"Do you mean he felt lost when he came to in the hospital or later?" I asked.

"Both," she said. "He always felt lost."

I'd heard about these experiences where people die and come back, but I didn't know anything about them. I wanted to ask her

232

more about what he said. Also, she'd just told me her relationship with Macreavy had unraveled, and Phil Troxel said she'd married a salesman. So how did she wake up with Macreavy in the middle of the night years later? She had a confusing way of telling a story, but I wanted her to keep talking, so I asked her, "What did you say to him?"

Dr. Bell reached for her coffee cup and took a sip. "I told him to empty himself. I told him to put everything aside and look into the darkness between the lights. I told him he had to find the balance in his body, between his spirit and his soul."

"That sounds interesting," I said. "I wish I knew more about the balance between the body and the spirit."

"No," she said. "Not the body and the spirit, the soul and the spirit." She shook her head slightly and raised an eyebrow. "You've heard of losing your mind, right?"

"Okay," I answered, and on the recording, I heard acquiescence in my voice.

"Well," she explained, "you can find your mind where and when you balance your soul and spirit, and they're not always in opposition, by the way. Your body will clue you in when you get close. Your senses will feel harmony."

She paused for a moment and looked at me. I got the idea she wanted me to respond somehow, and she said, "Thomas, you're looking at me like I'm crazy. This is nothing I dreamed up. The ancient Greeks and prehistoric people figured it out thousands of years ago. It's what we do in physics all the time. Start with nothing and look into the emptiness. Focus and ask questions. Ideas will occur to you. Patterns will show themselves.

"I'm not sure I understand," I said. "Did Macreavy ask you about this too?"

"Yes, he did," she answered. "Although I think he had a better grasp of it than I did. He just needed to be reminded."

I might have been able to get her to tell me more, but at that moment, Raphael knocked at the door. We both looked at him through the window, and she waved him in.

"I'm sorry to interrupt," he said. "But Gieles called." He held out a cell phone, and she took it.

"Thank you, Raphael," she responded.

Looking at me, she said, "Please excuse me for a moment, Mr. Strongtree. I've been waiting for this call."

"Of course," I said. "Please take your call." I needed a moment myself anyway.

"Thank you," she said. She looked at the phone and stopped to look at me again.

"Would you be so kind as to turn off your recording device while I speak with this gentleman?" she asked. "I promise I'll be back momentarily."

"Of course," I answered and touched the off button in full view.

"Thank you," she said and proceeded with her call. She spoke on the phone for about five minutes in French.

When she finished the call, she opened the door and waved the phone so Raphael could see it. He walked toward her, and as she handed him the phone. She smiled broadly and said, "Merci."

Turning back to me, she said, "Thank you, Thomas. It hasn't been easy to get through to that fellow. You may resume recording if you'd like."

She launched back into the story without prompting. "Another thing came out of the accident," she said. "The injuries took Mac out of contention for military service, so he didn't have to go to Vietnam." She settled into her chair and folded her hands in her lap.

She paused and said, "We didn't see each other for a long time after the accident. I suppose I could have run to his bedside and put off my degree, but I didn't. I had other things on my mind. He wrote his final papers from the hospital and mailed them to his professors. They appreciated the effort, gave him Bs, and he graduated despite himself. After he came out of the hospital, he began a rehabilitation program. I see now that he spent the rest of his life trying to rehabilitate himself.

"During that last semester he spent in the hospital, he met a girl named Karen Carlo. She did volunteer music therapy, and they hit it off. She played violin and studied at the Cleveland Institute of Music. I understand she had an amazing talent. Mac got dreamy once telling me about his 'Pennsylvania fiddler girl.' They both graduated that spring, and when he recovered well enough to travel, he brought her home to Jamestown to meet his folks. After that, they took off for New York City together. I happened to see her when she came to visit at that time. Small towns are like that. She had pale white skin, dark eyes, and short black hair. I also remember bright red nails and hippy clothes. Mac and I spoke on the phone once that summer. I asked him about his injuries, and he told me about Karen. Then we lost touch for years.

"In the meantime, I'd met Michael. He's the reason I didn't go running to Mac. In the last semester of school, the chemistry department assigned us to work as lab partners. I wanted to make a good impression on him, so I got to our first meeting at the lab early and made ashwagandha root tea in an Erlenmeyer flask. That's usually bad practice in a chem lab. It can be dangerous, but I'd used a new flask, and the tea gave the old lab a wonderful aroma. Michael walked in and sniffed the air. When he noticed the tea simmering over a flame, he said, 'Hey, if you don't know where your Erlenmeyer's been, you've got more trouble than sour-tasting tea.' He won my heart with that one.

"We passed our coursework and labs with high marks, finished together, and Uncle Dennis came up with a fantastic graduation gift. I told you about his infatuation with cars, and he'd recently bought a new one. He didn't want to lose the old one in trade, so he gave it to me. That summer, Michael and I picked up the Lincoln Highway in Ohio. It's a magic road full of hills and curves, and we drove across the country in a red, white, and chrome 1957 Chevy Nomad Station Wagon with a 245 horsepower V8 and Powerglide automatic."

I have to smile even now as I listen back to the recording of this elegant older woman reveling in the memory of her first automobile. The car would now be considered a classic hot rod.

"With college behind us, we hit the road for a grand adventure and spent months together. We took tourist cabins or slept next to each other in the Nomad. We drove to California and met up with some of our friends from engineering school. They had a lot going on, and it looked interesting. I can tell you now too, as it won't come back to harm us socially. They'd been experimenting with psilocybin. Michael and I tried it, and those experiences altered and defined our pathways in life. That whole 'crack in the universe' stuff they're talking about now at Johns Hopkins and Imperial College in London, there might be something to it."

The frank and casual admission of drug use derailed me momentarily. Listening back to the recording of our conversation, I realized I had missed the more interesting point. I should have asked her more about the pathways and "crack in the universe," but the moment had passed.

"As for sightseeing, Michael mapped out a tour of the Franciscan Missions out West. We drove around to these fabulous old Spanish shrines up and down the coast. Some of them go back to the 1700s. He taught me the rosary and mercy chaplet even though I'm not Catholic. They're lovely prayers, as beautiful as anything I heard in India. I still say them in meditation on beads he bought me in St Louis. Michael called them 'gateway prayers.' That made me smile, but he sold me when he told me they were best said for other people.

"The experiences in the churches had a profound effect on Michael. When we first got to know each other, he told me he'd been considering the priesthood. The semester before we met, he'd applied to the seminary at Franciscan University in Steubenville, Ohio. He said he had every intention of becoming a priest from boyhood through college, but the seminary ignored him, and he felt rejected. On the other hand, he took our relationship as a sign that God wanted him to do something else in life. He thought I might be what God had in mind for him. On a call home, though, his mother told him he'd received a letter from Steubenville. I'm not sure what happened. Either the school mixed up the paperwork or he had applied to the wrong office. Somehow someone figured out what happened and sent him a letter asking if he still had any interest. That evening, we sat with a cold bottle of California Chardonnay and looked out into the desert. He told me he wanted to go. He said he'd always regret it if he didn't try. He said he might not stay, or maybe they'd tell him he didn't have a vocation, but he also said it wouldn't be fair to ask me to wait. It stunned me, although maybe not as much as I thought. Deep down I knew. Michael had a spirit and a soul that attracted me, and what attracted me made him an excellent priest. He had a brilliant career.

"The day after he told me about this, he asked me to pray with him and took me to the Mission Santa Clara De Asís. Wouldn't you know, the crazy fool tripped on a step in front of the church and twisted his ankle. Our quest for a vision to discern the mysteries of "calling" ended up in the emergency room of a Santa Clara hospital. He'd sprained his ankle badly, and I've since found out this kind of thing happens to Franciscans all the time. He couldn't wrap it himself, so I had to keep his foot bound in an ace bandage for the rest of the trip.

"I can't remember how the timing worked, but I do remember the searing loss. What's crazy is I had to care for his foot and drive him across the country so he could leave me." Dr. Bell shook her head and breathed the word "ridiculous."

She got up from her chair, holding her coffee cup, and looked out the window again. She said, "Thomas, I begged that man. I got down on my knees, and I cried. I told him I'd go anywhere and do anything. He could have it all. He cried, too, but none of it made any difference. I drove us in the Nomad from California back east to Ohio, crying my eyes out and worried that I tied the bandage too tight or not tight enough. I pulled up in front of the admissions building at Franciscan University and took his suitcase out of the car. I helped him limp to the front door, planted the case on the sidewalk next to him, and drove away in tears.

"I have to say he did well in the priesthood. The church made him a monsignor, and we exchanged long beautiful Christmas letters until he died about ten years ago. He wrote a book once, and I went to a signing when he came here. I went out afterward for drinks with him and two of his priest friends. He introduced me as his college girlfriend. He admitted to them that he'd decided if I'd asked him one more time not to go, he wouldn't have. But I didn't ask. The men showed more empathy than you might expect. They had their own stories they could tell. They explained that a priest has to experience full-on compassion. Sometimes that comes from caring for another person, and just as often, it comes from accepting care. But true understanding comes from living for a time in a world where that's all that matters.

"Michael wanted everyone to know God delighted in people. He had a chapter that said sin is as simple as anything that separates you from God. He wrote, 'When you're searching for heaven, watch for connections and separations. Let the Spirit help you hold on or walk away. If whatever comes to you is good and brings you closer to excellence, do it with enthusiasm. The freedom is worth it.'"

Dr. Bell glanced down at her coffee cup and walked to the silver service to refill it. She motioned for me to have more also, and I did. She took her place at the table again, crossed her legs, and resumed.

"Talk about a miserable time," she said. "God Himself took Michael, and Mac had gone to New York with his fiddle player. I got mad and drove the Nomad back out to California again. I wanted to mope around with my friends from engineering school, but a few of them got jobs in Texas, and they wanted me to come along. They'd joined the space race to put a man on the moon, and I got caught up in the excitement. I took a job at NASA and never looked back. People needed me there. And Uncle Dennis couldn't get enough of telling everybody he taught me to fix cars and how I went on to build moon landers.

"Graduate school took five years, and NASA introduced me to my husband. I met and married Ted Hickman, a sales engineer who worked for Corning Glass. He knew about silica fibers, high-temperature microwave fusion, and adhesives, so he helped NASA develop heat-reflecting tiles for the space shuttles. Ted and I did well together. We had beautiful homes and expensive cars. We made excellent companions and traveled worldwide, making friends and contacts, but maybe we should have given more of ourselves to each other. As I explained before, I couldn't have children, so I spent all my energy on business. That led to this." Dr. Bell raised a hand, gesturing to the conference room and offices surrounding us.

Her second cup of coffee had cooled enough for her to take a sip. "Ted and I invested well," she said. "We made several fortunes, and anyone looking at us from the outside would say we'd won the game, but they couldn't see how we kept a lid on our passions." She placed her coffee cup on the saucer, put both feet on the floor, and recrossed her legs at the ankles. "As life got more serious during these years, I lost touch with Mac, but things didn't improve much for him after college. The car crash got him to quit drinking, and he married the violinist, which should have been good news, but he struggled in New York. After the accident, his father stayed mad at him, told him he had to 'scratch for himself,' and wouldn't release any family money. On the other hand, Karen did well with her violin. She got on the list of substitutes for Broadway musicals, which led to recording sessions. Mac told me sometimes she'd start recording in the morning and wouldn't finish with pit orchestras in the theaters until after midnight. She had trouble keeping up, and that's when someone introduced her to Benzedrine. Mac worked in restaurants and read books to stay busy, but she paid the rent. They ran into serious trouble when Karen picked up cocaine. Mac said he quit drinking because he knew he'd lose her if he didn't, so the irony is thick enough to cut with a knife. Maybe it's an occupational hazard in the music world, but I wonder. I think Mac could have helped more. Then again, perhaps it's the direction or coincidence of fate. While my husband teased me about reaching for the stars, Karen Macreavy sat ten feet away from them, next to the piano player.

"A night finally came when Karen didn't make it home. You've probably heard about Janis and Jimi and the 27 club. Well, the saddest part of the story here is Karen Macreavy joined the same club, and there aren't any testimonials remembering her. Her music ended, the world forgot her, and Mac got worse. I knew nothing about this at the time. He told me he wandered around the city after she died, looking for something to do. He said his experience after the car crash in Cleveland made it worse because he knew he should be doing something valuable, but he didn't know what.

"One night, while wiping tables at a restaurant where he worked, he saw a guy with a pile of criminology textbooks, and Mac started a conversation. The guy studied at the John Jay College of Criminal

Justice, and they became friends. This fellow told Mac to read *Serpico* by Peter Maas."

"I remember that," I said. "Frank Serpico, the cop who fought corruption in the NYPD. They made a movie about him too."

"Yes," Dr. Bell agreed. "Frank Serpico fought corruption, but a different conflict spoke to Mac. The young Frank Serpico wanted to grow up to be a policeman, but his problems surfaced as an adult when he confronted the realities of the department. That book brought Mac to life. He decided he wanted to go to the police academy, and by then, he'd recovered well enough to pass the physical.

"Mac found his being as a cop. It had to do with the purity of the law and the confusion of police work. He didn't mind seeing people on their worst days. He lived for moments when high ideals collided with flesh and blood. When he graduated from the academy, he worked on the streets for three years as a patrolman. He volunteered for holidays, off-hours, and dangerous jobs, and as a single guy, they took him up on it. He said those three years felt more like ten, but he finally did well at something.

"One morning, Mac's sergeant called him into the office. A phone call had come in from Jamestown. The department in Jamestown had located Mac through the state police. Both his parents had been killed in a car accident. He had no brothers or sisters, so Mac had to return to Jamestown, bury his parents, settle the estate, and decide what to do about the family homes and his father's businesses. Suddenly, Mac had a lot of money and a lot to do. He took a leave of absence from the NYPD and spent several years sorting it out. He sold the businesses and his family's home in town. They'd kept a summer place on the lake, and Mac took it on as a project. He wanted to live in the house all year round and had it insulated and upgraded with new wiring and heat. Because he never completely resigned from the force, he still received government newsletters from New York State. One day he noticed in the back of one of them that Jamestown had openings for patrolmen. Mac had come home.

"I hadn't seen Foraker Macreavy again after college until our fifteen-year high school reunion. A sales meeting had Ted tied up, so I went alone. Mac had changed some, but who hadn't? And thirty-three years old looked incredible on him. He wore a gray suit, had a fresh haircut, and looked strong enough to climb a mountain at a moment's notice. I'd just turned thirty-five and thanked God for every dollar and every hour I'd spent at the gym."

A memory of Eddie Moretti's description of the two of them flashed in my mind. I nodded and asked her, "Did you dance the night away at the reunion?"

"Oh, we danced all right," she said, "and talked with our class-mates for hours. Someone in my family told me his parents and his wife had died, but I hadn't spoken to him about it before then. The cop thing dumbfounded me, but I could feel his enthusiasm for being on the force and back in Chautauqua County. I remembered the lake house from our summers together, and he wanted to show me all he'd done with it. He asked me out there and said we'd have breakfast and catch up like old friends. I rescheduled my flight and drove my rental car to the lake the next morning. I think we talked that entire day. Sorry to sound cliché, but I felt like a kid again. It all came back. We both recognized the feelings, but, no, as a married woman, I didn't stay with him that night. He didn't ask me either. I went back to my hotel and left the following day."

Dr. Bell paused and raised an eyebrow. She said, "Here's another syrupy irony that fits into the story, Thomas. Going home one day later led me to find out Ted had been having an affair." With more than a hint of sarcasm she noted, "The simplest technologies some-times baffled the brilliant, world-renowned materials specialist. I thought the airline had overcharged for my rescheduled flight, and when I called to straighten it out, they told me about a $500 charge at a women's clothing store. He used one of our joint cards instead of his business card. When no fancy gift box arrived for me, I con-fronted him. He admitted it and didn't argue. In the next sentence, though, he also said he didn't want to leave me. I believed him, and aside from the hurt and embarrassment, leaving didn't make much sense to me either. I realize now I respected Ted for his talent and smarts, and he had a certain kind of honesty. He may have been unfaithful, but he didn't deny anything, and I had to admit it didn't upset me as much as I thought it should. It's as if I knew it could happen, and it did. Our partnership existed in the world of high-order thinking. We were great when we put our brains together, but we needed the kind of emotional passion I had for Michael. I kept asking myself if I wanted the marriage to end. It went on like this for two years and then I got my answer.

"Ted had a stroke," she said. "The good life caught up with him. He probably should have taken better care of himself, but it also shows how tenuous our places are in life. Forty-three years old, and everything stopped. Forget industrial marketing. The man couldn't walk or talk. I got him set up in an extended care facility and sold our house. I hadn't gotten around to divorcing him, which made things easier when he died. The miracles of modern medicine kept him alive, but the prognosis said total care for the duration, and he had no more reason to live. He'd had enough. He stopped eating. That kind of death is torturous, and he didn't deserve it, but it ended. Is that, or is that not better than just breathing for years? I don't know.

"In August, six months after Ted died and three years after our class reunion, I called Mac. I didn't tell him what happened with Ted. I asked him if I could come to the lake and told him I wanted to talk. I tried covering the big question I had with a joke. I asked if he'd finally been able to lure another woman out to his lake house. I wouldn't have gone if he had, but he said no. He didn't ask me why I wanted to visit, but I'm sure he sensed it must be something important. He said, 'I'll be here.' That's all he said.

"Summer had arrived on Lake Chautauqua, and we sat on the porch at his place. Beautiful old maple trees surrounded the house, and the porch looked out onto the lake. Seeing how much progress he'd made since my last visit impressed me. He'd renovated the house and made it a showcase. I told him everything. I admitted I'd figured out how much he meant to me, and I proposed an idea. I said I wanted to vacation with him at his place for six or eight weeks every summer. I would move to be with him all year round if we couldn't find any other way. I also told him I'd spent decades building contacts. I had millions of dollars on the line and didn't know how well the business would travel, but I didn't expect him to leave Jamestown and move west on account of me. I also told him we could break the deal if he met someone else. I know this probably sounds like an unusual arrangement for most people, but that's what I came up with.

"Mac didn't say anything for a long time. He kept looking out over the water. I'd said what I'd come to say, and I let myself dissolve into the warm afternoon and waited for his answer. He sat still for about fifteen minutes. I didn't know it then, but when I asked him later, he told me he wanted to pray and thank God first before answering me.

"After he finished whatever prayer he said, he looked over at me and stood up. He took my hand and walked me down to the lake. When we got to the dock, he took his shirt off. He told me I'd best take my clothes off too. He said they'd get wet if I didn't. We jumped into the water and swam around for an hour."

I couldn't help a surprised look on my face, and Nel Bell smiled. She said, "Oh, don't look so shocked, Thomas. Don't imagine anything evil. It's about honesty. Our arrangement worked out nicely, although he insisted we get married. His life had so much to do with laws and rules he said he couldn't just 'live like it.' I agreed. Living with honesty and passion had become important to me, and we had more of that over those summers than some couples ever have, whether they're married or not. We found a way to be together. We could count on glorious times every year. Admit it. Doesn't that sound delightful?"

I answered her, "Dr. Bell, you are one in a million. Good fortune came to Foraker Macreavy. So you were married then?"

Nell Bell smiled and continued, "Yes, I called Michael and asked him to marry us. He said he couldn't marry us in the church because we weren't Catholic, but he also said, 'If you two still want to get married after all you've been through, I'll officiate.' He also said he'd always wanted to learn to sail, so we had him out to the lake for a few days the following summer. We taught him how to sail, and he married us out on the water."

With a laugh, she said, "I amuse myself when I think of how swimming in the buff with Mac every summer kept me trim through the rest of the year. Looking forward to those weeks could make a girl nervous, or at least pass on dessert. I saw gray skies out conference room windows all winter, and I'd be thinking about the lake. At the same time, he'd be driving around in the snow as the Jamestown lawman or cutting wood for his fireplace. He kept in great shape right up to the end. We talked about retiring at the lake together. We thought we had years to go before that, but you know what they say—'If you want to hear God laugh, tell him your plans.'

"In late August, we'd start hearing about Labor Day on the TV and radio. Our lives before and after summer would begin again. I'd pick up in September where I'd left off in June. I'd fly in on Thanksgiving and Christmas and he'd fly out to see me at Easter. The rest of the time, we exchanged letters. He'd write to me about some of those kids whose records you found, and I'd send him notes from countries where I went for work.

"So you knew about the kids he arrested?" I asked.

"He'd give me the high points if they were funny or interesting," she said. "And I helped when I could."

That's as close as Nel Bell came to admitting involvement in Macreavy's activities, although I knew from my interviews how integral a part she'd been in many of them. Macreavy had an interesting way of working things out, but the brilliant ideas came when they took on difficult situations together. I wish I could tell you about what happened in Indianapolis.

"Say"—she paused—"did any of those people you talked to tell you about the sailboat?"

"Sure," I answered. "They told me a lot about it. Some of them had been out on it. One of the guys even raced with him."

I saw a flash of recognition in her eyes, and she asked, "Yes, how is the daughter? I got a big smile out of Condoleezza when she heard that story, by the way. I think she may have called the girl."

"I believe she's doing well," I answered. "But I didn't hear anything about a call."

"Oh well," she said, "I only spoke with her last year."

Her eyes lit up again. "That's right," she said. "Mac and his sailboat. He told me his uncle Henry built it out of Jamestown Rock Maple in 1932. Mac restored it and refinished it with modern varnish. He also bought new sails, but other than that, he tried to keep the boat as original as possible. He could have won more races if he'd sailed a new fiberglass boat, but he wanted to keep the old one going. That boat will tell you something about the Macreavy family though. In the thick of the Depression, with the rest of the country out trying to find a job and something to eat, Mac's uncle Henry bought a stack of premium hardwood and built a sailboat. But then I go back to what my uncle Dennis told me about Mac's family and the good they did through those years. That's the kind of family Mac came from." She pursed her lips and said, "What a flock of odd birds."

She clapped her hands together. "What fun though!" She said, "I got such a kick out of crewing for the races. One time he had me out on a heavy day. The wind hit hard. Whitecaps broke over the stern on a run. Mac close hauled so we could cut between the mark and two other boats. Then he told me to duck, and let the boat jibe. The sail shot across with a huge thwack. Mac caught the mainsheet, pulled hard on the boom again, and yanked the tiller toward him. The boat started to heel when the sails filled, and yelled, 'hike.' That's where you sit on the deck and lean back off the side. He thought I'd be scared, but it got me going. I shouted, 'Is this when I rip my top off?'" She laughed and said, "I don't think the guys in the other boats ever let him forget that one."

She returned to talking about their arrangement. "He had his pen going constantly and wrote excellent letters. I kept all of them. I still have them, and you've inspired me, Thomas. I'm going to take them out again. I want to reread what he wrote about Lent and mercy. We had a special place in our hearts for Easter, the week before and the week after. We made a point of observing those days and encouraging each other."

This perplexed me coming from a PhD, chef of science. "Am I surprised to hear this?" I asked her. "You mentioned the rosary and your young man who became a priest. You told me about the place between the spirit and the soul, and now you're telling me you and Macreavy celebrated Easter. I'm hearing more about religion than I expected."

"Are you?" she asked. "Surprised, I mean. Come to think of it, I haven't said much about religion. Religion doesn't concern me."

"Well," I said, pausing to find words for my next question, "I didn't anticipate you'd speak so reverently. Are you a believer?"

"In common parlance, you could say I'm a believer, but that's making too much of it. If you spoke with your wife right now, she might say, 'I'm fine.' That's 'I AM.' You wouldn't ask if you believed she existed. Please, Thomas, I am intimately familiar with the forces and materials in our world. I've met and spoken with the finest minds on our planet. The more we learn, the more we understand how little we know. Arrogance and hypocrisy have separated us from each other and the source of life. That's sin, and it's far worse than we can imagine, which makes Easter important. The gates are open. Let's not argue away salvation."

She'd confused me, and I didn't want to let it go. "I'm not sure I understand," I said. "Please explain it to me."

"Feel for the balance," she answered. "The body craves pleasure, the spirit looks for joy, and the soul wants happiness. Be careful. Watch your attachments. Trust God's Spirit to right the boat."

Nel Bell had taken me to task, answered my question, and given me hope, wrapped and delivered in a package. The implication followed. She might have said, 'Open the package, Thomas,' but she left that for me to tell myself, and my mind drifted.

I snapped out of it when I realized she'd picked up the story again. "Every year, sometime around Memorial Day," she said, "I'd send Mac a note about vacation. He'd put in for time off and call back. We'd talk for a minute or two, and that would be it until he picked me up at the airport."

She paused for some of her coffee, and I said, "I'd hoped you could tell me about the record cards and photos."

"Okay," she said. "What would you like to know?"

"Well," I started, "you told me how Macreavy came to the police and that he worked at the courts, but I don't know why he selected these kids for special attention."

"Ha!" she said. "It's a long answer, and it's only my speculation."

"Please, Dr. Bell," I responded.

She took a breath. "You may not have picked up his ambivalence to the law in your interviews. That's what I've been trying to show you. Rules and regulations frustrated him if he didn't know where they came from, and he never stopped asking questions. Where other people might ignore a law or try to find a way around it, he'd ask what the law attempted to accomplish. The way he saw it, virtue is found in the law, but following any particular law in and of itself doesn't mean anything. There has to be a reason. He'd be okay if he understood how a rule helped people or kept them from ruining something, but if it didn't make sense, he believed you had an obligation to look into it. He told me he thought some people obeyed laws to congratulate themselves on obedience, but compliance in and of itself doesn't bring balance. It makes you appear to be good but might be deceiving. He thought reason and rules came from the same place, but false reasoning resulted in arbitrary rules. Sitting on his porch at night, we'd sometimes listen to the wind and the riot of creatures calling to each other. Other times, we'd argue rhetoric and logic, and I'm sure we sounded like college kids in the dorms. And, yes, Thomas, it had to do with the body and the spirit and the soul, especially when he quoted Proverbs."

"Proverbs?" I asked. "As in the Book of Proverbs?"

"Mac had memorized the entire Book of Proverbs," she said. "He could recite them like Solomon himself, couplet after couplet." She looked away from me and out the window. She said, "Life doesn't get much better than those nights on the lake."

I said, "Dr. Bell, that's priceless. Late at night, philosophy and scriptures, by the lake and under the maples."

She repeated, "It doesn't get much better."

She continued her answer. "The way he explained it to me," she said, "when he started working at the Jamestown Police Department, he looked for anything the other guys didn't want to do. He took shifts on holidays and overnight. He emptied trash cans and picked up cigarette butts outside the courthouse. Several times he helped the janitor polish the floor in the holding cells. He didn't mind getting his hands dirty. Along the way, someone remembered he had a college degree, and little by little, he showed he could do scheduling and keep track of paperwork. He set himself up helping out between the station and the courthouse. The lawyers recognized his genuine interest in how the court worked, and they'd chat with him about their cases. Mac couldn't get enough of seeing people get their day in court. He saw everything and watched how different people reacted to their situations. The department might not have known this, but no one needed to pay him. All they had to do was let him stand around in court, especially in the Juvenile and Family Court. He only took the paycheck because he said it made him a real cop. Given the work schedule for a place the size of Jamestown, sometimes he'd arrest people one day, and a week later, he might be the bailiff standing by the courtroom door. He'd let people in and walk them out. All the while, he'd listen to their cases. When it came to juvenile offenders, I believe he wanted to hear something that signaled a kid had the same problem with the law he did.

"Every once in a while, Mac took an interest in one of those kids. I don't know if I ever cracked the code, but it had something to do with enthusiasm, acceptance, trust, or the kid's family. There may have been some root honesty and mental ability too, but out of a few hundred cases he heard over the years, those cards and pictures are probably for kids he felt had particular promise. Still, I'd be willing to bet a lot of kids who didn't show up on his radar also turned out fine."

"Speaking of the cards," I said, "how do you think they showed up at the flea market?"

"I have a rough idea," she said. "Do you have any of them here, by the way?"

I opened my backpack and handed her the remaining six envelopes. She put them on the maple table and opened them one by one.

"I didn't return these because the kids had died," I explained.

Dr. Bell reached into the pocket of her blouse. She produced a pair of glasses, paper-thin rimless lenses cut in the shape of hexagons held by thin silver wires wrapped around her ears. I sat in silence while she reviewed the cards.

When she looked up, she said, "I'm familiar with four of them, but these cards don't say anything. There's no accusation or sentence or fine or anything like that. So what's the big deal?"

"Exactly," I agreed. "And that's what I've been banking on. But I've been told just the mention of an arrest is bad in and of itself. The rumor of a problem with the police can bring questions. While that might not be fair, I have to admit it's probably true. That still leaves the question though. How did they wind up at a flea market?"

"That might not be much of a mystery," she answered. "I think I know how that happened too, but it shouldn't have."

"So how did it happen?" I asked.

"When Mac died on the bicycle," she paused and asked, "did anyone tell you how he died?"

"Yes," I answered. "Hit by a car near the Chautauqua Institution."

"Point Chautauqua," she corrected. "It's an enclave of cottages across the lake from the institution. I know because my grandmother had a place there. Nothing like the Macreavy place, of course, and it's probably been renovated or long gone by now. Anyway, along with the boat and the house, Mac rode bicycles."

I could feel another story coming on, but I could listen to Nell Bell for hours. I figured she'd get back to the record cards soon enough.

"Mac knew how to ride a bicycle," she began. "He could climb hills like a bug walking up a wall. He could gauge the landscape and shift into the right gear, hill after hill, all day long. He set me up on a bicycle, showed me how to ride, and he had me cycling around the lake in no time. There were days we'd get up in the morning and ride around the lake before lunch."

She stopped and looked at me again with her beautiful, sparkling eyes. "Did anyone tell you about that shower next to the house?" she asked.

"One of the guys I talked to said he helped build it," I answered. "It sounded like quite a construction project."

"I suppose," she answered. "But what a great idea! We'd get out on the bicycles and ride hard. I tried to keep up with him, and I'd hammer until I couldn't go anymore. I gave it my all and got to be pretty good at cycling. We'd drink water and sweat and laugh and charge up the hills. Who knows how badly we'd smell under the noonday sun, but it didn't matter. We'd cover fifty miles just as we turned into his driveway. With the shower outside, we didn't have to stomp through the house with sweaty cycling clothes and pedal cleats. We'd throw our stuff in the wash basket, walk into the shower, and let the warm soap and water rain over us in the sunshine. I never felt as clean as I felt on those days. That's the saddest part of how he died. An odd warm day showed up in September, and he probably thought he'd get out to make the most of it. I'm sure he had his heart set on one last ride and shower for the season."

"What happened?" I asked.

"A stupid accident," she said. "A woman in a van didn't see him in the late-day sun. It happened about two weeks after I'd left to come back here. Sixty-two years old, and he died at the scene."

Dr. Bell adjusted her posture to sit up. "At first no one knew what to do," she explained. "One of the paramedics recognized him, and the emergency people rushed him to the hospital. I'm sure they tried everything. He knew quite a few lawyers and had a hundred friends but no family. Mac and one of the lawyers made a will years ago, and he left it on file at the lawyer's office. Because of our odd arrangement, we didn't tell many people we were married. Too many questions. But when he died, officials at the police department knew, and they called me first. I spoke with his lawyer and signed off where I had to. I told Mac when we got together that I had no interest in his money. I had enough of my own, so I didn't contest what he wanted to do with it. He left some of it to charities around town, but most went to the Chautauqua County Juvenile Court and a rehab clinic in Buffalo. He only had one unusual request. He wanted the epitaph on his headstone to read 'Character is the first aim of education.' It's an old quote, but I'm sure he remembered it from the auditorium where we went to high school.

"By the way," Dr. Bell interrupted herself, "did you have a chance to meet Darla Rhinesmith?"

"Yes, I did. She's the one who gave me your home address. An impressive woman," I added.

Dr. Bell flinched. "Of course, that's right," she said. "Darla gave you my address. How did I forget that? Mac saw her as the daughter he always wanted, and she saw him as the father she'd dreamed about."

Dr. Bell went silent. When she spoke again, I noticed what Darla Rhinesmith had hinted at. Her speech slowed, and it took more breath for her to speak. She turned away from me, looked out the window, and focused on something in the field. She winced as if she'd felt a pain, and I heard her ask, "How do I see you? What did you tell me?" But I sensed these questions had to do with a conversation I knew nothing about.

She let silence hang in the room. When she spoke again, she said, "We saw the emptiness."

Dr. Bell had been precise and coherent throughout the morning. I'd had trouble keeping up with her at times, but now she sat still, looking out the window. When she looked back from the window, I repeated her words as a question, "The emptiness?"

She answered me slowly. "Yes," she said. "The emptiness. I had it with Michael. He had it with Karen, and I had it again when Mac died. It's a paradox. We've been given emptiness. The mistake is thinking we've found nothing."

I didn't know how to respond to this. When I didn't say anything, she circled back to the subject of Macreavy again. "Since he had no family," she said, "I went back and took care of things. I called the police department and got telephone numbers for his friends. They went through his things, and I told them to take whatever would help them remember him. One of the guys took his boat, and Darla said she wanted some bicycle wheels he'd built. A school principal in New Jersey sent a truck for the books, and I had the Volkswagen shipped out there."

"He had a Volkswagen?" I asked.

"No, I did," she answered. "A '62 Karmann Ghia ragtop, candy red with canary yellow fenders, Dayton wire wheels, and not a spot of rust on the chrome bumpers. Someone had even reupholstered the interior in natural tan leather. That fellow with the daughter, Sergeant Cook, grew up around people who restored cars. When he heard it came up for sale, he bought it and sent it to Mac to give me. At first I couldn't accept such an extravagant gift, but Mac convinced me the man had given it from his heart. He'd offered me a part of himself, and he knew I'd appreciate it. I made it my summer car and drove it around Jamestown and Chautauqua County during those years I spent the summer there. Sergeant Cook's family kept it over the winter and got it ready for me every spring. They wouldn't take money for the service, so I gave them business instead. I talked to my car buddies and sent them so much work they had to open a second garage.

"Sounds like fun on wheels," I said.

"Absolutely," she said and continued, "Some of his furnishings found good homes, and after that, I called a place that does estate sales. They had an auction and sold the rest online. Mac probably never intended those record cards to see the light of day, but no one thought he'd been keeping anything that required discretion. I didn't know to look for anything like police records, and apparently, no one else did either. The whole place went on the block. The guy who sold you those cards probably bought them from that auction. I flew back and forth to sign papers and hired an agent to sell the house." Nel Bell finished her coffee, and it didn't look like she would pour another cup.

"How is your health, Dr. Bell?" I asked.

"I'm not well, Thomas. It won't be long now, but you've given me strength for today." She stood and looked unsure on her feet.

I stood as well. The interview had come to an end. I wanted to say something meaningful, but I couldn't. I fell back on the old standby. "Dr. Bell, it has been a pleasure to meet you. I'm honored that you've spent your morning with me. Thank you."

"Mr. Strongtree," she replied, "you've made my heart sing. I appreciate your interest. It's been a pure delight to remember those years. Please give me a minute. I have to pass by my office and then I'm out of the building. I'll meet you by the elevators after I collect my things, and if you'll be so kind, please walk me to my car."

"I'd be delighted," I said.

I picked up my backpack and left the meeting room. As I stood by the elevators, Raphael came over.

He looked at me with a curious stare. He said, "She's touched your heart, hasn't she?"

"Is it that obvious?" I asked.

Raphael laughed. He said, "She has that effect on everyone."

"I suppose you're right," I agreed. "She's touched me and touched the world."

Raphael said, "Nel Bell is one of the finest women I've ever met."

The woman herself rounded a corner, smiling and carrying her briefcase with some of the energy she'd displayed earlier. Raphael pushed the elevator button, and the doors opened as if they had been waiting for her.

As we rode in the elevator, I thought of another question. "Dr. Bell, you told me Foraker Macreavy memorized the Proverbs. Did he have a favorite?"

"Hard to say," she answered. "But his favorite verse came from Isaiah."

She recited from memory, "They rejoice in thy presence as men rejoice at harvest, or as they are glad when they share out the spoils. For thou hast shattered the yoke that burdened them."

The elevator door opened, and she took my arm as we walked through the front doors. She leaned toward me and said, "Your questions tell me you have been given ears to hear, Thomas. Listen. You will hear harmony."

She'd asked me to walk her to her car, but she meant we'd wait together in front of the building while her driver came around. A black Tesla pulled up and stopped in front of us. She said, "This is me. Wonderful to have met you, Mr. Strongtree."

The driver came around to the front passenger side door and opened it for her. I thought of one more question. "And you?" I asked. "Do you have a favorite verse?"

"Oh yes," she answered. She took her place, and the driver reached in to help her with the seat belt. After the buckle clipped, he backed out and held the door open.

"Mine is a Proverb," she said. She looked at me with her beautiful eyes, touched her hair, and said, "Gray hair is a crown of glory, won by a life lived loyal to God.

"Put away your fear, Tom. Believe and accept your life. Let it resolve."

I looked it up. She'd quoted Proverb 16:31.

The driver closed her door and returned to his place. She smiled at me through the window, and the car edged away.

EPILOGUE

I thought my days with the people in my project had ended when my flight home from Seattle touched down in Ohio about a year ago. That is until last Tuesday afternoon. A truck pulling a car-haul trailer parked in front of the house. The driver knocked on our front door and asked me to sign for a delivery. When I told the fellow I hadn't ordered anything, he showed me a shipping manifest from Associates and Light with my name and address printed on the top. A stamp at the bottom said, "Paid in full." We walked to the trailer together, and the man opened the back. The trailer door opened down to make a ramp, and we looked in. I had to smile. She'd sent me the Volkswagen. The license plate on the back of the car read "OOH LA LA."

I signed the paper. The delivery man jumped into the truck and loosened the straps holding the car to the trailer's floor. He reached in, shifted to neutral, and released the parking brake. He had a winch chained to the chassis, which allowed him to roll the car out of the truck and onto the driveway. I asked him if it started, and he said he didn't know, but I'd find the keys and all the paperwork in the glove compartment.

Along with the title, transferred and notarized, and a registration card, I found an envelope she'd addressed to me in the same beautiful script I recognized from before. On the back of the envelope, at the point of the fold, she'd written "SWAK." I sat down at our kitchen table, and again, I opened the envelope with a blade. I recognized her scent.

Dear Thomas,

> The sun came out a few days ago, and I felt strong. I took the car and drove it to look at the ocean. I'm afraid my left foot isn't up to the clutch

255

anymore, and the shifter almost put an end to my wrist. Even so, I didn't want to go back, and I imagined Mac riding next to me. I returned to a phalanx of doctors and nurses who informed me my driving privileges have been rescinded. I must have given them quite a scare.

If you're reading this note, know that I have passed. Please accept the car as a token of my gratitude. You made my final months delightful. Following your kind visit, I brought out decades worth of letters I'd been saving. Life has been such a gift! What wonderful people I've known! I allowed myself to drift into memories of the joy I felt at receiving their letters then, and I am so looking forward to seeing them again soon.

You came to mind as I thought about what to do with the car. You took an interest and cared about the lives of the kids Mac came to know. You have heard their stories, and I cannot think of anyone who would appreciate it more. However, even though they will not let me drive it, I cannot let it go just yet. Perhaps I'll coax one of the young doctors or nurses into taking me for a ride. (As soon as I find one who can drive a stick.)

As part of my advanced directives, I am leaving instructions to ship the car to you. All fees will have been taken care of, and I will also keep the registration current for the time being, albeit in Chautauqua County, for sentimental reasons. I have an excellent mechanic who has looked after my cars for years. It drove well the other day, and I am sure you will find it in tip-top shape.

You are a good man, Thomas. Take rides with your wife. Find someplace to drive together.

Laugh and smile. Care for her and accept care from her. Look forward. And when you're searching for heaven, watch for connections. Let the Spirit help you hold on or walk away. We'll be waiting.

Au Revoir,
Nel Bell

My wife had been grocery shopping and got home just as I finished Dr. Bell's letter. She walked into the kitchen with two armloads of sacks from the market.

"Who's here?" she asked. "There's an old-time sports car in the driveway with New York plates."

"It's ours, Boo," I said. "I'll tell you about it while we put the groceries away. There's a letter that goes with it. I'll read it to you and then I want to take you for a drive while we've still got some of the day left."

ABOUT THE AUTHOR

After graduating from Case Western Reserve as an English major, Paul Martin spent the last forty-four years fixing bicycles, making violins, restoring furniture, assisting patients as a nurse's aide, writing hospice life journals, and collecting stories. As a Third Order Franciscan, he has used the Lectio Divina and Ignatian meditation to listen to God. Married for over forty years, he and his wife have two grown children and three grandchildren.

www.ingramcontent.com/pod-product-compliance
Lightning Source LLC
Chambersburg PA
CBHW020440130626
46549CB00001B/227